SWIM WILD

Swim Wild
Dive into the natural world and discover your inner adventurer

Jack Hudson
with Calum Hudson and Robbie Hudson
the Wild Swimming Brothers

This paperback edition published in 2020.

First published in Great Britain in 2018 by Yellow Kite
An imprint of Hodder & Stoughton
An Hachette UK company

3

Typeset in Bembo by Palimpsest Book Production Ltd, Falkirk, Stirlingshire

Printed and bound by Clays Ltd, Elcograf S.p.A.

Hodder & Stoughton policy is to use papers that are natural, renewable
and recyclable products and made from wood grown in sustainable forests.
The logging and manufacturing processes are expected to conform
to the environmental regulations of the country of origin.

Yellow Kite
Hodder & Stoughton Ltd
Carmelite House
50 Victoria Embankment
London EC4Y 0DZ

www.yellowkitebooks.co.uk
www.hodder.co.uk

Contents

President Obama: 'What is it that led to such a deep fascination with how the natural world worked?'

Sir David Attenborough: 'Well I've never met a child . . .'

President Obama: 'Who wasn't fascinated?'

Sir David Attenborough: 'Who was not interested in natural history. So, the – I mean just the simplest thing, a five-year-old turning over a stone and seeing a slug, you know, and says, "What a treasure – how does it live and what are those things on the front?" Kids love it. Kids understand the natural world . . . so the question is how did you lose it? How did anyone lose interest in nature?'

Transcript from *David Attenborough
Meets President Obama* (Atlantic Productions)

Preface

Little brother Jack has tried his hand at all kinds of content writing. He was editor-in-chief of a digital watch magazine, a movie critic, a travel writer and a copywriter for several animal and educational charities. He now writes mostly about wild swimming and has written for various adventure-centric publications, including Another Escape, the Outdoor Swimming Society and Red Bull UK, where he worked as the guest Adventure Editor.

Middle brother Calum spent five years in the London tech start-up scene, until he became business development manager at the ticketing and event management company, Eventbrite. He is also a veteran of endurance triathlons and open-water races, having competed in the UK Iron Man, Double Ironman, Nettle Warrior and Celt Man triathlons. Driven from his urban confinement, Calum first proposed a wild swimming expedition to his brothers as a way of getting back in touch with the natural world.

Big brother Robbie is an artist who's exhibited his work around the world from Istanbul to Toronto. After securing a bursary from VARC (Visual Arts in Rural Communities), he launched a solo gallery exhibition displaying sixty large-scale abstract paintings at the Kendal Art Centre, inspired by his seven-and-a-half-mile swim across the length of Lake Ullswater. He now works as editor-in-chief at BOXROX, a leading digital magazine for competitive fitness.

This book has been written by Jack Hudson, including contributions from Calum Hudson and contributions and illustrations from Robbie Hudson.

It was late that night and Calum was sitting at the kitchen table in his sparsely decorated London flat. Above his head the wall was covered by a torn map dotted with notes written in pink marker. He leant his elbow against the table, tousled his hair with a clenched hand and rested his phone against his cheek. His careworn face began to sag as Mum's voice came quietly and slowly through the earpiece.

'I am the only mum in the world who has watched all three of her beloved boys swim across a whirlpool,' Mum was saying. 'I didn't say anything – I was smiling and shouting words of encouragement.'

Calum conceded that this was true. It was very likely that Mum was the only parent in history who'd ever watched her three children swimming across a maelstrom at the same time. She was no stranger to the anxieties of raising three boys, but this was different – this time she was serious.

'Heck lad, last night I made the mistake of googling Saltstraumen before I tried to go to sleep. Nope, did-nae fall into a comfy, snore-y, relaxing snooze. Can't think why?'

'It'll be okay, Mum, I'm being extremely thorough,' Calum insisted.

3

'I'm working through all the details and dangers, going back and forth with the most experienced ship captain in the region.'

'Did you see the YouTube video of a kayaker talking about crossing it?' Mum asked, ignoring him. 'He said there was no defined start or finish. He said it was very wide. There's lots of whirlpools, chuck, not just one or two. Any swim would have to be at Olympic twenty-five-metre record speed. If not, the slack tide disappears.'

There was a moment's pause before Mum went on: 'I'm just asking you to please consider this one as a no-go. Think of the tidal drift and length of time needed to make the crossing. There is too much potential for actually losing at least one of my lads. It's too far to make the distance during slack tide.'

'Would you like to come with us?' Calum asked.

'I couldn't go with you. I'd die of nervous shak-ery. I want to keep all my darling boys until I'm old and decrepit. Adventure should be difficult, unique, sometimes dangerous and exciting — but this one is too dangerous . . . Cally, I am saying all this because you are too precious for me to keep quiet.'

'I know, Mum.'

'Okay, chuck, 'nuff said . . . for the time being.'

There had only been a handful of times in our lives when our mum had asked us not to do something. Usually, she was pushing us outdoors and supporting our mischief. And yet this was one step too far — she just couldn't get on-board with the idea of us all risking our lives. That being said, after a month or so of quiet fretting, she finally let us know that we were permitted to attempt our world-first swims across the two largest and most powerful maelstroms in the world: the Saltstraumen and the Moskstraumen, in Norway. The only problem being that, by this time, Calum had been stopped in his tracks and was starting to question his plan. It had come to our attention that Mum had been having recurring nightmares, which involved the three of us being sucked into the vortex of a whirlpool. Suddenly the expedition seemed to be laced with peril. Perhaps it was a stupid idea. After all, as far as we knew, no one had ever attempted these swims before – there had to be a reason, right? Were we putting our mum through stress for the sake of our own selfish goals? Or, even worse, our egos?

When the person you love more than anything in the world starts to fear for your life, there has to be something wrong with the path you've taken. Meanwhile, Calum was also getting flak in several interviews with the Norwegian press. One conversation with a journalist at Dagsavisen (an online publication we were introduced to by Nina Jensen of WWF Norge) ended on a rather sour note. Calum thought they wanted to discuss our motivation, namely the plans to drill for oil in the Lofoten Islands, although the journalist had other ideas in mind. It soon transpired that he thought we were going to die. Supposedly, he'd spoken to local scuba divers who described the Saltstraumen's currents as being too powerful. They said that any swimmer who entered those raging waters would be wrenched down to the bottom of the ocean, whereupon their lungs would fill with water and the leaden pressure would wrap around them until they drowned. Needless to say, when the article surfaced it was less than encouraging and the headline, which we Google-translated, seemed to foreshadow a catastrophe.

It read: Do Not Kill Ourselves.

In the end Calum decided, after wrestling with the idea for some time, that he could stomach the responsibility of endangering me and Robbie. In other words, he was happy to get rid of us both, which supports a suspicion I've been nurturing since childhood. He also said that Mum was one of the wildest and strongest people he knew, and that her mum, our Grandma Wild, would be proud of us if we went through with the swims. He was certainly right about our grandma: she had always been our staunchest supporter and a very fierce ally indeed. Mum once told us that Grandma had moved up to the Highlands after her husband, our grandpa, was killed in a traffic collision. She stayed there for the rest of her life, during which time she became something of a local legend along the loch-side. They called her the Wild Lady of Loch Broom. She was a former belt-wielding English teacher turned Wildling, often sighted charging up and down the hills, wielding a machete as she hacked her way through the tangled bracken. Her strength and fortitude ran in all of us.

Secretly, I suspected that Mum had never intended to stop us from attempting the Norway swims. Led by example, she had, perhaps unconsciously, permitted us to disregard the rules, while forgetting to genuflect to figures of authority because they, being human, can also sometimes be wrong. Ironically, the lessons we'd learnt from Mum encouraged Calum to defy her early pleas. Her middle son was showing the same wild ability to be stubborn and put stock in his own ridiculousness. Then again, while the burden of responsibility still rested heavily on his shoulders, Calum was sure that we would all be strong enough to make the crossings.

'As long as we're together,' Calum said to Robbie and me, 'we'll make it across and Mum won't have anything to worry about.'

1

'Don't Forget Your Cap'

Into the Maelstrom Expedition, Day 1 (Saltstraumen)
Monday 22 August 2016

- *Point-to-point 250-metre swim.*
- *All swimmers to swim diagonally against the current to head for the opposite bank.*
- *Currents – if a swimmer is travelling downstream faster than the others then the priority is that swimmer.*
- *DO NOT swim up against the current – swim in a diagonal line and exit water further down.*
- *If a swimmer is dragged under the water by a whirlpool or current then this is immediately a priority. Spotters on the boat are to keep their eyes on their swimmer but the boat is to head for the swimmer and their buoy immediately.*

My girlfriend Beth was standing in the doorway, half hidden among the puffy folds of her waterproof overalls. Across the table my Scottish friend and kindred uni goof, Dave, was attaching his camera to a chest rig. We were the last people

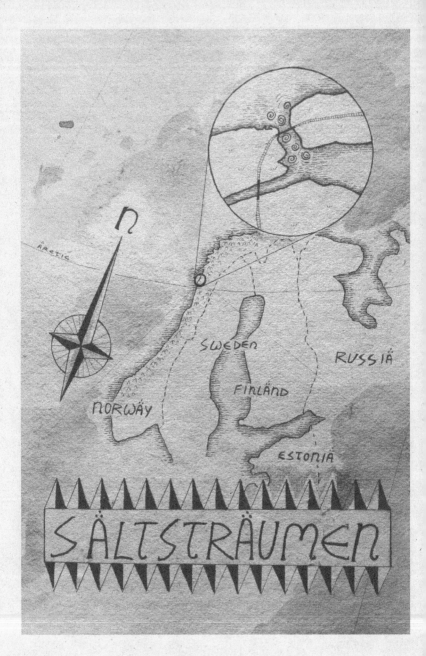

left in the conference room, on the top floor of the pristine Thon Hotel. At this point the long tables, usually assembled at the behest of tidy business groups, were cluttered with empty water bottles, sachets of energy gel, cables, laptops, towels and all manner of swimming paraphernalia. On a nearby whiteboard there were two rules scrawled in blue marker – reminders of our recent whirlpool conference.

The first rule was simple: *Do not drown.*

The second was a little trickier: *Do not get killer-whaled.*

For some reason we felt obliged to use everything the hotel had given us. That's why the whiteboards were covered in whirlpool doodles and a huddle of laptops sat hooked up to the projectors. The hotel had lent us these meeting rooms for the whole nine days we were staying in Norway, as well as four bedrooms and a wholesome dose of Scandinavian warmth. When we first saw the rooms, with their giant, mounted screens, retractable projectors and panoramic views of the harbour, we couldn't believe our luck. Admittedly, it did seem a little excessive at the time. As it happened, though, the addition of a large space to collect and store our stuff had proven quite handy. Especially now that we were rushing out the door, on our way to swim across the world's most powerful maelstrom.

In Bodø, the Norwegian town where we were based, the Saltstraumen is a source of income for a few boat captains and a source of wonder (and sometimes fish) for everyone else. It also possesses the world's strongest maelstrom, which made it the more dangerous of the two we were planning to swim across – the other being the Moskstraumen, which is the largest maelstrom in the world. Swirling in a narrow gulf south-east of Bodø, the Saltstraumen is often glimpsed by cars that tear over the highway, crossing the sloping cantilever bridge that overarches the water. If you were to look down from the peak of that bridge you'd see the criss-crossing currents forming odd, spiked waves. You'd also see scattered eddies swirling through the white-frothed water. By all accounts that is the heart of the maelstrom, packed into a narrow strait that creates a rugged, rock-strewn funnel beneath the surface. Into this funnel flows 400 million cubic metres of water, four times a day, as though it were pouring down the throat of a huge, thirsty leviathan.

For those who aren't familiar with the word, a maelstrom is essentially an area of turbulent water in which whirlpools form. This phenomenon occurs when opposing currents collide over an unusual rock formation. Maelstroms are particularly common in places where undersea mountains (or seamounts) have abruptly changed the elevation of the seabed, disrupting the tidal flow. In these conditions the rising tide can be disturbed by an inflow that sweeps in before the preceding tide has settled. This stirs the currents into a circulatory motion, creating whirlpools and eddies that are unpredictable in nature, and not to be taken lightly. It's important to remember that you also find whirlpools under waterfalls, where they often possess a force that pulls you directly downwards. This experience of being wrenched underwater is what makes whirlpools so terrifying to wild swimmers. The Saltstraumen alone has claimed around sixty lives over the past thirty years. Of all those who've drowned in the maelstrom, only three bodies were found, which gives you some idea of how strong and dangerous the deep currents can be. In fact, fishermen recently hurled a dummy into its raging currents, equipped with a GPS/depth tracker. The dummy was dragged down to a depth of 200 metres in just three seconds. Consider the fact that we had just twelve minutes to swim from shore to shore, before the maelstrom would gain a similar force. More than anything else, it was going to be a test of sheer efficiency.

It would be late summer and the weather would still be warm. We would have to start swimming the moment the clock hit 6.28 p.m. Then we would sprint the 225-metre crossing, without stopping to rest or take in the scenery. Otherwise . . . well, let's just take the dummy's example and assume that it would be suicide for us to stay in the water at high tide. At that point the crushing wash of currents would suddenly smash together and spur the maelstrom into motion.

In fact, we'd met our boat captain, Knut Westvig, the day before and he'd quickly clarified these dangers. If you could trust anyone's judgement it would be his – Knut has been visiting the Saltstraumen since the age of twelve. He now makes his living running *Stella Polaris* and leading tours to see the maelstrom when it's in full force.

'Crossing when it's at its strongest,' Knut had said, reclining in his office, beneath the taxidermic figure of a yellow-eyed sea eagle. 'It's really strong. So, we want you to see what you're up against.'

A ripple of nervous laughter suddenly circled the room, causing Knut to smile and add: 'I mean, crossing the current when it's at its strongest, that's madness – complete madness.'

As you might expect, I was growing increasingly nervous as we left the conference room and headed down the hotel corridor, passing a cleaning trolley stacked with towels. Dave followed me with the camera and tried to shoot a quick interview when we were crammed inside the lift. We had just enough time for me to admit that I was feeling the pressure. Then we met the others in the lobby and took the short walk to the harbour together, under the cool Norwegian sunlight.

One of the many welcome surprises, after we landed in Norway, was the warm temperature. It wasn't what I'd expected at all. When Calum told me we were heading into the Arctic Circle my first thought was to pack for an igloo interior. If I'd studied the Gulf Stream and strong westerlies I might've known to expect warmer climes, not the subarctic tundra of Svalbard. But that was part of the excitement, I guess – none of us, except Calum, had any idea what to expect. For example, we knew that from May to late July the sun never sank below the horizon. That's why some locals refer to Norway as the Land of the Midnight Sun. Conversely, from late November to the end of January, the sun never rises and the northern-most communities are forced to live in perpetual darkness. In Bodø, a 745-mile car journey north of Oslo, we thought we might experience this strange, unending daylight. However, as it happened, the sun set on our first night together and we all watched as it dipped slowly behind the hills, feeling slightly cheated.

By now it was late in the afternoon and most of the boats had been tied to their berths and covered for the night. We stood on the dock for a while and watched them as small waves lapped against their bows. Occasionally Luke – one of our support team – would pluck a fresh shrimp out of a bag he held dangling from the crook of his arm. I watched him as he picked the shells apart and tossed them into the water, enticing fish of varying sizes, which snatched them quickly from the surface. They were swimming through the clearest water I'd ever seen – the kind that you'd expect to find in some glacial pool hidden on a Himalayan mountaintop. In fact, if you picked a nearby boat and followed its docking rope, you could clearly see the concrete blocks that anchored it to the seabed. We'd already been advised to wear dive masks for the swim, which would increase our field of vision, but it was only now that we were beginning to see why that advice was so pertinent.

Just then I sighted our captain, Knut, as he came cruising up to the jetty in his black RIB (rigid inflatable boat). Calum was wearing a huge grin, with his balled hands stuffed inside his jacket pockets. Beside him, Robbie cut a calm figure, half hidden behind a patterned pair of wooden sunglasses. They were talking about the moment when Calum first pitched this trip to Norway:

'I thought you were joking,' Robbie said, smiling. 'The thing before this you suggested was you wanted to swim with a camera strapped to your head – crawl, really fast, off a waterfall and go into, like, a huge swan dive. In your head, you imagined some 400-foot swan dive.'

I started laughing and turned away from the water to face them. 'In the future it will just be Calum in a barrel,' I said, 'and we'll be watching from the sides.'

'Houdini did that,' Calum chirped. 'Houdini went over the Niagara Falls in a barrel.'

'Did he survive?' I asked.

'No.' (In fact, Houdini didn't *actually* go over Niagara Falls in a barrel at all.)

It was time for us to go. Luke wrapped his shrimp into a sealed bundle and slipped them into his pocket for later. Then Beth hurried down the metal gangway to the jetty, where Dave was setting up a shot. Finally James, an army captain who went to school with Robbie, tucked his little white drone back into its box.

'Matthew Webb,' Calum went on, bending over and lifting his sagging swim float from between his feet. 'The first person ever to swim the English Channel – he, erm, he tried to swim the whirlpool at the bottom of Niagara Falls and he died.'

'This has taken a morbid turn,' Robbie said, with a slight smile.

'Well, it's just – it's the history of swimming,' Calum insisted. 'An iconic British swimmer – he's like the Hillary of swimming.'

I cast a dumb look at Calum, my pursed lips flickering with the hint of a smile.

'Hillary Clinton?'

We all started laughing.

Meanwhile, Knut edged the boat up alongside the jetty, and Luke, Beth and James climbed on-board and slung their kit into the gaps between the seats. We'd given ourselves enough time to get to the maelstrom and watch it gradually slowing and calming before we crossed. This also meant that we could take our time getting out there. It would take just under an hour for Knut to drive his boat around the headland to the narrow inlet where we'd find the Saltstraumen.

As I walked down the clanging gangway, behind Robbie and Calum, I felt the sudden immediacy of the moment. This was what we'd trained for and now here we were, inside the Arctic Circle, about to attempt something more dangerous than anything we'd done before. At that point we'd been dreaming about swimming the Saltstraumen for just over a year. For us it was a matter of diving into the chaos and finding out how well we knew ourselves and each other. We wanted to see how far we could push ourselves. Joking aside, Calum had worked intensely to get us there and the fact we were even on this adventure was mostly down to him. You've gotta have a hell of a lot of confidence to carry out such an idea. Come to think of it, I reckon most great ideas must've sounded crazy when they were first brought up in conversation. Imagine the Soviet Sputnik boffins, sitting in tight circles, discussing the prospect of launching a satellite the size of a beach ball and sending it on a mad maiden orbit around the circumference of the Earth. Or think of the Norwegian explorer, Thor Heyerdahl, telling his assembled team that he wanted to ride a balsawood raft from Peru to Polynesia, without any modern equipment, save the odd essential radio, chart or sextant . . . I guess we should be thankful that crazy sometimes seeks out company. Otherwise these mad folks would all wind up alone in dingy states of isolation, scrawling their ideas over the confines of their enclosures.

I don't think Calum would mind too much if I said that

he deserved to be counted as one of those mad ones. As a kid, he was always the first to ruin a pleasant photo, usually sticking his tongue out and pretending to eat something, like my head or whatever I happened to be holding. As he grew older it became apparent that he was also prone to vagaries of brilliance. He quickly learnt to talk like an academic and became very fond of challenging adults to debates. Sometimes it was difficult to separate his madness from his brilliance. It's that old cliché, you know? Like when he proposed this expedition to Norway, with the intention of swimming across the world's largest and most powerful maelstroms. My first thought was that he'd lost it. This was a step too far – it was just too dangerous. Now I realise that I was mistaken. I had underestimated our need, as brothers, to stick together and not be singled out for having held the other two back.

Calum looking sober on our way to swim the Saltstraumen.

In that little boat I began to think about who I was there with and who they were to me. I realised that I had Luke, with whom I'd travelled to India; Beth, my girlfriend of four years; Dave, my closest uni mate; James, who'd supported us on our last few swims; and my two brothers. It was hard not to feel at home in their company. Suffice it to say, I used their presence to calm myself while the boat engine sputtered and the motor vibrated with a low, continuous growl. Then Knut slowly steered us out of Bodø harbour and a moment later we were rocketing towards the horizon, bouncing out onto the open sea. In a matter of minutes, we'd left the mountains and the squat buildings behind us. Suddenly we were hurtling into orca and porpoise territory, far out beyond the coastline, at which point our surroundings were revealed as a snaking, green landscape of epic proportions.

I stared straight ahead as the boat veered away from the offing and turned back towards the mainland. As we picked up speed again the wind hammered my face and rattled my gums. Sometimes a gust of salty spray would whip over the prow and lash us in our seats. Instead of turning away, I began to savour the feeling of these cold, gentle lashings. All the while I kept my eyes half closed and didn't open them again until Knut began to slow the boat and move us into the shallows. It was then that we came to a stop close to the shore and sighted an expanse of asphalt belonging to a military base. Knut called to us from the wheel and pointed to a partly concealed fence, where a pair of sea eagles sat perched on two posts. The eagles were busy being harassed by an angry seagull, although they scarcely acknowledged the nuisance, like two

elephants swatting flies with their tails. After a while we left them to their gull-swatting and followed the coast inland at a relaxing speed. I took the opportunity to lean back and take in the vista, admiring the views on all sides, which were truly wild and spectacular. Wherever I looked, my eyes were met by forested slopes and rolling fields. Yet my attention always returned to those distant, pointed mountains, huddled close together in stances of fellowship, framed by the cloudless sky.

I dare say Norway is everything you dream of when you're cooped up in the city – a rugged, edge-world archipelago, which spans the western flank of Scandinavia and extends to the far-flung islands of Svalbard and Jan Mayen. On one side the country is flanked by a storm-beaten, green coastline, hewn by the mighty Barents, Norwegian, North and Skagerrak seas. Further inland, sprawling expanses of unpopulated scenery are split by deep, glacial fjords that shape the sculptured mountains.

Most British children know this country as a land of horned warriors and gnarled trolls. The population has enjoyed a recent period of prosperity, owing to an abundance of natural resources, namely petroleum, as well as natural gas and minerals. Norway is now the world's number-one producer of oil per capita, excluding the Middle East. It is also one of the leading nations in terms of its environmental performance, setting a high standard through progressive policies centred on the maintenance of national parks and the strict regulation of powerful conglomerates.

I felt a great affection for Norway as we continued our journey to the Saltstraumen, following a long promontory patched with farmland. There was something very welcoming about the isolation and the relaxed, retiring locals who enjoyed it together. Coming from Newcastle, I know exactly how loud and rowdy folk can get. Especially when it's derby day and no one, not even the police horses, is exempt from being involved in a brawl. So, for me, it was very settling to experience a culture that values quietness and a people that keep drinking on the periphery of their everyday. I'd warmed quickly to this far-flung world, which was still untamed and unspoilt. Sadly, that warmth began to fade as we rounded an outcrop and swerved towards the scariest thing under a bridge since the Three Billy Goats Gruff.

'Calm – before the . . .' I said, trailing off as I turned to Robbie, who was still hidden behind his sunglasses.

Robbie nodded. Then we both looked ahead at the ruffled waters of the Saltstraumen. I could see the calm channel, close to our starting point, which would take us several minutes to swim across. I reminded myself that this would give us time to acclimatise and prepare ourselves. Then there was the rocky island, which shielded us from incoming currents. When we passed that island we knew we'd be hitting the toughest part of the swim. Immediately after those rocks the wrap-around currents swept into the heart of the maelstrom, criss-crossing and thrashing together to create scattered eddies and whorls of froth. At that point it was likely that we would have to sprint to keep our course. It was also likely that we'd be separated.

The previous afternoon we'd all gathered in the meeting room and discussed the likelihood of this happening. Since then the thought of finding myself alone in the maelstrom was lodged in my mind. Despite what I told myself, I couldn't shake it. I knew it was ridiculous, but that didn't seem to matter. It's like when you hear the *Jaws* crescendo while you're swimming in deep water. It was just one of those irrational fears that prey on your insecurities. I knew this, and yet it didn't help to settle my stomach. Instead I was reminded of a time, before we flew to Norway, when I was fearfully staring at my coffee as I stirred it, watching the little, brown whirlpool forming as it swept around my spoon. I must say the idea of being sucked into the downward spiral of that swirling cone was quite terrifying.

Unfortunately, there just wasn't enough time for me to unpack my fear – we had to get ready instead. Without speaking, we all climbed out of our overalls, sealed our wetsuits and attached the floats to our waists in unison. It seemed like mere seconds had passed since we'd been sitting in the hotel. Now it was almost time to go. Approaching the side of the boat, I puffed out my cheeks and pushed the air between my lips. A knot was tightening in the pit of my stomach. I began to feel sick, although I tried to dodge the feeling by telling myself that I was ready. Then I stared into the water and focused on that exact moment in time. At once a pleasant thought entered my mind: in an hour we'll be riding the boat back to town. It seemed so close – so tangible – only first we had to get in and swim.

Suddenly a weight dropped into the pit of my stomach. I felt trapped, chained to each agonising second that carried us closer to the maelstrom. Meanwhile the boat was gripped by a stillness as the engine quieted and the currents dragged us towards the bridge. I could hear Calum talking to Knut behind me and I could sense his excitement. We were finally here.

This was the culmination of two years spent chugging up and down pools, lakes and tarns.

Breathing slowly, I leant over the side of the boat and dipped one of my booted feet into the water. I could feel the cold through the neoprene. I could also feel the tug of the little eddies as they splashed against the boat. Now and then I thrust my foot into the centre of one of the vortexes and tested its strength as it pulled me inwards. I was conscious of the fact that I'd been the one who'd asked the most questions and shown the most fear in the build-up to this moment. And yet I was quietly confident that I wouldn't give up. I just needed to keep my head and control my breathing. Panic is a sure way to open a hatch beneath your feet, and I didn't want to fall – not now.

With a sharp jolt, the boat was nudged into a spiral and a shiver shot through me as I tightened my grip on the bar above my seat. I've noticed that one thing I'll do, on the brink of something that scares me, is to take a moment and allow the atmosphere to sink in. Sometimes I listen to the people around me. I catch snippets of muffled conversation, but I notice them less and less as I sink through my thoughts, extending my mind towards the job at hand. Soon I'll feel a wave of emotion that rolls quickly over me. Then the hairs on my arms all stand as a cold chill sweeps through my body. I see the faces of all those folk who make me happiest. It's like they've gathered for some solemn communion. Their faces are vivid in my mind and I can hear their voices, too. Finally, I focus on the condition of love that is everywhere and in everything. I remember the kind folk who I might never see again. I see family members. I relive old jokes. I don't think about anything that makes me less. Instead I ride on an upsurge of positivity, which lifts me through my little self, to a height where there is no pain, and no fear either. This ride sparks subtle pricks of electricity that spike my body and cause pimples to appear on my skin. At once it feels as though I've found my place and planted both feet firmly on the ground. I'm ready to stand at full height and give testimony to what Hemingway said: *Man is not meant for defeat.*

'Ready Calum?' I called.

'Yeah,' he said. 'Let's go boys.'

I pulled my goggles down over my eyes and rolled onto my stomach, hugging the side of the squeaking boat, with my legs dangling over the water. Calum and Robbie leant over me and watched from above as I let go. I could feel the cold rushing over my shoulders and stinging my cheeks as I hit the water. I suppressed a gasp and floated for a moment, until I'd steadied my breathing. Then the other two crashed through the surface on either side of me. There was a moment of quiet gasping and treading water before we reached out and began to swim. The next thing we knew we were sitting on a nearby shelving, among tangles of kelp and seaweed, ready to begin our swim.

In those slow moments I was silent. I just waited and strained to hear Luke's signal over the low roar of the maelstrom. My hands were pressed against the rock and the water lapped against my bare wrists. Everywhere else I was covered by neoprene. Breathing slowly, I peered into the shallow water and thought about the sprint ahead. I could feel that it was cold, but it also looked clear and somewhat inviting. Then I noticed little fish darting over my black socks, while a nearby red jellyfish – the kind that can sting – wrestled with the fronds of bronzed kelp.

Remembering what'd been said about the water clarity, I dipped my goggles in and cleaned the whorls of spit from the lenses. When I pulled them on I could feel a faint burn as the chilled water forked down my cheeks. It was then that I heard raised voices on the boat and looked up to see if we'd been given the signal. It was a false alarm. The seconds slipped by. The tension tightened. Neoprene snapped, seagulls cawed and waves sloshed against the side of the RIB. We only had twelve minutes to make it across. The currents being as they were, spinning in connected discs, you could never predict how fast you would move. We'd talked about the likelihood of being separated or taken by the current. Calum had insisted that we shouldn't waste energy trying to fight it. If the maelstrom wanted to whisk us off in a new direction, we had to let it. After all, it didn't matter where you climbed out on the other side, so long as you made it across.

'All right lads,' Luke called to us. 'Good to go. Yeah.'

Quickly I shimmied down the rock and dove forward into the cold water. I wasn't going to waste any time. Feeling my way through the kelp, I clambered over the rocks until I was deep enough to begin my crawl. No sooner had I started swimming than I was enveloped by and in awe of the lucid water. I glimpsed silver fish darting beyond my extended fingers and patches of colourful coral, clothed in a greenish veil. I could also see Robbie and Calum clearly as they came up on either side of me. Then, as the boat swerved and headed out towards the island, we all began to gather speed and tighten our formation. Bubbles coiled around my goggles as I pulled back through the water and slid over the sinking seabed, watching my shadow and noting the shape of each stroke. Whenever I came up for air I was met by the sight of Robbie beside me, digging hard into the water and kicking quickly. Over his shoulder, I could also see the boat easing forward and shepherding us across the channel.

As we'd predicted, the first currents gave us little resistance and we soon found our rhythm and forgot about the cold. A little while later I pulled my head up to see if we were nearing the island. In doing so I snatched a glimpse of the underside of the bridge, which towered over us. Coupled with the mountains behind it, the sight reminded me how very small we were. Fortunately, I could also see the tiered rocks that surrounded the island. We'd come further than I thought. In the moments that followed we were shielded by these rocks and blessed with a stretch of still water. It was a brief respite, during which we held our formation, while I was lulled into a relaxed state, almost forgetting what was around the corner. My mind had found the stillness that we swimmers treasure. It's that sweet spot – that point when you forget you're swimming. Then I began to think: if I could just sneak out of this moment, but keep on reaching and kicking, maybe I'd be able to forget what I was doing and come around at the other side, unfazed. It almost seemed possible, until we passed the island and a strong current ploughed into our strokes, slowing us all to an agonising halt.

Now the island was behind us, but, much as we willed it to, it just wouldn't recede into the distance. Instead we seemed to be moving backwards, groping at ranks of waves as they spun into a frenzy and began to encircle us. At once we knew we'd hit the sweeping currents at the centre of the maelstrom. I could hear myself releasing pained sighs as I came up to breathe. I tried to keep a steady rhythm, for fear of losing my strength. At the same time, I was becoming frustrated. I couldn't put enough into my strokes to beat the current. I kept pulling my gloved hands back, grasping handfuls of water and flicking them behind me. I kicked harder, but while the boat was inching forward, we were slipping backwards and rapidly losing energy in the process. Each time I extended my arm, my eyes lifted towards my fingertips, watching as they gripped the water. Once, I even noticed a thin vortex that spiralled down into the deep like a silvery woollen thread.

Fighting the whirling currents at the heart of the Saltstraumen.

The others told us later that we were struggling in the face of an inflowing current, which was manifest in a sudden swathe of choppy water. To us, it felt like we'd lost control. Rolling over onto my back, I noticed where the water was being whipped into faint whirls. Then I spun around and saw the rubber prow of the boat as it swerved alongside me, guiding me back towards the bridge. I used the boat as a point of reference and reminded myself that the current was driving us towards our support team – not out to sea. Reassured, I plunged back underwater and extended my arm. *Just a little further and you'll make ground*, I told myself, as I dug my hand again into the greenish murk.

It's a strange feeling when you're reaching with everything you have and still gaining nothing. What made it even worse was the fact that our ten-minute window was almost up. Also, Robbie was now several metres behind me, caught in the worst of the inflowing current and veering towards the boat. Looking back, I realise that this was one of those moments when I thought we might not make it. It was a thought that suddenly flashed inside my mind, although it was quickly replaced by the sound of Beth shouting my name. It was the same sharp tone she'd used when I killed her plant by leaving it on the electric heater.

'Jack.'

I lifted my head, rolled back and recoiled as the rubber prow of the boat came looming over me. Then I spotted Luke, waving his arm and calling to us.

'Further this way guys,' he said, pointing us in a new direction. 'Aim for that bit there.'

They'd spotted a patch of calmer water. I altered my course and followed his finger, outstretching my arms to their full extent. This time something had changed. I could feel the water sliding past me. Then, suddenly, I felt my whole body lifting through the sluggish backflow. It was like stepping onto a conveyor belt. With gritted teeth, I cut my hand hard into the water and heaved myself onto a gentle eddy, which redirected me towards the shore. It was then that I heard Calum's voice, pushed myself upright and began treading water.

'Let's wait for Robbie,' he said.

I looked back and sighted Robbie as he crawled towards us, making painstaking inches against the current. Behind him the island had finally retreated into the distance and, dare I say, it looked as though we were going to make it. Uplifted, I watched as Robbie kept his pace and struggled through the chop. You could tell that he was starting to tire. He kept poking his head up to see how far away we were, although he didn't stop.

'Keep going, Rob,' Luke called from the boat. 'That's it, good man Robbie. There we go.'

The strokes kept coming, one after another, as Robbie shortened the gap between us. Afterwards he said he wasn't happy with how he'd swum. Like all good athletes, he has a habit of being tough on himself. I just think that having the squat physique of a weightlifter didn't do him any favours. After all, long arms are the secret weapons of almost all professional swimmers. Nevertheless, Robbie reached deeper into his reserves of grit and went on battling through the current. He'd assured us the day before that he'd keep swimming until his body dropped beneath the surface. I must say I believed him. I think he would've sooner drowned than turned towards the boat, away from his younger brothers. All the while I watched him, hoping that it wouldn't come to that, and, of course, it didn't – he kept up the unending fight, like Sisyphus with the boulder lodged between his shoulders.

Meanwhile, Calum and I bobbed slowly seaward, drifting past the prow of the boat as it moved back to accompany Robbie. Even now, having just made it through the worst of the maelstrom, I could feel this immense force around me, seizing my chest and legs.

'The current's taking us,' I called, turning to Calum.

I remember how, in *The Day the Whale Came*, Lynne Cox described the sensation of having a grey whale pass beneath her. She said the whale displaced so much water that she could feel herself being tugged downwards. I'd always wondered how it would feel to share the water with something so huge and powerful. I might've experienced something similar in that moment. It was just this encompassing mixture of awe and terror. I could almost hear an ominous growling in the water, like the guttural purr of a powerful sports car. Then I realised that our time was almost up and the tides were beginning to change, slowly whipping the whirlpool into full force. Soon we would be in the grip of an immense movement – an almost godlike motion, like the leaden march of tectonic plates. Even worse, we were about to discover nature's true potential for destruction.

'Let's get out of here,' I cried, the moment Robbie caught up with us.

With that I was determined not to stop again. I trusted that my brothers would both make it, but I also knew that I needed to get to the shore. The feeling of losing control, gradually, was starting to get the best of me. My power increased with my first few strokes and I thrust my hands hard through the peaks of the waves and felt my body rising as I lunged over the troughs. On several occasions, I mistimed my breathing and had to stomach gulps of salt water, but I was unreservedly fixed to my rhythm – the knowledge that at any moment we could be brought to a halt had centred my focus.

Before long I was swimming at full speed, extending my fingers to pull back as much of the water as I could. For the first time, I felt like I was nearing the shore. Then I pulled away from Calum, who was close behind me, and threw all my strength into the remaining distance. In doing so, I abandoned my form and wound up battling awkwardly with a barrage of waves. It was a mad scramble for a reprieve, but eventually I did glide into the glassy shallows, where the rippling seaweed could be seen rising from the murk. Then my momentum carried me to the shore, until I finally gripped a rock beneath me with both hands and pushed my dripping body up through the water.

That moment when I stood up, wobbling slightly, and looked over at Calum as he clambered onto the shore, is one I'm sure I won't forget.

'We did it, like, eh,' Calum panted, affecting a broad Cumbrian accent.

Gasping for air, I laughed, threw my arms up and shook my fists. I could hear our support team clapping from the boat and I turned back towards them and spotted Robbie inching into the shallows. I knew then that we'd all beaten the currents and made it across the Saltstraumen.

Relieved, I hugged Calum and watched as Robbie stumbled to his feet and peeled the goggles back over his forehead. He was breathing hard, but his bluish face was also alive with a mixture of joy and exhaustion. Finally, we climbed up onto the shore together, fastened ourselves into a tight circle and exchanged our disbelief while James's drone wheeled slowly overhead. That was when Calum and I noticed, between fits of laughter, that Robbie was still wearing his shoes. Dumbstruck, Robbie glanced down at his feet, like a public speaker noticing they'd forgotten to put their trousers on. Then he lifted his head and a disbelieving grin spread quickly across his face. It turned out he'd been so caught up in his preparations that he'd neglected to take them off.

We could've hung out on the rocks a lot longer, laughing and catching our breath, but Knut had kept his eye on the maelstrom and he wanted everyone safely back on the boat before it gathered its force.

'We'll come to you now,' Luke called, as the boat edged closer to the rocks.

Even from where we were standing, we could see the sluggish currents being dragged under the bridge and gradually swirling together into a violent frenzy. By now the gulls, which had been sitting happily on the water, were all taking flight. I spotted them drifting away beyond the bridge in squawking flocks. I could also see more eddies forming – the very same ones that would soon suck the boat into a gradual spiral.

Spurred into action, I hurried down from the shore and dove back into the icy water. My eyes unpeeled, momentarily, before I began to kick my feet again and pull myself towards the boat. Seconds later, I resurfaced under a wall of rubber padding and grabbed Luke's hand as he leant down to meet me. One after another he pulled us up and James helped roll us onto the floor, like the most ungainly fishing haul you've ever seen. As soon as we were all on-board, James turned back to his controls and guided the bobbing drone down to Luke, who caught it with his arms outstretched. While they packed the drone into its case, Knut began to accelerate, spinning the wheel as he steered us back towards the sea. Meanwhile, the three of us sat side by side, propped up by the rubber, and watched the tall bridge receding as we pulled away.

Calum, Robbie and me, looking red-faced and knackered, after our sprint across the Saltstraumen.

We didn't speak much, yet we often smiled at each other and repeated the words 'we did it' with increasing degrees of disbelief. I was so relieved that we'd made it – not alone, mind you. The sense of accomplishment was unanimous and everyone was in high spirits. Our support team had been with us whenever we'd looked up. They'd guided us through the currents and called to us when the heart needed to kick in. I was so glad to have had them there. I gained a great deal of inspiration from their different characters and the fact they were willing to travel so far on our behalf. Luke said later that he felt responsible for us. The fact that Beth kept close contact with Mum and James and Dave provided encouragement at every turn, and assured me that they all felt the same. You should never underestimate the importance of good friends like that. I dare say nothing of any note is ever accomplished by any lone individual.

That night we opened a bottle of Scotch whisky and sat up in the conference room, watching the drone footage on the projector screen. James muted the video and played some Sigur Rós instead, which meant we could watch the crystal water and relive the short journey, while also listening to those otherworldly Icelandic strings and vocals. It's funny, I thought we hadn't met any red jellyfish during the swim, but just a few minutes into the video I could be seen cutting my gloved hand right through the middle of one, which then wrapped its tentacles around my wrist, unbeknownst to me at the time.

Later, I spoke to Calum as we walked out onto Bodø harbour to look at the stars and drink in the night air. He told me that some of the guys he'd spoken to thought the prospect of crossing these maelstroms sounded like insanity.

He said it always struck him as odd when naysayers spoke like that. To him, he explained, the daily city grind felt insane, whereas swimming maelstroms with his brothers seemed to make a lot more sense. It's difficult to explain, but these maelstrom crossings were turning out to be an extreme form of water therapy for us. They gave us a respite from the city – room to breathe and think. They also gave us time to reconsider what is important in our lives.

Looking back, I've warmed to the idea that you should tend to your mind in the same way you would tend to a garden. In the end, your soul should be peopled with friends and happy memories. For me, I always go back to the lakes and rivers I used to swim in when I was a kid. Sometimes I go back to the forests too, where we hid and ran and fought with sticks. Then I find the fields where we camped and I remember the Lake District and the piers and cliffs we jumped from. Inevitably, I'll think of the River Eden, which once cradled the village where we grew up together. When we were kids that river was our favourite playground and our first great escape route into the big, wide wild.

Get To Know Your Fears (Rob's Tip): Cold water, currents, sludgy riverbeds, defensive wildlife… There are many things that can make you think twice about swimming outdoors. You have to work on your relationship with wild water. Fear is natural. Just know that feelings of gratitude, confidence and achievement are linked in proportion with how scared you were when you started. The more you experience the post-swim high, the more you'll search for it and the less you'll be in conflict with your earlier fears.

2

Matriarchs

It was a beautiful morning and Uncle Mike's car wound slowly down the road as we followed the pebbled shores that edge Loch Broom. I remember looking over at the water and seeing the grey surface, unruffled and peaceful, with the little waves catching glints of early sunlight. On either side of us the bracken-patched Scottish Highlands rolled like sleeping giants. They had an ancient quality too – a sort of primeval wildness that is at once endearing and overpowering. Sometimes their outcrops would stand as stages for stags that roared their songs into the wilderness. The ragged slopes were also striped with scars from the recent floods and landslides. The very same ones my Grandma Wild had talked about the last time I'd spoken to her – the last time I would ever speak to her, in fact.

At that point Grandma's cataracts were so bad that her world had become an array of near-hallucinogenic visions and distorted mixtures of light and shadow. I asked her what the floods had been like. She told me how she'd heard a great roaring above the house. Then she assumed the role of ol' Mother Nature, as she often liked to do in the middle of a story. She started making fierce whooshing sounds, no doubt throwing her free hand into the air, while she sat on her stool beside the fireplace, where she always used to sit to take calls.

*Me listening to Grandma Wild tell stories about
her adventures on the* Star Clipper.

As we drove on, Grandma's house slowly came into view on the other side of the loch. It was a little white bungalow adjacent to a coppice, with steep fields below, leading down to an old boathouse. On the hill above her bungalow was Lexis, a stone house she renovated.

My mind drifted back a few days earlier to when we'd visited that house to say goodbye. Chances were, a lot of us would never go back after that last visit. Never again would we sit on the long *chaise longue* by the window, using binoculars to pick out the dog-like faces of seals bobbing in the loch. Never again would we while away our holidays in that wild bastion of peace, which was such a great wellspring of creativity.

It was strange to see the old house we'd visited since we could remember, and to take the walk up from Grandma's gate, without her rushing down to greet us. A quiet, travelling man named Alan was living there at that point. He'd taken care of Grandma in the last years of her life and kept her fire going and her wood stocked when she was unable to do so herself. They were two people who seemed to have escaped the world and found each other. Suffice it to say that they had become very close. In fact, it was Alan who was there with Grandma at the very end. He later told us how he'd walked in on that last morning and seen her staring into the fire, seeming more despondent than she'd ever been before.

After we'd seen the house we walked across the hill to look at the coppice. We found the rugged gully where the river had broken its banks and upturned huge clods of mingled earth and rock, bundling them down the hillside. We were amazed to see that the water had carved a deep swathe through the coppice, splitting the canopied war-grounds where we used to play when we were kids. Mostly we would hack at each other with sticks and invent elaborate fantasy games, inspired by table-top *Warhammer* battles. I still wander into those memories from time to time. They are reminders of the boundless imagination that we possess as kids, which is so difficult to protect and keep intact.

The three of us as youngsters, in Scotland, when our heights matched our age order.

As we walked through the coppice I kept back from the others and explored the familiar patches, under the antlered branches, where we used to stage those gruesome scenes. I remembered waking up early and putting on my coat and midge suit, imagining they were armour. I also remembered when Robbie helped us carve the bark off long, flexible branches to use as longbows.

Suddenly I noticed Calum out of the corner of my eye. He was holding a long stick like a spear and prowling through the bracken. Over a decade had passed since we'd stopped hunting each other and abandoned those *Warhammer* fantasies. Yet at once I could see that he too had drifted back to the same place as myself. We'd returned in unison to the heart of our childhood, only now there was an air of melancholy, which made the ensuing stick-fight much shorter and less vivid than the ones we remembered.

The car jolted slightly as Uncle Mike changed gear. Stirred from my memories, I watched Grandma's house as it swept out of view. Then I turned from the car window and allowed my daydream to fade. Calum was busy talking in his cool, confident manner. We both knew that soon we'd have to stand up in front of the congregation, along with Robbie, and say a few words for Grandma. He seemed to be very settled, although I was worried for him because he hadn't written anything down. I was also trying to compose myself. I could already feel the weight of what was about to happen and I knew I had to keep my head up for it.

Presently I sat in the front of the car, beside Uncle Mike, who also provided a soothing presence. He talked intermittently and told us about his first visit to Grandma's house, long before either Robbie, Calum or I were born, when there were Russian fishermen who worked all night on the loch-side. He described how he used to lie awake listening to their foreign patter and the calm rumbling of their boats.

Before long we crossed a river and turned onto a familiar road that split two fields crowded with sheep. The dreary grey church could be seen in the distance, jutting up over a tangled bramble thicket and several stone walls, close to the loch. By contrast, the sky shone pale blue and no clouds could be seen save for a few faint wisps that drifted over the hills. We approached the church down the straight road and found a gathering beyond the last cattle grid. Some of our close family members were yet to arrive, so we parked and stood in circles, talking occasionally, but mostly just listening to a young boy playing his bagpipes outside the church's pointed vestibule. All the while I kept one eye on the silver hearse, with its front wheel mounted on the grass. I could see the coffin inside and the wreath of flowers rested upon it, but it wasn't until I heard Mum's quiet sobs, muffled by a familial shoulder, that I fully accepted it was Grandma who was laid inside it.

After we filed into the church we took our pews and listened to the gentle vicar's introduction. Soon Calum and I were called up. Then we stood side by side, confronted by the sober silence of the black-clad congregation. We were wearing the Murray of Atholl tartan of our Scottish ancestors. It was Grandma herself who'd bought us those once-outlawed outfits. She'd always been immensely proud of how we took to our Scottish blood – or how it took us, I should say.

Directly in front of us there was an unused and boarded column of pews. I focused my attention on those empty places. I guess I was afraid of seeing someone I knew and suffering their reaction. I paused. The silence seemed much quieter now that it was mine to break. I glanced around the church. Our close family were seated to the left, and Grandma's local Ullapool cronies and loch-side friends were seated to the right. Both sides were crowded with people. Some of them looked familiar and others were strangers to me. Judging from the turn-out, I guessed that Ullapool must have resembled a ghost town at that moment.

'It seems fitting to me that this should be a celebration of life,' I began, holding out the words I'd written in my little black book, 'because that's what Grandma's life was . . .'

Without warning my voice suddenly cracked and disappeared. I was utterly taken by surprise and couldn't speak. A trapped wave of fear reached up my throat and my head lowered as I stared at the jumble of words – the words that would save me from silence and defeat, but also the words I couldn't say. Suddenly I felt my family shifting in their pews. I felt the weight of their eyes and their overwhelming presence, willing me to speak.

Determined to keep going, I let out a breathless sigh and rallied my senses to try again.

'It seems fitting to me,' I gasped, 'that this be a celebration of life, because that's what Grandma's life was. She stayed in the Highlands. She was exactly what she wanted to be. She was happy. She always backed my brothers and me in whatever we did. She wanted us to travel and get out into the wild unknown. Also, she wanted us to be smart and know how to argue and stand up for ourselves – just as long as we knew we'd never beat her in an argument. More than that, she never neglected to say how proud she was of us . . .'

My voice broke again, only this time I paused and took a deep breath. Then I felt Calum's hand as it dropped onto my shoulder. He held it there as I went on.

'Her three bodyguards,' I said, with force, 'linking arms with her when we walked the docks of Ullapool, or the bracken-tangled paths of her coppice. The great thing about my grandma, though, was that she didn't really need bodyguards. We were holding on to her, gripping her tough, wrinkled arms like the mast of a ship. To us she was someone who never wavered and never failed to show us that age doesn't have to mean fatigue.'

I felt the momentum of what I was saying, and now the breathless stammer was gone and the words rolled out from somewhere deep inside me. I could still feel Calum's hand on my shoulder, lightening the gravity of the moment. I could also sense the coffin behind us, dressed in flowers.

'Sometimes, often in fact, we went for a late dinner at the Morefield. Then we used to drive back afterwards, taking the road that cradled the ruffled loch – keeping an eye out for deer, or winding the windows down, slowing the car and quieting the engine to hear the stags roar. At times like that my grandma often yawned, her head rested against the window. And whenever I asked if she was tired she always replied, with an unfailing smile, "not tired – just satisfied".'

Again I breathed the air into my lungs and reached into the pit of my gut for that last gust of wind.

'Engraved on the beam that hangs in Lexis is the mantra: "Rest and be Thankful",' I said. 'True rest is achieved at the end of a life that has been well lived, for what is there to be thankful for, if you never gave it your best? From what I saw, my grandma's life was a ride that peaked and swerved, and she held on, despite adversity, and let the winds hammer her soul, but never leave it misshapen. And when the cart finally shuddered to a halt, I could imagine her drawing in that rare breath of satisfaction, such as only the wildest feel – and having the liberty of looking back on a family that love and will cherish her.'

After I'd spoken, Calum wiped the tears from his eyes and

stepped up beside me. He spoke with the unfailing strength of a good and honest man. What's even more impressive is that he managed to tell a funny story after what was quite possibly the worst set-up in history. Keeping his composure, he recalled how Grandma had taken both oars and rowed her boat out onto the loch when he and Luke went fishing. Even though they'd offered to help, stoic old Grandma kept insisting that she could handle it, which later instilled a very rare sentiment in Luke that he called: *Grandma envy*.

Later that night, after the wake, we gathered at our campsite and drank by the loch-side. I remember I'd just filled the dog's bowl with water and placed it on the lowest step of our campervan. Then I looked up and saw the silhouetted figures of my family, framed by the moonlit surface of the loch. Earlier that day I'd been thinking about a church I'd been in that used the 'God is Love' slogan to adorn the pulpit. Now I was reminded of the prayers we'd said at the funeral and how, when I'd heard mention of God, or the word 'Lord', I'd recoiled and pulled back from the moment. Yet there I stood, staring at the members of my family, and suddenly I was hit by a passing thought: what if the word 'Lord' was changed to 'Love'?

With a slight smile, I closed the campervan door and walked towards the shadowed figures, leaning side by side against the fence.

When I look back at the people who've inspired me, I usually see Grandma and I *always* see Mum. To my memory, Mum never made a point of trying to teach us any lessons. She never jerked us to one side and stooped to tell us that what we were doing was *wrong*. I guess she didn't want us to act in an approved way, or to present ourselves in accordance with some prude-elected version of propriety. That isn't to say, though, she didn't teach us anything, nor that she was soft in any way – it's just that the lessons she had for us were always kept close to her heart. In fact, they were almost undisclosed, hidden in the way she talked and lived day by day, in a perpetual struggle to re-wild herself and, in doing so, to escape the mundane particulars of the everyday. She would often make these microcosm gardens crowded with towering plant-life. She'd build huge vegetable patches and revel in the unearthing of rude potatoes. She'd carry twigs and leaves in her unbrushed Medusa coils. She'd train dogs, cats, and always used to rush out to save the prey they caught. To me, all her subversive, wonderful weirdness was evidence that it's okay to be yourself, instead of hiding in the comfort of a crowd.

After my mum I often think of my brothers, Robbie and Calum. The three of us were good friends growing up, separated by just a couple of years on either side. Calum was the central antagonist and self-confessed sufferer of middle-child syndrome. He used to push me around a bit, while also keeping Robbie on his toes, as head of our little trinity. Out of all the adventures we had together, I always remember the ones that involved water. One of our favourite summer pastimes involved us forming a ragtag band and exploring coastlines, feeding limpets to the crabs we found in still rock pools, rescuing splayed jellyfish and seeking out chilled, secluded swimming spots, cradled by the overhanging crags. When we moved to the Lake District we couldn't believe our luck. Suddenly the doors were flung open to the sprawling playground of the natural world. There were these huge bodies of water on our doorstep, like little, contained oceans, and rivers too, cascading secretly through the forests. Soon, wild swimming became more and more accessible. You didn't have to worry about being swept out by the tide or snatched from below by the shark from *Jaws*. Also, there was something quite irresistible about swimming in cold open water – a fresh dip was the perfect way to work up an appetite for a barbecue or to celebrate midnight in your campsite.

Those childhood memories often surface in my mind and when they do I'm always surprised by how clear they seem. I can still see myself and this old mate, James, floating down the Eden rapids on a hunk of wood we found. No matter how long it's been, that memory still remains vivid. I can also watch Sandy as he plummets from Kirkoswald cliff into a small plunge pool and I can see Watson bombing across a furrowed field on his new quadbike. That feeling of being out in open space, among the trees, or under the beating sun, is one that stays with you. You get withdrawal symptoms if you neglect it for too long. It's an itch you've got to scratch – an addiction lodged deep among the roots of your unconscious, where it won't be ignored.

In her book, *The Mindful Art of Wild Swimming*, Tessa Wardley refers to an interesting brain phenomenon called *synaptic pruning*. She explains how, occasionally, the brain engages in a kind of spring-clean, whereby information is removed to make room for new experiences. Supposedly this happens most extensively at three key points in our lives: during our time as toddlers, our adolescence, and our late forties and early fifties. At these different key stages of development our brains light up, hungry for new experiences, which is manifest in bouts of emotional instability and radical decision making. When we're young, our brains overproduce the synapses connecting our brain cells. During puberty the threads of these myriad synapses start to be cut, allowing others to strengthen in turn. Then, over the next few years, the number of synapses is continuously cut, until eventually the adult brain emerges. This kind of synaptic pruning occurs in many different mammals and ends at the point of sexual maturation, when the brain is fully formed and has relinquished all the weakest neural connections.

I thought this discovery had wonderful implications – the idea that our brain disposes of unwanted memories in order to gain greater clarity and strength in other areas. Perhaps it is true, after all, that we carry some experiences with us, unaltered, and they remain strong and clear and can light the way through the uncertain caverns of our futures.

When I look back, I realise that growing up close to nature also helped to stoke our creative aspirations. In short, we made things when we were happy and to us nature was pretty much synonymous with happiness. It's a realisation that reminds me of something Leo Tolstoy once wrote: 'if you want to be happy, be'. I think, essentially, Tolstoy was referring to the value of mindfulness, which is a discipline that necessitates the space and stillness of the natural world. After all, there is a reason why Buddhist temples are hidden on mountains, close to forests, rivers and plunge pools. The silence of an open mind is found in such company and therein lies the simplicity of being – the raw feeling of riding an impartial current. When nature washes over you, you also begin to feel the diversity of life and the relative insignificance of our own species. You feel that you are part of something much larger than yourself, which allows you to cut the bindings of the ego, even just for a moment. That's what playing is. That's how intimacy is created. When you're in the wild you're forced to play the game of survival. You can't opt out or fall into an existential funk. Even if you're suspended in soberness the system continues without you – a system that has often been disrupted by the arrogance of glorified Man. Just think of all the myriad species we've wiped out. In our bloodlust and our greed, we have seen to that. Rather than continuing to make these mistakes, perhaps it might be time to find a less resistant place in our little kingdom – to seek stillness in the forests, hills and all the other natural monasteries waiting within our reach.

Growing up, there was never any doubt in my mind that I wanted to create things. At school I used to doodle obsessively and write stories featuring recurring characters, namely gnarled old men who imparted wisdom, and orphans too, which I should probably thank Roald Dahl for. It was the kind of stuff you'd expect from a kid with vague creative dreams, like maybe being a writer one day . . . or a filmmaker. Before long we got our first taste of the establishment when the brass tried to ban the game of Tig. I guess that was when health and safety was starting to become all the rage, propelled, no doubt, by a few hypochondriac parents who coddled their kids like Ming vases. At our school that Tig-ban went down like the prohibition. We kept chasing each other and bending the rules as much as we could. We'd attract the teachers' attention with flamboyant displays and make a point of never actually tigging each other, being the little smart-arses we were. I also remember there was a forest close to the tennis courts where we were taken to play football every lunch. It was a short distance from our playing boundaries. Sometimes a stressed kid would make a dash for freedom and spend several minutes living like a feral Mowgli, before a teacher had to go in among the trees and drag them out.

A decade or so later, I'd become what you might call an adult, disconnected from everything that once made me feel wild and happy. One day, I was sitting at work writing some e-commerce blog about jewellery that no one would ever read. I remember leaning back in my chair and turning towards the window. In our office, we had these criss-crossing bars over the glass, supposedly to keep burglars out, although the more I looked at them the more I thought of those multi-storey sweatshops in China – the ones where they fix nets under the windows to stop workers from committing suicide? I was being overly dramatic, I know, but it was a particularly morbid experience to peer through those bars and stare across the car park, past the rows of company cars all crammed together in their usual spots. On the other side of the asphalt there was another office surveyed by several white security cameras. Usually I'd look up at the face of this building and drag my eyes over the dim windows. I'd see square ceiling lights shining faintly from the inside. If I squinted I'd also make out stacks of folders next to oversized grey printers and bloated filing cabinets that some poor sap had taken the time to fill up. Finally, I'd see the dimly lit figures, hemmed in among the sharp right angles and papery clutter.

You know the first thought that usually came to my head, when I looked at this scene?

This is shit.

That small suffrage was fuel I used to get back to the Eden and seek out the former thrills of my childhood. The dreary memory still tugs at a part of me that feels each passing day. It's a friendly reminder that life is ending one second at a time. Not only that, but as it disappears so too does the greatest opportunity any of us are ever given, which is the opportunity to *live*. Mum was always a fierce advocate of us breaking loose and fanning the embers of our past. That's partly why she was so thrilled when we told her about our plan to swim the River Eden.

You see, fortune had it that while I was wrestling with blogs in Newcastle, my brothers were similarly dissatisfied and looking for adventure. Separately, we'd all arrived at a meeting point in our lives when each of us wanted to escape – if only for nine days. There was also the advantage of it being a reunion of sorts. Everyone seemed to be going their separate ways. The time had come for us to sell the family home in Langwathby. Mum and our long-term friend and guardian, Iain, were separating. We were about to lose the steep bank that dropped down to our shallow little bend of the River

Eden. Meanwhile, Calum was selling tech software in Conrad's *Heart of Darkness* and Robbie was working remotely in Berlin. Discomfort be damned! We were fast becoming the coffee-swigging, buckled-down champions of working life. And yet, something in us had decided to resist the change. Gradually, I began to realise that many things would never be the same again and that, from now on, any time we spent together would be much more valuable.

It was during this period that Calum came to us with an idea – or, I should say, he came to me and said that he and Robbie were planning something. He told me they wanted to swim down the full 145 kilometres of the River Eden. I was understandably excited. I think 'That's awesome' were my exact words. Then he asked me to be a support kayaker. Suddenly I had an image of two brothers slicing through the choppy water, their gasping breaths sounding together as they sucked the air hard into their lungs. I saw their shoulders rolling in time when they ducked back under, their jaws clenching and muscles aching, with nothing but green water in sight. Then, all at once, I saw them creeping around the bend for that final 100-metre stretch.

They've made it this far, the onlookers would be thinking, *they've only gone and done it!*

Then – *wait, who's that?*

A slightly pot-bellied, lanky fella on a kayak comes sliding into view. He turns his paddle lazily and eases onto the current. He looks tired.

'That's the other brother,' someone says. 'The youngest one.'

To his credit, Calum asked me, albeit quite half-heartedly,

if I wanted to do the swim as well. I guess he was thinking what I was thinking at the time, which was that I certainly wasn't up to it. I mean, he was fresh from an Iron Man, still in shape and drilled into the right mind-set. Meanwhile, Robbie had recently swum Lake Ullswater and, being the eldest, had always been very proud and inclined to approach physical stress with the same attitude Joe Frazier had in boxing. You know: he'd just keep moving forward – inexorable is the right word for that, I think.

And then there was me . . .

Now, I could do with the cold weather and harsh conditions. I lived in Newcastle for God's sake. My nearest beach was roamed by muscular seagulls that'd do you in for a strip of greasy cod batter. It was hardly idyllic. Big freighters lined the offing and the wild, grey ocean was cold enough to get a gasp from Lewis Pugh, UN Patron of the Oceans. The cold wasn't the problem. The problem was that I was physically unfit, and in case you're expecting some miraculous *Rocky* turnaround, I'm still quite unfit. The only thing that gave me any confidence whatsoever was the fact that my brothers were going through with it. The two people I know best – the exemplary guides who've always been there to provide inspiration and foil my wordy flourishes.

Needless to say, I decided I wasn't going to be the only brother kayaking. The first step, before training started, involved looking at the maps of our old country haunts. We were surprised to find that so much of the River Eden was unknown to us. In fact, together we'd only covered a tiny fraction of its full flow. This meant we had a lot of exciting new ground to cover. Our journey would lead us for ninety miles across the wide, rolling river basin known as the Eden Valley. This valley stretches all the way from the feet of the Pennines to the roving slopes of the Lake District fells. Once the medieval staging ground for the raids of the border reivers, the scenery is still scarred from old battlefields and scattered with sites of historical interest, including the ruins of well-kept pele towers and castles. No one could deny that it's a meaty slice of English countryside, swathed in green ribbons of forests, fields and hillocks. In our opinion, there's no better way to enjoy it than by using the river networks that weave in secret among the hills, passing · through wheat fields, overgrown nettle thickets and tall forests. There are many different waterways you can follow, but one is perhaps more famous and better loved than the others. It runs like a main artery connected to the heart of the Eden Valley and it is called the River Eden.

In its infancy the Eden bubbles up from peaty bogs and tumbles down the gorges of Black Fell Moss. It leaves the rugged high ground to snake thinly along the forested boundary between Cumbria and North Yorkshire. Then the river plummets down the steep dale of Mallerstang and arcs and bends and opens into the green Vale of Eden. For several miles the waters run among sandstone cliffs, farmed fields and little forests. Suddenly villages and parishes appear and the town of Appleby jumps out from the widening banks. All the while the Eden is filled by brooks and rivers, carrying the cold runoff from the Pennines and the western lakes. Finally, it passes through the city of Carlisle and stretches out over the squelching tidal flats of England's eastern coast, where it joins the River Esk and enters the Solway Firth.

Once we knew exactly where we were going, we wrote out our routines and started training. There were a few milestones I remember from that period, starting with the first time I swam a mile. Walking back afterwards, I posted a selfie with puffy chlorine-eyes and added the caption: 'just swam my first mile, if I can do that nine times a day for nine days I'll be laughing . . . until then better keep a straight face'.

After that, the next few months were churned into a watery blur as I increased my distances, bouncing up and down the little, dimly lit indoor pool that was close to my house in Newcastle. It was a slow start. That pool was less than twenty metres long and it took me over a hundred lengths to make up the mile, during which time I continually lost count of how far I'd travelled. When it came to the winter season, Robbie, Calum and I all took a special trip to the Olympic Pool in London. It was the first time I'd swum long distances out of my depth. It was also a chance to compare our techniques and work on our rhythms together. Calum told me to keep my eyes ahead of me, just under the surface of the water, and to extend my strokes more. I started to watch my hands as they reached out, stretching my fingers and straining my deltoid muscles to ensure I was reaching far enough.

The following year, when I got back to my pool in Newcastle, I started to focus more on developing my crawl technique. Over time, the awkward, muddled distraction of my flailing feet began to fade and kicking became an almost unconscious aspect of each swim. I started to move more smoothly through the water, my feet paddling gently as I focused on the strength and shape of my strokes, feeling the sharp tug in my latissimus dorsi and triceps as I scooped back handfuls of water. I found that the more time I spent in the pool the easier it became to get lost in the activity of swimming. Mind you, the first fifteen lengths or so were always a drag. My head would be filled with thoughts and I'd keep mistiming my breaths as I tried to find the rhythm. Every now and then I'd think about stopping and calling it a half-day. I'd wonder what time it was or what I was going to eat after I left the water. These were recurring disruptions that I quickly learnt to ignore. I knew that I couldn't cut corners or cheat myself. Every individual swim was a small battle. I had to keep digging in until I broke through that bubbling wall, after which the strain faded and the leaden, lazy thoughts all disappeared. I found that this was the key to improving my endurance. I just had to keep getting through those walls and reaching a relaxed and quiet place inside myself.

Out of the water I developed a semi-regular routine of body-weight exercises. I used different variations of press-ups to develop my upper body strength. My favourite involved holding my hands in a triangular position and dropping until my nose dipped between my fingers. This was great for shoulder strength and I think over time it had some pay-off in the pool as well. I also went out on short runs in the wooded dene, ending with a hill-sprint to improve my aerobic fitness. The only thing I didn't get on-board with was the idea of cold showers. We had to acclimatise ourselves to being in the river for prolonged periods of time, but I just couldn't bring myself to give up those steamy showers. I'd rather end the swim floating inside a giant ice cube. Luckily, I was also gaining a layer of doughy blubber, which would later prove invaluable.

As the swim neared, I started heading out with Beth to visit the local coasts, lakes and rivers. I'd only swum out in open water a handful of times and I was dealing with pangs of Deep Water Fear. I decided to take it slow and ease into it. I distinctly remember the first proper wild swim I tried. We drove to a cove in Tynemouth, just behind an outcrop that conceals the far-reaching curve of Longsands beach as it tapers northwards, towards the lighthouse. The water there was shallow and calm. I knew I'd be able to stand up at any point, so I decided to keep close to the beach, swimming lengths from one side of the cove to the other. I was nervous about being alone with the unknown currents. There have been a couple of times in my life when I've gone out too far while surfing and I've felt the rip tide pulling me out and had to swim back hard against it. I'd never forgotten the feeling of panic as you're dragged out by that uncontrollable force – more powerful than anything you've experienced before.

I kept going back and slowly inching further out, until I could no longer see the white sand beneath my fingers. Then we took a trip way out to an inland lake called Broomlee Lough in the serene Northumberland countryside. We had to take a short walk over the hills and down onto a patch of squelching marshland, although we were soon rewarded with a view over this long, uncovered stretch of water, overlooked by one of the crag-mounted forts of Hadrian's Wall. Then I was paddling out from among the reeds and making my way into the middle of the lake. I spent several minutes just floating, kicking and turning as I tried to get used to the feeling of being alone with the murky depths, without any aid and without any nerves.

Another time, Beth and I went out and found the Low Force waterfalls in the leafy Tees Valley. Upriver there was this series of steep cascades where several brave kayakers were taking turns bombing over the falls. We decided to find a secluded, shaded patch further downriver, where I went in without a wetsuit and learnt to relax and slow my breathing as the cold wrapped around my pale, pimpled body. It was a feeling I knew from a childhood spent leaping into rivers and sprinting into lakes and seas. Still, it was one that shocked me into taking the cold water more seriously.

On the way home we were driving down this rough country lane when Beth had to veer down a side track to make way for a tractor. In a few seconds we wound up stuck in a muddy trough, at which point the farmer kindly leapt out of his tractor and rushed back to help us. Clutching the towel round my waist, I hopped out of the car and stumbled up to greet him.

'Not really dressed for this,' I mumbled. Then, together, we pushed the bumper with all our might and trudged uphill, while Beth reversed, pounding us with tyre-pummelled clumps of mud.

While I was getting into the swing of things, helping farmers to move cars, my brothers started to accelerate ahead of me. From what I'd heard they were both training more regularly and spending more hours in the water. Mind you, trailing in the wake of my brothers was something I'd grown used to. Being the youngest means doing everything last and it's hard not be influenced by the examples set by those before you. I mean, I've certainly been changed by the stories they've told me or advised me to read. I've also absorbed something of their tastes in music and film. So I didn't really mind having to dig in to catch up with them – that was partly what I'd wanted from the Eden swim in the first place.

Another important source of motivation was the idea of going back to revisit our childhood. It was something we all felt we needed. I guess the idyll of home had wilted slightly, in our minds. We were also growing increasingly aware of the time we'd spent apart. To me, it felt like there was something to reclaim – something we'd had when we were kids, but had since forgotten about. Perhaps it was an urge to play and spend some time together. Maybe we just selfishly wanted to reap the rewards of having siblings. After all, close, lifelong company is a valuable blessing. It's also good to know you've shared your formative years with others, and that they, like you, have been shaped by all those little absurdities that pave the road to adulthood. Out of the folk I've spoken to, almost everyone, without exception, is thankful for their siblings. They might feign disinterest or even contempt, like they wish the womb had been sealed off after their exit, but mostly I think that's just a safeguard – a guise designed to replace any mawkish displays of affection, which might lessen the other-wise grounding influence of a familial connection. In my mind, when all the fighting and competition subsides, and when all is said and done, you know that you inevitably need each other.

The last time we left our childhood cottage it was Beth and me in the car together. We were driving over the Pennines behind Langwathby. Sometimes you'd see those hills smoking as the fierce mists of the helm wind rolled like a waterfall over their spines. That day we were following the snaking Hartside road, chasing a group of Country Angels on their guttural low-seated bikes. Then we came to the point, beyond the hilltop café, where the whole of the Eden Valley was laid out far and wide behind us, like a verdant patchwork quilt. A moment later, the whole vista disappeared, but not before I stole one last look through the rear-view mirror and felt a sudden heaviness inside me.

I think I'll always remember the open fire in that house and the black piling stove, beside which I used to lie after hard rugby games or long days at school. I also remember the day when we first went to see the house – how Calum came up with this impromptu song about the fact we had two toilets and danced around the place. Another time, he couldn't make the house viewing because Mum was forcing him to finish a bowl of Linda McCartney's veggie mince, which he hated.

I have a lot of odd moments like that appearing in my inward eye, but the thing I remember most clearly, because we were so excited about it, was the river that ran past the bottom of our garden. We just couldn't wait to get into it. The cold didn't faze us, nor did the depth or the slight current.

We wanted to fight and play in our ever-changing patch of the Eden.

Now, within this ebb of sweet silence, I see all those little adventures spent riding broken trees down the river or finding lopsided stacks to jump off. It's funny, the relationship you can have with something insensate and utterly oblivious to your presence. We'd kayaked down the Eden's rapids, learnt its bends and yawped in the echoing arches of those tall railway bridges. In hindsight, the river had provided me with some of the happiest moments I've had – something my brothers and I will always have in common. We had all whiled away summer afternoons cycling shirtless to our swimming spots, pedalling until the sweat was crawling down our backs, and then, once there, diving in and floating, carried by the ripples, thoughtless and entirely at peace.

We all loved that river.

Trust Your Body (Rob's Tip): Deep-water fear is a very natural reaction both physiologically and psychologically. It exists to help your body cope with the water. Cortisol and adrenaline are released and this causes your heart rate to elevate. Then, more oxygen is being transported to your muscles and used, alongside glucose, to produce adenosine triphosphate (ATP). This provides your body with more energy. Your central nervous system is also stimulated and, together, these physiological reactions supply you with the means to overcome adversity. So those butterflies in your stomach are simply the result of these hormonal changes. Whether you like it or not, nerves and fear exist, but you can use them to enhance a swim. You just need to accept and understand that these are reminders that your body is reacting to help you.

3

Corryvreckan

Corryvreckan Expedition
Saturday 1 August 2015

- *Point-to-point 1.5-kilometre swim.*
- *Swim together in a staggered formation with Calum leading the way and Robbie and Jack on either side. The swim is abandoned if anyone has to leave the water.*
- *Sea captain Duncan will judge the weather and make the final decision as to whether or not we enter the water.*
- *Minimum swimming speed: 35 minutes.*

Before we swam the Eden, there was a single word we used as inspiration for our training. For me it was a word that evoked a wilder and more ancient Britain – the Britain that cartographers drew in the early sixteenth century, when the coastlines were wrapped in inky seas populated by writhing leviathans and Hebridean sirens. It was also a word preserved in Viking legends, one that drew the mind to the west coast of Argyll, where a collision of tidal pathways intersects and

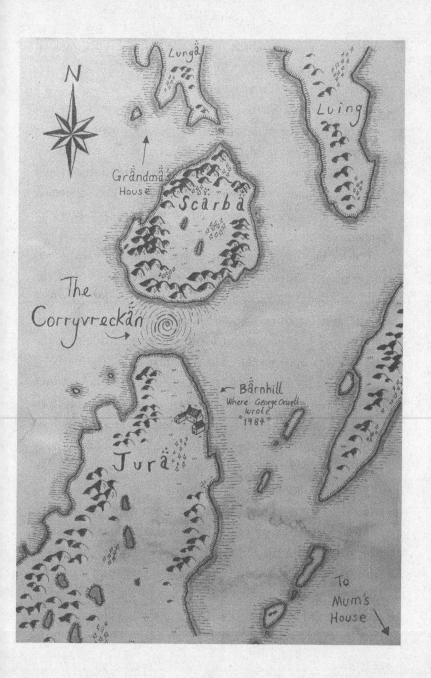

sends manic waves to smash against the jagged, limpet-studded rocks that edge the Isle of Jura . . .

That word was *Corryvreckan*.

Locals say that for ten miles in every direction you can hear the gurgling roar of this monstrous phenomenon – Corryvreckan, the third-largest maelstrom in the world. We'd heard that it possessed such currents and whirlpools as could tear boats asunder and enrage the Sound of Jura, churning and swirling the froth-speckled water over a 200-metre pinnacle of undersea rock.

Calum had already told us several stories to inflame our imaginations. One involved a Norse king, Coire Bhreachain, who attempted to show his mettle by anchoring his galley in the gulf for three days and nights. Oddly, he used three different anchor lines, one made of wool, one made of hemp and one made of virgins' hair. The first two lines broke as the waves jostled the galley, but the virgins' hair held strong, until the very last hour of the final night. Eventually torn loose, the ship was quickly dragged into the gurgling whirl-pool and Bhreachain disappeared with it, until his lifeless body was later hauled ashore by his dog.

There was another reason Calum came up with the idea to swim the Corryvreckan, uniting our training for the first time in a year, to prepare us for the Eden. It had to do with a young man named Eric Blair who, in 1947, was riding a motorboat with his sister, niece and nephews, when they strayed into the fierce, amorphous clutches of the maelstrom. Soon the outboard motor was wrenched off the boat and the whole family was thrown into disarray. It was Blair's nephew Henry Dakin, a young army officer, who seized the oars and defiantly rowed them out of the raging currents. However, the tides eventually got the better of them and they capsized close to a smattering of little islands dotted across the gulf. As the boat overturned, Richard disappeared beneath it and had to be dragged out by Eric, who then led the group onto the serrated shelving of a nearby island. Supposedly they were stranded there, cold, exhausted and half drowned, until a passing fishing boat finally caught sight of them and came to their rescue a few hours later.

Shortly after this near-death escape, Eric returned to the Isle of Jura, and it was on this far-flung, stormy refuge that he wrote arguably his most incisive work. Today, Eric is known around the world as George Orwell, and the book he wrote on Jura, titled *Nineteen Eighty-Four*, is now regarded as his masterwork. When I read it at school I found that the story got under my skin and entered my bloodstream. Working through that final page I felt like I was slowly starting to drown. The hopelessness. Big Brother's total victory. It was a feeling that scared and angered me. In fact, it was the same one I was fighting as we drove across Scotland, towards the coast and the source of Orwell's greatest work.

We read and talked a lot on the way through Scotland, towards the Corryvreckan. Occasionally I wielded a GoPro out of the window, blasted by the wind, while Calum barked at me, desperate to preserve the battery. The further we travelled, the narrower the roads became, winding and carrying us through the hills like tarmac snakes. All the while the bracken-swathed landscape rolled around us, shrouded in the mist that stroked the valleys. Then lochs started to appear through breaks in the paling trees and all the while the scenery seemed to grow more and more familiar. Coupled with the fact that we'd been apart for so long, it made us all strangely nostalgic. Mum began to talk about Robbie being a cartoonist at a very young age. She recalled how he'd wound up in the papers for his witty and often satirical drawings. I remembered that some of the panels were parodies of celebrated historical events, like the 'War of the Noses', which had two men jousting with lance-like honkers, and the 'Battle of Hammock-burn', which depicted, unsurprisingly, a man setting a hammock on fire.

Just then Calum chimed in from the back of the car. 'Small Human Beaver Manages To Hold Pencils,' he joked, referring to the oversized denchers Robbie sported at that age.

Later, Calum told us how some of the folk in his London office had asked him how you went about wild swimming, as if it were some outlandish fad they couldn't comprehend. He simply told them, with as little irony as possible: 'You find a body of water, outside, and go swimming.'

The thing I've found through talking to different folk is that they either seem to be on-board straight away, ready to follow you over waterfalls and into the churned rapids, or, in the other corner, they just seem entirely unmoved by the idea, as though nothing short of uncontrollable misfortune would ever get them out into wild waters. For me, wild swimming is simply a way of getting my hands dirty and digging up the cold, gnarled root of this sport we call swimming. I love the fact it delivers you to the rough palm of the natural world. For a while it *does* feel primal and the sense of freedom that this instils in you is very addictive. The best example I can think of to illustrate this point is a story Calum told me about his extreme Celtman triathlon.

The Celtman event takes place annually in the Highlands of Scotland, close to where our Grandma Wild lived. It involves a gut-wrenching 3.8-kilometre loch swim, 202-kilometre bike ride and a 42-kilometre mountain run across the rugged spine of Ben Eighe. When I spoke to him afterwards, Calum said that it rushed him right back to the bed of his childhood – a time when he used to run through Grandma's tangled coppice, wielding a big stick, hacking at dead branches and pretending to be a Celtic warrior. He described the morning when all the competitors arrived at the loch-side, before the sun had risen, and walked down over the dew-soaked grass in a big clump of neoprene, some chattering excitedly and others sealed in silence. He said that the sea loch was laid out ahead of them, ringed by mountains and eerily lit by fire torches and flaming pyres that were scattered along the pebbled beach. Piercing the quiet, cold calm, the mountain music of Celtic bagpipers and drummers standing by in their kilts reached his ears. The deep drums pounded, the nasal-sounding pipes soared and a Celtic symbol glowed in flames in the distance, wreathed in smoke.

I immediately understood how Calum felt when he described that scene. There's nothing quite like escaping the safe and organised modern realm and plunging back into a world of magic and natural wonder.

While it might seem like a cultish ritual to some, to others wild swimming has become a way of life. Recently Calum had been on TV in London talking about how we were in the grips of a *wild swimming revolution*. It certainly felt to me that this was true. The deeper we dove into this current the more we became aware of a widespread community of British wild swimmers. Then we made contact with Kate Rew, founder of the Outdoor Swimming Society, who helped to draw attention to our Swim the Eden charity, the Swimming Trust, which is devoted to getting swim teachers for kids who otherwise couldn't have afforded them. She'd spoken to Calum on multiple occasions, telling him that she really liked what we were doing. Support like that really helped us and we were very grateful that likeminded folk were interested in our adventure. Also, we had just been backed by Speedo (which later became Alpkit when we attempted our icy Norwegian swims) and were travelling with our brand-new, matching wetsuits. This followed sponsorship from Ascendancy Apparel, Buff, High 5 and a whole host of other major swim brands that supplied everything we needed, from woollen headgear to chewy caramel sports bars. Throughout that period of promotion, Calum had been a force of nature, and I was thankful for the perks and publicity, although I didn't really let on that much.

Around midday we arrived at Craobh Haven, a secluded, mist-soaked marina where Calum had arranged for us to meet our captain. We rolled into the car park early and decided to while away an hour or so at the old pub, which overlooked rows of white boats rocking in their berths, and which was rather grandly named The Lord of the Isles.

Growing nervous, we sat on the terrace outside and nursed our pints. I remember Mum began talking about how her threatened teaching position was, in her words, hidden at the end of a twig. A half-drink or so later she moved on to our other grandma (Dad's mum), who'd once sailed from Palestine to England. I'd heard that she'd also helped to run a sailing school in the Caribbean and was very familiar with the far-out wrath of the deep Atlantic. Fixing us with her kind, steady eyes, Mum described how Grandma Martin often used to stay at relaxed yacht marinas, just like the one stretched out in front of us. She told us how they'd occasionally encounter rich yuppies who waxed lyrical about their various noble adventures.

'Yah, yah,' they used to say. 'I've crossed the Channel five times. We're planning our sixth next year if we can find the time.'

One by one they'd all tell their stories with the same affected air of grandeur, like they were each of them a veritable Ulysses carved by the elements. Then, eventually, they'd turn to Grandma, this little old, unassuming lady with bouffant white hair, and they'd ask her condescendingly whether she'd ever sailed before. To which our grandma would have to reply, in her quiet, polite voice: 'Well, yes, I've crossed the Atlantic three times.'

Damn straight, Grandma.

She didn't talk about her adventures too much. In fact, I can only remember a single instance in which she revealed the magnitude of what she'd done. It's another one of those clear memories. We were sitting at the kitchen table and she was holding her second cup of tea while my auntie and dad washed plates and cutlery and chatted out of earshot.

'It was good that we did that,' she'd said, concluding our conversation.

I remember how her eyes lifted above my shoulder, towards the large map tacked to the wall behind me. In awe, I watched her, repeating those words in my mind – *it was good that we did that.*

Of course, it was good. Imagine if they'd never set sail; what kind of conversation would we've been having? What if she'd stayed in that cosy country house she had, surrounded by friendly animals? What if she'd held her little nugget of retirement with quiet resignation? Well, she would've had her tall hedges and her enclosed garden and her neatly ranked vegetables and latticed windows that beguiled dozy bees. She would've had her marriage and her work and year-round security and *blah, blah, blah* . . . Yet at the same time the unattended longing would've eventually been extinguished. With it her wildness would've faded too. She would've been tamer, my grandma, and happy, perhaps, but these wouldn't just be hypotheticals that I've spouted – they'd be the little realities that subdued her spirit.

In front of us the marina hummed with the murmuring of local sailors, backed by the caw of the gulls that wheeled overhead. When our drinks were empty, we walked together across the gravel car park, holding our wetsuits slung over our shoulders, with our swim caps stuffed in our coat pockets. Mum followed close behind with our excited spaniel, Marlin, pulling on her lead. Our captain, Duncan, greeted us on the grass verge above the harbour. At once he struck me as a maritime veteran – the kind of stoic sea-hand for whom pleasantries are an afterthought, since he only remembered to give us his name after he'd discussed the weather conditions.

Above us the sky seemed calm, reflecting the slow movement of the water, which was ruffled by gentle, lapping waves,
caught amid the dreary doldrums. Eager to make good time,
Duncan soon walked us down onto the jetty and led us to
where his little boat bobbed in one of the outermost berths.
Once there, we immediately stepped on-board and collected
our kit together. Then the clouds began to clear as the engine
rumbled and spluttered in the water, causing the deck to
tremble underfoot. Next, Duncan untied the thick rope from
the moorings and the boat jolted slightly as we pulled away.
Immediately the jolt tested Marlin's sea legs and her big paws
parted as she strained to stay upright.

A moment later we were watching the marina recede into
the distance as we weaved out onto the ocean, through scattered
huddles of green islands. Sunlight came streaming through the
breaking cloud. The rays warmed our faces, caught the waves
and dazzled us. Then, suddenly, we were hurtling and leaping
over the ocean, headed for the distant gulf between the Isle of
Jura and the Isle of Scarba. The steady drumming of the engine
drowned out any attempts we made at conversation. Eventually
we retreated into our thoughts. I rested slumped over the side
of the boat and watched the Lost World islands sliding by, with
the sprayed mist gently whipping my cheek.

We made good time and arrived early at the maelstrom
while the tides were still thrashing together and creating peaks
and troughs that toyed with our little vessel as though it were
a fisherman's float. In fact, Duncan repeatedly expressed his
disappointment at how big the swells were. I began to think
about the night before – how we'd cooked a foil-wrapped

sea trout on the bonfire. Calum joked that it was an offering to appease Poseidon. Apparently, the gesture had fallen into an abyss though, since the maelstrom was still raging, spinning whorls of froth and bending the horizon.

For some time, we waited for the slack tide and used Duncan's binoculars to spot seals and scan the gulf between the two islands. It was about the same distance I'd swum across Lake Montriond in France a week or so earlier. The only difference, really, was the temperature of the water and the fact it was being whirled around in a gurgling frenzy, as if controlled by an unstoppable washing machine.

Soon Duncan served us steaming cups of tea and we drank slowly, our eyes flitting onto the point where we'd begin our sprint – a distant, jagged outcrop on the furthest island.

'Thirty-five minutes in the water,' folk had said. After that the whirlpool starts to gather its strength again, whipping the water into a frenzy. Other concerns seemed to pale in significance. I asked if we were likely to encounter any basking sharks. Unfortunately, Duncan told me that the local phytoplankton (an ocean buffet feeding everything from zooplankton to whales) had all but disappeared. He speculated that this had something to do with – among other things caused by our blundering species – the rise in sea surface temperature. It's another one of those curious and abrupt phenomena that seem to foreshadow something grave in our future.

To allow us to see the whirlpool in full swing, and to also reach the starting point, Duncan slowly steered the boat out into the heart of the crossing tides. The wind was strafing over the choppy water and shaving mist off the crests of the waves. We knew it was less than a mile between the two Hebridean islands. The difficulty wasn't the distance, though; it was the unique tidal currents, which were strong enough to send us all off on wandering courses, like drunks stumbling home after a lock-in.

Robbie, Calum and I stood together facing the open sea and holding the railing. I could see them both gritting their teeth, twisting their faces and saying 'yes' repeatedly, like they just couldn't wait to throw themselves in. I was slightly more reticent, releasing quivering bursts of laughter as they turned to me with wide grins and eyes that bulged with adrenaline.

By the time we reached the opposite shore the tides had calmed and the boat swayed as little waves clapped against the bow. My eyes darted to the black, froth-speckled ocean. Then the engine stopped and we collected our wetsuits, swim caps and goggles. Suddenly the boat was gripped by a pensive silence. Without speaking, we each pulled off warm clothes and struggled into the wetsuits and caps. Once the Speedo armour was on, we danced on our toes a little, stretched our shoulders and receded into our silent preparations.

It wasn't long before Duncan gave us the signal and gestured to the ladder. Then Mum gripped my cheeks between her hands and beamed at me.

'I have absolutely no doubt that you can do this,' she said.

Her outright belief struck me and shot through my body like a bolt of lightning. Reassured, I stepped up onto the back of the boat and planted my foot on the top rung of the ladder. Robbie followed close behind me, while Calum was at the back, shooing us into the water. I must confess to a moment's hesitation, in which I looked over at the rugged, black escarpment, ending in blades of fissured rock, before I leapt out and plunged into that dark and icy world. Dropping through a greenish blur of coiling bubbles, my first thoughts belonged to the cold salt water. Then, bursting through the surface, I sucked the air deep into my lungs and rolled over onto my back to regain my senses. When I felt comfortable I began to swim and my first slow strokes were punctuated by the thump of my brothers dropping into the water behind me.

Suddenly we were all conscious of the short window we had to make the crossing. Soon the tides would change and the maelstrom would regain its full force. We rushed together to the starting point and climbed up onto the outcrop as the boat bobbed slowly to one side and cleared the mile-long path to the Isle of Scarba. In a fever of mingled nerves and excitement we counted ourselves down and gripped the sharp rock, poised to dive forward into the barrage of waves.

The first sprint started with a mad dash away from the wave-beaten outcrop, eased into a fevered triple-beat rhythm – stroke, stroke, breathe – and ended with Calum and me treading water and searching for Robbie. Suddenly we were suspended in a moment of panic. Then we sighted him crawling in an arc and veering away from our course, into the wake of the boat. We didn't know at the time, but he'd swallowed a mouthful of seawater and, between breathing and spluttering, was still unable to find his rhythm. The mad rave of the relentless waves slowed our approach, raised the cost of each second and, worst of all, led to us being slowly separated. I could barely speak. We were about halfway between the two islands, right at the heart of the maelstrom, and the ocean was starting to punish us. I told Calum we had to wait for Robbie, but he wanted to push on. We had no idea whether we were making good time, and the prospect of the whirlpool starting up again, coupled with our exhaustion, induced a dangerous shadow of doubt.

Duncan had told us that if we wanted out we only had to raise, extend and cross our arms to signal the boat. It was *that* easy. A sudden urge came from a quiet voice inside my mind – the same voice that is always assuaged by comfort. This time it was manifest in an enticing murmur that, to me, can sometimes be a source of jaded nihilism.

Give up, it said, as I dribbled strings of salt water and struggled to keep my head above the waves. But I wouldn't, not because of some 'Eye of the Tiger' bullshit, but because at that moment Robbie suddenly realigned himself with Scarba and headed back in our direction. Now I think of it, we were probably wrong to doubt that he would catch up with us. We already knew that he was *The Unstoppable Turtle* after his sluggish breaststroke swim, several years ago, across the whole seven and a half miles of Lake Ullswater.

Collected, for a fleeting moment, in a neat spearhead formation, we began our crawl again, digging hard into the water and kicking out against the weird currents. It didn't last long though. Soon Robbie and I forked in opposite directions, leaving Calum alone in the middle. Later, he told us that the experience of trying to keep us both on course was like 'shepherding cats'. Neither Robbie nor I could find a direct line towards the island – half of the time, we couldn't even see the island for the ongoing barrage of salt water. Frustrated, I finally rolled onto my back and was immediately lifted onto the swollen crest of a wave. Feeling the weight of my aching muscles, like anchors calling me to the seabed, I angled my head up at the sky and shouted out between breathless gasps. It was a mixture of anger and exhaustion, not the kind of emotional cocktail you want when you're halfway across the Corryvreckan.

Then Calum swept out in front of me . . .

'Follow my feet,' he cried, and with that I gritted my teeth, spun back over and sliced my leading hand into the water.

I picked each breath carefully, feeling the water hitting my cheek and spitting the salty intake out whenever I could. It became harder as my breathing quickened and I began to hyperventilate. I kept poking my head up above the water, half crazed with disbelief at the distance we still had to travel.

I'd be reaching now if I tried to recall and write down my thought process during that last ten-minute sprint. The overwhelming memory is one of dogged concentration in the face of being absolutely knackered. Every so often I'd switch to breaststroke to catch my breath and calculate the distance still separating us from Scarba's outcrop – our salvation – where we could finally plant our feet on dry rock and collapse.

When we did eventually reach the island, the waves carried us hard onto the sharp shelving and I ripped my numb fingers and tore my feet trying to keep hold, before being washed out and bundled back in again. I won't soon forget how it felt to finally scramble clear of the waves, roll over onto my back and gaze up into the sky.

We'd done it. My brothers were strewn across the ragged rocks around me like shipwreck survivors. Together we took a moment to acknowledge what we'd just accomplished, snatching the odd note of happiness between arduous breaths. I could've curled up there and slept, but then I heard Calum planning to dive back in again and swim to the boat, which bobbed a short distance from the rocks. A moment later he and Robbie jumped in with little hesitation. Meanwhile I caught my breath and waited until an incoming wave broke, swept in and flattened. Then I leapt out into the rip and was pulled into a thrashing mixture of froth and fronded kelp. Believe me, it was the last place I wanted to be. Nevertheless, I reached into my final reserves, kicked upwards and crawled towards the ladder with a pain-stricken grimace.

I look on as Robbie dives into the roiling Corryvreckan, following Calum back to the boat after our successful crossing.

'Good show,' was all Duncan said when we stumbled back onto the swaying boat, exhausted. His words immediately hammered the moment home. Then we shook his hand, hugged Mum, congratulated each other and that was that – we'd crossed the Corryvreckan.

The return journey was buoyed by good feeling. Mostly it was just the relief of us all having made it and in good time (twenty-five minutes) too. We talked, interspersed with peaceful intervals, and stared at the ocean and the islands sweeping by. Mostly I sat with my brothers on the back of the boat and we dried ourselves in the wind, feeling suddenly warm now that we were out of the water. Inspired by the occasion, I decided to sup some of Robbie's whisky and secretly made repulsed faces that were later found in photographic evidence. All the while the weather reflected our mood and the sun beamed from its throne in the vacant azure. At one point, we began to joke about Grandma Wild's involvement in the forecast. Mum started to describe her in angelic company, standing on heaven's clouded eaves, looking down at us. We guessed that she'd be keeping the Almighty in his place.

'No [God], I'm speaking now,' Robbie quipped, quoting Grandma's favourite line when she was in the heat of an argument.

We knew that she would've given anything to be there with us. Mum said she probably would've got into the water – that *Wild Lady of Loch Broom*, who used to pull spears of bracken out of her shins without flinching and could beat us all in arm-wrestles until we were adolescents. There was no denying that we could feel her, and we could see that missing smile and hear those swollen words of pride. Yes, I'm an atheist, but in the end I do believe in soul. I think an essential part of who we are survives death, intact. Anyone who knows you has, to some degree, been you, by which I mean they've felt enough of your pain, shared enough of your experiences or heard enough of your thoughts, to, in some way, preserve your character. Both of our grandmas are in our blood and they urged our strength at times like that. If someone tells you enough times that you can do something, eventually it's going to stick. In their cases, they'd spoken to us and looked at us throughout the entirety of our lives, as though we could do anything. To say now that they'd been supportive would be doing them a grave disservice – they'd been in our corner since the days we were born.

Now that I think of it, the Corryvreckan swim just wouldn't have been possible without the examples they'd set. Like me, Robbie had struggled and even encountered the same voice I'd heard, begging him to stop and give up. It wasn't surprising, given how he'd swallowed a lungful of seawater several minutes into the swim. He later explained how the waves had made it difficult for him to find a breathing pattern. Then, suddenly, he came up for a gulp of fresh clean air and instead was met by a slab of cold water. Panicked, he'd sucked the saline deep into his lungs and struggled to control his strokes. That voice inside urged him to get out of the water, but his body was still going through the motions. He took in another gulp of water and again the voice called out and told him to quit.

'You know the usual internal dialogue you have?' Robbie asked me. 'This was different.'

Out of his depth and disorientated, Robbie decided he had no option but to swim on. So he dug in. He fought his burning chest, his rapid breathing and his muddled strokes. To make matters worse, he then hit a backflow and started veering off in the wrong direction. It wasn't until he heard Mum shouting from the boat, pointing to where Calum and I were treading water, that his mind slowly cleared, his strokes strengthened and he regained his focus.

Back at the B&B, Calum was laid sprawled across our bed, waiting for someone to vacate the hot shower. I remember him saying how that was his favourite feeling, having tested yourself and pitched your grit against your own limits and, more importantly, your previous misconception of who you are and what you can achieve. I later realised that hard-earned rest is not only redemptive – being a form of expiation for pent-up guilt and laziness – it's also revelatory, you know? It brings you closer to the truth that limits are nothing but conventions. You can go further than you ever have before, so long as you can conceive of doing so.

The more I thought about it the more it seemed to be true. Then it brought me back to thinking about Grandma Wild again and the saying she'd engraved on the wooden beam in Lexis: 'Rest and be Thankful'. I guess this is the closest thing we have to a family motto. It was also something we didn't understand at first, although, saying that, perhaps my brothers, who'd fetched and carried most of the rocks used to build Lexis, had more of an inkling than I, who'd lazily ducked to one side.

As we drove back home, Mum talked at length about her

life in Scotland and told us where the saying came from. She said that Grandma had once seen it written on a signpost positioned at the top of a hard track trudged long ago by horses and carts. It was a notice for weary travellers, used to inspire them to take a moment to rest and reflect. The only time I ever really felt its meaning was in the aftermath of serious physical exertion. I related it to sitting in the shower after a hard rugby game, warmed by the jets of water. I remember how I used to watch the mud washing off my legs, revealing bruises and fine scratches left in rows by studded boots. More recently I'd had that same feeling after two of my mates and I climbed the dormant volcano Rinjani, in Indonesia. On the return descent, I was one toenail down, badly blistered and exhausted. We'd been up since two in the morning, in the cold hilltop night, and the trek was starting to take its toll. Then the slopes began to level when suddenly we were caught in a tropical downpour unlike anything I'd ever experienced. An hour or so later we were forced to make this very precarious river crossing. Even the Sherpas were hesitant. They stopped us at the banks, having run a mile or so under the beating rain, stomping through deep, muddy puddles. We had some oldies and young 'uns (their children) with us, but my friend Sandy and I were desperate to make it to the bus.

'Just like the Eden,' I said to him, as we waded waist-deep through the coffee river, widening our stances and rooting each step like lumbering, lanky Ents. Without hesitation, Sandy led the way and I followed. Then we formed a kind of human bridge and helped the others across.

By the time we made it back onto the bus I was soaked to my bones. The white wrinkles around my toes had hardened and frozen and my infected bites looked like the onset of some grotesque disease. The point is, though, that on the bus, when we were heading back to our hotel and watching the scenery sweeping by, I rested my head against the window and remembered what we'd done. I thought about where we'd been that morning – at the summit of Rinjani, watching the pale sunrise warm the ancient, misty jungles and volcanoes of Lombok.

Rest and be thankful.

Maybe you should keep that line in mind next time you plan an adventure, or, if you want to take a leaf out of my book, wait until your siblings exclude you from something and then obstinately latch on to it. After all, I do think it's something we all need. I'm not sure how much time you spend in front of a screen, but, if you're anything like me, it's probably an unhealthy portion of your life. It's tempting to want those dopamine rushes that social media offers. Just remember that you're not alone. We're all grappling with the same light-speed technological growth – the fastest in the history of our species. It's no wonder society is now siring a zealous array of travellers and tearaways. Everywhere you go you'll meet folk like Christopher McCandless, the young man who hitchhiked his way to Alaska, became stranded and finally wasted away in an abandoned bus.

I learnt about Jon Krakauer's book, *Into the Wild*, through Sean Penn's film. That was how I discovered Chris's story. When I eventually found a copy it was half hidden in a cluttered bookshop in Chang Mai, Thailand, which was run by an old balding expat.

'I don't get everyone's obsession with this kid,' the expat had grunted, as he turned the book over in his hands and grimaced at the title – I might as well have been buying a copy of *Mein Kampf*.

Nevertheless, I kept quiet and shrugged, as I usually do in the face of brash exclamations, as a way of being ingratiating. Then I went away to brood and confirmed how I resented the idea that Christopher was arrogant and stupid, as the expat had gone on to say at the end of a fervent and utterly one-sided rant. Of course, I recognise the arrogance of ignoring the advice of the locals, who knew the area, and the ironic fact that there were hunting lodges so close to where Chris died. However, it's difficult to criticise Chris for walking away from the veneer of his parents' marriage and the false, white-washed dome of suburban America. He did something very few of us can claim to have attempted. He recognised the battle we're all locked in and started fighting, with all his mad energy, to win. He went searching for that which many of us feel and know to be essential, but are unwilling to pursue, for fear of becoming lost in the unknown.

What did he find? Of course, there are numerous answers, depending on who you ask, but I think his most valuable epitaph was left scrawled in the margins of a *Doctor Zhivago* book, which was later found in the bus where he slept. It read: *happiness only real when shared*.

I'd heard something similar from one of our uncle's friends, Niall, who we met in India. He was one of those hippies who'd ridden Hunter S.Thompson's wave and felt the crushing weight when it finally broke and rolled back, leaving, in its wake, a valley of washed-up souls. Done with society, he'd decided to find a place for himself in a fecund valley of the Himalayan foothills, where he built a rickety, two-storey cabin, hidden in the midst of an orchard of fruit trees and overgrown cannabis plants. Robbie, Calum and I, along with our cousins, Gareth and Owen, and Luke, went to visit Niall one afternoon when we were travelling through Northern India. We all sat together on his balcony and smoked as the sun fell, poring over old maps of the area and stealing the sound of a nearby river to use as music.

Over time the smoke gathered and we began to slide down onto the floor and spread out into languid positions. I think it was Robbie who eventually said how much he envied Niall's refuge, hidden in the mountains.

'Well, if you're gonna do something like this,' Niall replied slowly, 'make sure you do it with somebody.'

I've never travelled on my own, so I'm not the best authority on the pros and cons of isolation. That being said, when I reflect on the things that Chris wrote and Niall said, I can't help thinking that nothing eats at the soul quite like loneliness. And I would say that love, whatever it is, is something we need to survive. Maya Angelou said that it 'may be that which pulls the stars in the firmament. It may be that which pushes and urges the blood in the veins.' I would also like to say that anyone who criticises Chris, who hasn't taken that first step to entering the wild, behind the fancy curtains of society, is undermining the importance of such a venture. You can say that it is silly and sentimental to romanticise what he did. Just don't forget that all romance ends with tragedy – that's what makes something romantic. We know that ultimately, for us, love is unfulfilled because it doesn't last forever, as it yearns to. Blink and you could lose the meaning of what Chris saw and wrote, as well as the worth of what he did. Granted the ending was miserable, but there is some solace to be found in the fact the wild today has no shortage of adventurers. Many still survive who seek counsel from the natural world and who go on choosing their own trails by studying the footprints of their wild heroes. Just first try to find a partner in adventure and then you won't have to go it alone.

Looking back, I realise how fortunate it is that we found a sport that could return us to our childhood. Little did I know wild swimming would also become a new source of creative inspiration, not to mention the positive effects it would have on our health. And it's funny; the thing most folk think should reduce the appeal of swimming outdoors is probably the most beneficial aspect of it. I'm talking now about the cold water. I've heard that the colder it is the higher its oxygen content will be. That's why you find such an abundance of marine animals in the Arctic Circle. In fact, all the evidence I've seen has reinforced my appreciation of water, particularly the colder variety, as an elixir, nourishing all life on Earth.

So, why do we take it for granted? Bubbling up from seemingly infinite springs, cold water continues to flow from our taps and spatter from the showerhead, and we think nothing of it. What some of us are perhaps forgetting is that this was once the element we lived in. We may have evolved to survive on the land, but that isn't to say the ocean has dried up in our souls as well. On the contrary, swimming in cold water has been proven to help us both psychologically and physically. It fortifies the immune system, decreases your blood pressure, causes your cholesterol levels to drop, burns fat, boosts your metabolism, combats cellulite, releases endorphins and even improves your fertility rate (imagine a band of swim-trained sperm shimmying along like Michael Phelps).

I'm not sure if it had to do with these benefits I've just mentioned, or the sense of accomplishment, but I did feel very different when I got home, after the Corryvreckan. Suddenly I was uplifted, confident and I couldn't wait to dive into the River Eden and follow its course with my brothers . . .

I was ready to immerse myself in the experience.

The idea of going for a wild swim can seem slightly daunting, especially if you've never tried it before. If you don't feel confident in open water it's important to remember that all the obstacles you'll face are manageable. However, you do need to know what these obstacles are.

First, there are many different drop-offs at the water's edge. One moment you might be wading through shallow water with sure footing, and the next you'll step over an abrupt precipice and suddenly wind up out of your depth. One way to avoid this is to start off in shallow, clear water, in which you can easily see the bottom. If you take your time this will also protect you from stumbling on loose or slippery (usually moss-covered) rocks. We lost count of the number of times we slipped and fell on the rocky riverbed in the Eden. At times we must've looked like a drunken gang of all-nighters stumbling home.

Currents are another danger that wild swimmers have to consider. Fast-flowing water or undercurrents, commonly found close to waterfalls or weirs, increase your risk of drowning. Super-stylish fluorescent swim floats can be used to counter this. Another thing that creeps up on some wild swimmers (especially the less blubbery variety) is the early onset of hypothermia. Cold-water swimming drains your natural body heat and sometimes causes you to shiver and shudder. If this happens to you, you're probably showing signs of early hypothermia. Get out of the water and warm your body by throwing on dry clothes. Maybe bust out a few star-jumps and go for a brisk jog. That should do the trick! To avoid this problem you should allow yourself time to acclimatise. Test the temperature and take your time getting in. Doing the ol' headfirst bull charge is great 'n' all, but it doesn't quite work if the water is much colder than you expected. If this happens, you run the risk of involuntary *cold-shock*, which causes your heart rate to increase rapidly.

Sometimes a pristine plunge pool might scream for you to attempt a dive. Just be aware of potential obstructions underwater, like branches, boulders and roots. While you're swimming you might suffer from sharp bursts of cramp (I've had this recently in the arches of my feet and in my quads). This is usually brought on by over-exertion. Dehydration and poor dietary habits can make you more susceptible to cramp as well. If you feel yourself starting to cramp up, it's best to call for help, lean back and paddle to safety. This is a good reason to avoid deep-water swimming without a support kayaker.

If you venture out into coastal waters, you should always be wary of the surf. The undertow often rolls deep under breaking waves and it's easy to be pulled out if you're too ambitious. Always check that you haven't strayed too far from your pre-determined route and be sure to have precautions in place like a support kayaker, lifeguard supervision or a nearby exit point.

The last few things you should take into account are the plants and animals. Weeds are quite common in slow-flowing lowland rivers and lakes. Several times, while swimming, I've suddenly found myself floating over the snaking tendrils of a weed forest. Sometimes these weeds can wrap themselves around your legs and disrupt your stroke. It's best to stick to open water and to avoid any greenish patches where the anaconda-weeds are waiting. If you do wind up passing over one of these forests, simply slow down, stay calm and use your arms to paddle back to open water.

Blue-greenish algae can be found in lowland lakes as well. During the late summer, algae blooms form as the algae multiplies, which can cause a green scum to gather around the lakeside. This scum might give you a bad skin rash if you go dancing and splashing around in it. It can also irritate your eyes and stomach, so, if you have dreams of one day becoming a wild algae swimmer, I'm sorry to say you might be in for some disappointment. Similarly, if you enjoy wallowing in bogs like a hippopotamus, you might pick up *swimmer's itch*, courtesy of little snails that collect on reeds in marshland and around stagnant ponds. It's also not advisable to swim in urban rivers and canals, especially after heavy rain, when the outflow from sewers and storm drains might be joining you in the water.

If you still have questions, you might benefit from joining the community of swimmers who belong to the Outdoor Swimming Society. They have a great, interactive Wild Swim map as well, which is available online. I know it sounds like a lot of hassle, but these obstacles I've mentioned are seldom encountered and largely avoidable. I guess the important thing to remember is the reassurance that was inscribed in friendly letters on the back of *The Hitchhiker's Guide to the Galaxy*: *Don't Panic.*

In our varying states of isolation, many of us have grown afraid of nature. One question we're often asked when we take our pals for their first wild swim is: 'What if I touch the bottom?' If you touch the bottom you'll likely feel either loose pebbles, sand or that dreaded sludgy muck. Yes, it might feel a little like having sausage meat pushed between your toes, but remember that medicine doesn't always taste sweet. Flies, sludge and algae are a reminder that you're not in a pool. This is you toughening up – getting closer to your wilder, much more resilient ancestors. In a pool you could plant your feet on clean tiles freshly scrubbed by a lifeguard. It might feel more comfortable, but it isn't anywhere near as good for you. In time, you might even come to enjoy these seemingly irksome details. Indeed, the act of swimming wild will take you on a journey. Gradually you'll begin to understand the value of the natural world and how essential a relationship with nature is to both our physical and psychological survival. Your history, your biology, your soul: all these things depend on you putting time into this connection. Someday it might become your salvation, beyond the safe confines of whatever routine it is you've accepted for yourself.

Of course, it's important to keep all these dangers in mind, but it's *very* important not to let them put you off your wild swim.

Read The Water (Jack's Tip): *When you arrive at a new swim spot the first instinct is often to do as The Hoff does and sprint for the water. This isn't always the best approach. Cold water shock is a very real consideration. Respect for undercurrents (strongest closer to waterfalls), and other obstacles like an unsteady entry point or an abrupt drop-off, is also essential. Take some time to check the water. Where is it darkest and deepest? Are there patches of disturbed water? Are there submerged rocks or trees just beneath the surface? There are always tell-tale signs to look out for when you scope out a new swim spot.*

4

The Source

The connection we, as humans, have with water can be traced back to the earliest records of our species. The accepted theory, for many years, stated that humans eked out a nomadic existence on the African savannah. However, some remains of our fossilised ancestors have raised suspicions about how dependent we were on the oceans, rivers and lakes. More recently, scientists have posited the idea that we are, in fact, related to an *aquatic ape*, which once descended from the trees to discover the bounties held in tracts of water.

This theory of an aquatic ape was first proposed in 1960 by the marine biologist Sir Alister Hardy. Hardy presented the scientific community with this new evolutionary paradigm, centred on industrious foraging and opportunistic hunting. It was an idea that was then supported by the late writer and anthropologist, Elaine Morgan, who also dismissed the male-centric idea of hunters peering over tall savannah grass, spearing big cats and chasing down large prey. Unsurprisingly, Morgan took issue with the implication that we owe the survival of our species to a single gender. She drew attention to the fact that the savannah theory neglected to offer any discernible evidence of female adaptation and contribution. Morgan also helped to expound Hardy's theory for why we evolved to stand upright. Hardy had previously pointed to the fact that as apes we would've been quadrupeds, walking on our hands and feet, suggesting that the development of a bipedal posture would have been a hindrance if we were hunting four-legged prey on open grasslands.

Now, this question of how we evolved to walk upright is one that has vexed scientists and delighted cartoonists for centuries. Morgan, Hardy and fellow proponents of the waterside model, including David Attenborough, have collated evidence that sheds new light on the mystery. By studying their eating habits, field scientists have discovered that all monkeys walk upright when they're wading through shallow water. This has become a salient example of prolonged bipedalism among primates. Chimps and bonobos – the latter species possesses a genome that's 98.7 per cent identical to the human genome – are also known to forage in forest pools, tugging water plants up from the mud, then returning to the banks and reverting to the four-legged gait of a quadruped.

If this was how we learnt to walk upright, it stands to reason that there would be many examples, throughout our history, of humans continuing to interact with shallow water in this way. Morgan often referred to fossilised evidence of early hominids, traced back almost two million years, which supported this supposition. These fossils revealed aquatic hunters who once hauled slimy, wormlike clarias catfish from the wallows at the water's edge. This huge, nutritious fish, which sometimes grew up to two metres in length, used to spawn upriver in the shallow flood banks, where opportunistic predators could simply wade in and drag them to the shore. Marks of incision were also distinguished on the remains of these fish, suggesting the meal had been carefully prepared and filleted. Isn't it amazing that the bones discarded by our ancestors, like the cave walls that bear our ancient paintings, invariably offer clues and tell us stories?

What's also interesting about the fossilised remains of *Homo erectus* is their surprising bone density. Scientists have examined these bones and found that they show signs of pachyostosis, which means they are hardened by layers of lamellar bone. This condition is especially common in both aquatic and semi-aquatic vertebrates. Scientists have gleaned from this evidence that our ancestors were built for shallow diving and ill-equipped, physiologically, for long persistence hunts on the savannah. Another clue, pertaining to the mystery of our intelligence, has to do with the nutritional value of the marine food chain. In many cases, advanced cognitive development is found in the animals of a marine-based system. Sperm whales, for example, have the largest known brain mass of any animal alive today, while the brain of a bottlenose dolphin is four times larger than that of a chimpanzee. My favourite champion of sea-smarts, however, has to be the humpback whale. These big barnacled bruisers have even been proven to practise philanthropy in a way that puts all other species to shame. On many different occasions, humpbacks have been observed rescuing smaller sea animals from orcas – a single humpback combatant can fend off up to ten orcas at a time, rolling and diving in powerful engagements, which sometimes last up to seven hours.

While it's very unlikely that *Homo erectus* ventured far out to sea, the waterside model suggests that we would've hugged the shoreline and followed the course of rivers, sometimes wading into the shallows for tasty morsels. We already know that *Homo erectus* migrated along the fecund coasts of China and Indonesia. Several fossil sites have been uncovered that mark the course of this migration, while also validating the waterside model. We can use the location of these sites to make educated guesses regarding our primordial diet. It's possible that our ancestors also progressed from plucking mussels in the tidal shallows to swimming in deeper water, where they might've dived down over coral reefs and burrowed for crabs, sea urchins and sea snails. However, mussels would've probably been the easiest and most edible prey, owing to the fact they can be snatched up close to the shore, cooked fresh inside their shells and then prised open to reveal a tasty and healthy package of meat.

Before I move on, I want to offer you one final ancient clue that I found quite remarkable. This clue concerns a distinct condition called auditory exostoses, which causes protective bones to grow within the outer ear canal. What's amazing is that this condition only ever exists in swimmers – a doctor can even tell how often a patient has been swimming by observing these little bones. Funnily enough, archaeologists have found proof of auditory exostoses in both

Neanderthal Man and *Homo erectus*. This specific pattern of bone development could only have been caused by prolonged periods in cold water. The same condition was also found in the 700,000-year-old Peking Man. It seems apparent that at least some of our ancestors were swimmers after all.

Swim the Eden Expedition, Meet-up
Friday 14 August 2015

- *Source-to-mouth nine-day/144-kilometre swim.*
- *Dad and Mum will provide support. Each day we will arrange a rendezvous for lunch. The rest of our supplies will be taken in dry-bags. James Silson will join us in the water and will get into a kayak on the third day.*
- *Rapids, gorges and waterfalls will be treated with due caution.*

In the run-up to our Eden swim I became quite obsessive and thought of little else besides water and swimming. Nevertheless, after all that time spent focused on the river, the reality of our adventure still arrived with a sudden jolt. One moment I was sitting in an office in some remote business park. The next I was standing at a train station, sucking the country air into my lungs, surrounded by the sprawling hills of the Eden Valley. At once it seemed as though the sky had grown and in this upturned, black ocean the stars emerged and burned faintly in trailing bands, like shoals of fish frozen in space. Meanwhile, I paced up and down an empty track alongside the railway and thought about the journey ahead of us.

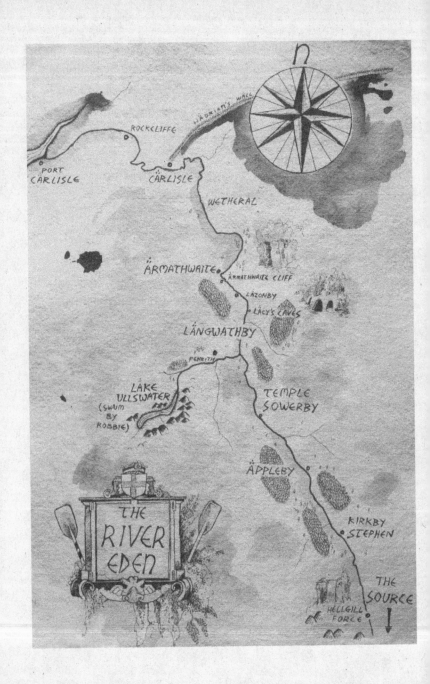

Eventually I got to thinking about some of the animals we had to watch out for in the Eden. They didn't pose any real danger, but long, tubular lampreys are known to lurk on the riverbed, using their suckered mouths to cling to the rocks. These strange jawless fish hunt by latching on to passers-by, boring into their juicy flesh and feeding on their blood. One of my friends once pulled his arm out from a snarl of river weed and found one of these big bad boys wrapped around his wrist. I think that nightmarish image stayed with me. Then there was the sharp-toothed, torpedo-shaped pike, although we knew how rare they were – it was much more likely we'd bump into grayling, trout and salmon. Aside from a few of these more dangerous critters, I was very excited about the prospect of meeting the local wildlife, especially the idea of spotting darting kingfishers and long-legged, courtly herons that swoop in and strut their stuff at the water's edge. If we were very lucky, there was also a chance we'd find ourselves bobbing through the fishing grounds of the resident otters.

It was exhilarating to think that we might soon be meeting such creatures in the water. The idea of having such rare country encounters reminded me I was home. An hour or so earlier, I'd been sitting with my forehead pressed against the train window, watching the trees and shire villages sweeping by. Half dozing, I'd dipped intermittently into a world of lamp-lit living rooms, cushioned conservatories, black stoves, Tibetan flags, tall plants, vegetable patches, allotments, chickens, apple trees, playgrounds and everything else that reminded me of home. Then I'd seen the River Eden from above, as the train hurtled over high ground, and I'd traced the muddy current through gaps in the trees, thrilled by the reminder that it would be my companion for the next nine days.

After I'd paced the track for a little while longer, my dad arrived and crammed me into his red Beetle packed with tents, bags and all kinds of outdoor paraphernalia. Then we drove a short distance into the hills outside of Kirkby Stephen. It was already dark by the time we reached our campsite on a slope traversed by crumbled dry-stone walls. As we pulled up, Calum, Robbie and our friend, James, came walking towards us down the road. They looked like a trinity of gangster yokels, their faces hidden behind woollen balaclavas used to fend off the midges.

After we hugged, my brothers told me about their radio interview that morning and said how fast flowing the river had been when they'd done their short swim for TV. It was clear they were growing more and more excited that word was getting out, and I was too, although I hadn't done much to contribute on that front. In the end, it was Calum who'd headed the whole marketing campaign, enabling us to take the place of the latest giant vegetable in the Cumbrian papers. He'd also worked through the logistics of what we were about to do, calling various landowners and associations and reading up on the local legislation. He told us that the 1968 Countryside Act described both riverside and woodland as open country, which meant we were free to roam, as far as they were concerned. The only problem was that we were swimming through the territory of the fishing authorities.

We'd all experienced the reprimands they often fling at supposed outsiders. It wasn't uncommon for local river wardens to see a group of youths and assume the worst. Once, I'd been out on the Eden, kayaking close to our garden with a few mates, when a grumpy gnome of a man appeared through the tall grass and climbed down to the water's edge.

Red-faced, he called us over and asked what we were doing. I greeted him cheerily and pointed to my garden across the river.

'I can't actually do anything unless you're on the bank,' the man grumbled, maintaining his line of attack. With that, he turned away with an awkward shrug and left us floating on the current, confused as to what had just happened.

Before Dad left, I took my bag from his car, slung it over my shoulder and headed off into the dark field. As we walked I could see the tent ahead of us, lit by blades of moonlight that shivered through the coiling mist. It was into this mist that we then disappeared, drawn to the fluttering sight of our new wind-beaten homes, which held the rest of our kit. Later, we cooked dinner on a little foldable stove and sat hunched under the tent cover. While we ate, my brothers decided to tell the nightmarish story of how they'd wandered down the hill to the nearby farmhouse, behind a fence of withered trees. Apparently, when they'd walked through the yard they'd met a farmhand with a scar on the crown of his bald head and snub features pinched into a perpetual grimace. They described what followed as though it was a scene from *Deliverance*, replete with mangy dogs lurching out from the dark and rattling their chain leashes, gnashing the air and lunging with frenzied eyes, as if caught in the drooling clutch of rabies. Their intention had been to greet the landowner and make sure their arrangement still stood, but the only people inside the house at that time were his son and his surly, mute friend.

'Aye, we know why you're here,' was all the son said, as he stared into the fire with grim resolve. After that, the three of them, my brothers and James, turned and hurried off the premises, chased uphill by the barking of the chained dogs.

Having eaten, I went back to the tent I was sharing with Calum and carefully sealed the door to keep out the relentless swarms of good-for-nothing-bastard-midges. Then I lay in my sleeping bag, my eyes half closed and my padded coat bunched against my cheek. Slowly I began to drift into a state of pleasant anticipation. I knew what lay ahead of me: not in the sense that I knew what to expect or how hard it might be; I just knew that it was going to be nine days in the Eden and, better still, nine days with my brothers.

Swim the Eden Expedition, Day 1
Saturday 15 August 2015

The following morning brought a slow warmth to our misted spot on the slopes of Mallerstang dale, above the *Deliverance* farm. While the mist began to dissipate, we wrestled with our wetsuits and pulled them up to our waists (we'd be walking uphill for a couple of hours to find the source of the Eden). Next, we filled up on knotted porridge and a few energy bars and Robbie quickly knocked back a pint of milk, which he insisted was essential. Then we disassembled the tents before our dad finally arrived and charged triumphantly over the hill in his camp red Beetle. We'd joked about the fact his car was clearly designed with women in mind. He kept insisting that what was undoubtedly a flower holder on the dashboard was intended for drinks. Of course, the only glasses that fitted into it had to be as narrow as a bunch of flower stems, but that didn't stop him from clinging to his masculinity, like a geriatric clutching their purse during a robbery.

With typical fatherly gusto, Dad helped us unload the car, gather our essentials and map the route up through Mallerstang Valley to the peak where the Eden began. As it happened, that early hike ate up a large portion of our morning. For the most part we trudged uphill with our bare backs to the sun and flocks of sheep bleating around us as they jumped through the bracken. It was a luxurious start to the swim, interspersed with moments of stark glamour. At one point, we all had to stop for our first communal bowel movement. I remember looking back from the river – the image is still seared into my brain – and seeing all three of them squatting on the crest of a tufted hill, like feral pink bears. It reminded me of something Calum had said about true adventure, which related to SAS fieldwork as Lewis Pugh had described it. Pugh's version of armed adventure involved a full-grown soldier in camouflage, crammed down a rabbit hole for a week, instead of some Chuck Norris type abseiling from a helicopter with a knife between his teeth. Similarly, real adventure might evoke a man scaling a mountain, pinching a crevice with his trembling fingertips and defying the laws of gravity. However, if you wanted a complete picture, it also had to evoke that same bloke hunched in a wind-beaten cave, with his trousers around his ankles, peering through the icy night as he empties his bowels into a freshly dug hole.

Safe in the knowledge that we were getting into the swing of things, we pushed on and followed a narrow stream – the infant Eden – and took the time to enjoy the morning sun and catch up, while jumping between rocks and traversing the gentle, wooded slopes. Eventually, we came out from among the trees and followed spirals of barbed wire into open fields dotted with stone ruins. At that point Calum and I dropped back a little while Robbie quickened his pace and moved to the front.

'Do you think just swimming would cure depression?' I asked Calum, as we began a slow uphill amble through the fields. 'Like – what do you guys think about when you're swimming?'

'I just kinda switch off,' Calum said quickly. 'It's my time. If I'm in a lido in London, if I'm outdoors, it's my time to just relax. I can be thinking about the problems of the day – if I've had a stressful day at work, I'll just completely zone out.'

'I try and get to that point,' I replied. 'But I have sort of . . . lots of weird conversations and thoughts that crop up every now and then. I'll have like, ahm, I'll have the stroke thing that I'll use to try calm myself down, like – one, two, three, breathe – I'll try and use that to get really relaxed.'

'Yeah, you meditate.'

'Yeah, kinda,' I conceded.

'Zen mode.'

'I'll try to get into that state 'cause then it's a lot easier to swim as well.'

Just then Robbie stopped, turned back and rested his foot on a mound of grass. 'For me,' he began, 'I just zone out after a while, but it takes time to get into it. For the first bit I think about my stroke, all the time, as much as I can and concentrate on the tiny details: your hands and arms. Doing that a while, when your breathing is nice and regular, you start zoning out.'

'D'you find it gets much easier the longer you swim?' I asked.

'I think it's like anything,' Robbie replied. 'If you're doing something creative, you have to graft if you want it to pay off. When you're making—'

'Don't say the "A" word Rob.' Calum grinned, stopping Robbie in his tracks.

Calum liked to play the philistine when it came to Robbie's art. He also stuck to the idea that it wasn't art if *he* could do it. That's one of the reasons he liked to criticise abstract squiggles and unmade beds and elephant dung splattered over walls.

After a while the conversation began to trail off and we grew tired and began to focus on the walk. Eventually we left the open fields and climbed out of the valley onto a squelching peat bog. Ahead of us we could see a wide stretch of marshland dotted with spiky tufts of grass. We tried to take it in our stride, although we soon found our legs were being swallowed up to the knees, forcing us to crawl for some time on our bellies. It looked like the Dead Marshes from *The Lord of the Rings*, where the murky depths are littered with the pale corpses of elves, orcs and men. In time, the slow, crawling pace became quite punishing and we often sank into bogs and coated ourselves in the wet mud. That being said, the views on all sides did help to assuage the drudgery somewhat. We were right up against the roof of the world, looking out over the sheep-spotted green spines of the fells. The morning mist collected behind and below us, like a vapour tide, ebbing and flowing through the rugged valleys.

'I think I've become cynical,' Calum said, his eyes on the rocky path we'd just used to leave the valley. 'Too long in a shit job. I used to sit with a spreadsheet in front of me making the same call over and over. Then every time I was on the tube, I used to ask myself what the hell I was doing.' His voice sagged with the fatigue of three years spent at the heart of the London start-up scene. 'None of them know what they're doing,' he sighed, 'no matter how high up they are. They're all just winging it. You shouldn't take anything seriously.'

'You said you wanted money so you could take your kids to all these exotic places,' I said, remembering the reason Calum had cited for going into sales in the first place. 'Say you took them to the Galapagos Islands – I bet you'd take that bloody seriously.'

To which Robbie added, 'That's a good point.'

Calum didn't think so though. 'I wouldn't take it *seriously*,' he said, raising a quizzical eyebrow.

After several false celebrations, we eventually reached the source of the Eden and clambered onto it in a fit of excitement. It was unlike anything I'd seen before, yet at the same time it looked exactly as I'd hoped it would – a tall, mossy volcano issuing a shallow trickle of water that cascaded down the grass. Zipping up my wetsuit, I climbed into the hole straight away and crammed my feet into the natural earthen pipe that pumped water up from somewhere far beneath us. The source was so deep that the rim of the volcano encircled my waist. I could feel the cold, bubbling water biting my ankles, but it wasn't enough to make me uncomfortable. The wetsuit helped to hold any water that seeped in, which in turn was warmed by my body heat. The only problem with wetsuits is that they do restrict your movements when you swim. Also, nothing quite beats the freedom of going genitals to the wind and skinny-dipping.

Me standing in the source of the Eden.

*Me, Calum and Robbie having a laugh up in the hills at the
start of our Swim the Eden adventure.*

At that moment, while I was testing my wetsuit, there was
an unusual bird call somewhere overhead. It sounded like a
cross between a firework and a creaking door. Robbie lifted
his head and gestured to the sky. I followed his line of sight
and spotted a buzzard hovering on the wind, its head tilting
from side to side as it surveyed the tufted peak on which we
sat. The buzzard squawked again; this time the call was longer
and the lilt more distinct.

'Sounds like Jabba the Hutt's sidekick.' Robbie grinned.

We treated the buzzard's call like a starter gun and decided
to get going. From that point onwards we'd be heading
downriver. We had nine days ahead of us. Nine days of riding
the river, pitching tents and being close to nature. James was
going to be walking and swimming with us for the first two
days, after which he planned to jump into a sea kayak and
paddle alongside us. Any food or drink we needed would go

into that kayak. Just before the halfway point we also had Sandy and Dave joining us in kayaks, and Beth was going to be along for the ride at various different stages as well.

Eager to test the water, Robbie and Calum pulled up and zipped their wetsuits in unison. We didn't want to kill too much time, given how long it'd taken us to scale the boggy Hugh Seat and find the source. Then they both joined me in the volcano and we crammed ourselves into a tight circle, with our feet wedged inside the earthen pipe. Next Calum shimmied onto the slope and crawled through an outflowing trickle of dirty water. After that the three of us were sliding like penguins and scrambling excitedly through the first trickling rivulets of the Eden. Around us belching puddles dotted the swampland and gurgling brooks split tufted islands of tall grass. Like veritable commando-eels we slid over the soggy, swollen mounds and inched head-first down little waterfalls, plunging into cold black pools with fits of excitable laughter. We also squeezed through narrow gaps between the mounds, groping the rock and hardened peat and altogether savouring our last adventure of the summer.

Further downriver, when we'd dropped back into the valley, we found that traces of copper gave the water a blood-red hue as it rushed over sandstone chutes into bubbling eddies and frothy black swirls, carrying us down the hillside in a mad, cold flourish. It wasn't long before we'd left the peat bogs behind and were heading onto the sinuous single waterway of Red Gill Beck, which later became Hell Gill Beck when the streams joined and the flow widened, at which point larger, serrated rocks jutted up through the current and forced us to start walking.

The second portion of the beck took its toll on our bodies, particularly our feet and ankles, which we twisted several times, stumbling in every direction when little rocks gave way beneath our clumsy steps. This hurt Calum especially, since he took the brunt of the uneven riverbed after forgetting to bring his padded wetsuit shoes. Basically, he was barefooted, stamping on the rounded crowns of piled rocks and sharp edges that bruised our heels and bit hard between our toes. Every now and then you could hear one of us growling through gritted teeth when we lost our footing and fell hard in the stream. At one point, I slipped back into a seated position and slammed my tailbone into an unforgiving spear of rock. A bolt of rough electricity shot up my spine and my insides clenched, as though I'd just been sodomised with an iron bar. It was one in a series of bruises and rolled ankles that left us hobbling and vaguely demoralised.

Fortunately, the awkward stretch of stumbling ended when we neared the flatland woods, where we were also greeted by the mouth of Hell Gill Gorge. Calum had already told us all about this exciting obstacle – a tight canyon hidden under the trees, which snaked downhill like a deep scar, splitting the moors and swallowing steep billows of water that plummeted at intervals through the 200-foot gorge. It sounded like one of those wild, arse-clenching rides that test your nerve and ultimately nourish your soul.

Edging closer, we saw how the water had carved the limestone into smooth cascades. Each pool dropped at intervals and disappeared into the shadow of the rugged cliffs on either side. I looked up and saw the precipice overhead, crowned with trees. Then, chattering to each other between bursts of excited laughter, we all shimmied into the thrashing current and edged to the start of a long succession of little waterfalls. James found a position on an outcrop above us and started filming as we leapt down the cascades and plunged over vertical drops into little, swirling pools, shouldered by sprouts of dripping foliage and veils of ivy.

It took us a while to realise that we were, in fact, on a canyoning course. The first indication came when we found a heavy flow of water that tugged us to a sudden edge and then hurtled directly down into a black pool several metres below. Above us there was a rope that connected to a sheer face ahead of us and acted as a kind of static zip-line. Filled with adrenaline, I pulled myself along it, hand-over-hand, beyond the precipice, until I felt a sudden twinge of pain – the rope had burned my hand. Instinctively (at least according to the instincts of a squeamish little kid), I let go and plunged fast into the deep pool below. As I sank through a coiling pillar of bubbles I felt a sinister current that gripped my feet, like the hand of some lost, drowned soul pinned to the underworld. Immediately my gut was hit by a horrible dread and yet one strong stroke was enough to pull me back up to the surface. Then, as I burst up through the water, I heard the falls rushing behind me, turned, and let out a triumphant 'yawp' as I swam away on my back.

Having taken note of my inglorious example, Robbie, Calum and James all followed and managed to climb down the rope until they were clear of the waterfall. Then they lifted their legs and dropped into the pool with mighty splashes. After that, there were several more cascades before the gorge began to narrow and the trees, coupled with the overhanging rocks, enclosed us in a shaded sanctuary. Suddenly we were alone, left with the knowledge that we had to continue going forward, no matter what was around the next bend. Insects flitted through our line of sight and the water soon became much deeper as the riverbed gradually disappeared beneath our treading feet. I remember looking up, with my arms outstretched and my ears dipping under the cold water as it lapped against my swim cap. I could see the leafy canopy glowing a luminous green and beams of filtered sunlight hitting the surrounding rock formations and arches, many of which formed sculpted shapes, which I admired as we floated by. As our worries faded, there was nothing to do but enjoy the flow and to kick and turn our hands in the slow-moving current, as it bore us through the sinuous single vein of Hell Gill Gorge.

When we emerged from the gorge we found a wide, flat arm of the river ahead of us, warmed by the afternoon sun. For some time, we scrambled and waded through the shallow water, while also trying to make up for lost time. Then we came to an abrupt stop at Hell Gill Force, an eight-metre waterfall – the highest on the Eden – which marked the boundary of Yorkshire and Cumbria. We looked at the dizzying drop and talked about that scene in *The Beach* when Françoise runs and leaps over the falls while Leo and his compadre are arguing. Below us, the newly formed river snaked out of sight among a stand of sunlit trees. Soon it would join with Aisgill Beck from Wild Boar Fell, at which point it would become the Eden. By then we were desperately hoping that the river would be deep enough to swim in – maybe after the next bend, or the one after that . . . So far, we'd only been able to paddle a few metres through the gorge, and walking on the uneven riverbed was less than satisfying. I was now nursing a bruised coccyx and Calum had torn several holes in his flimsy, unpadded wetsuit shoes.

As we continued to make our way around the wide confluence (in case you were wondering, it was too shallow so we didn't jump from Hell Gill Force) the pace began to slow even more. Looking back, I could see Calum wincing and grimacing with every step. Rounded pebbles and slabs greeted his blisters whenever he stumbled, which was often. James offered to carry him, but Calum manfully refused. Before long the sun started to dip, at which point we realised that we were almost four hours late for our rendezvous with Dad. In fact, when we arrived at the castle where we were supposed to meet him, stumbling out from under the forest canopy into the clouded light, it transpired that he'd already left. He later told us that he thought he'd somehow missed us, having waited four hours, unable to check the satellite tracker we'd been using. Our painfully slow pace resulted in us having to forgo lunch and trudge on like river zombies, letting out the occasional frustrated growl as we slipped and fell sidelong onto the rocks.

The last few hours of the day were particularly gruelling. A covering of bleak clouds concealed the sunset, and the water became suddenly cold again. Luckily, I had a secret weapon – no, not a hidden pair of flippers, but a simple layer of subcutaneous fat, or blubber, as I affectionately called it. By that point, Calum had also tried to duct-tape his shoes back together, but the makeshift bandage couldn't withstand the water, which meant he was left pretty much barefooted. Soon, every step had become a cruel insult to what had become the tenderest parts of his body. You could see the pain written across his face. Still defiant, he gritted his teeth and kept to the back of the group, out of sight. It wasn't until the sunlight faded that something finally happened to raise his spirits.

I remember we were talking about the likelihood of Mum driving all the way down from her new home in Dumfries. 'I really don't think she'd come all the way out here,' I was saying, but before I could finish my sentence a familiar silver car suddenly lifted into view on a nearby road.

A moment earlier we were ready to throw our exhausted bodies into the several inches of water we'd been kicking through that past hour. Now, our mum was calling to us from her car and we could see the white tail of our spaniel, Marlin, wagging in the boot.

Together we quickly clambered up the bank and rushed over the field, scattering a bewildered flock of sheep. Mum's wide grin was like a beacon, and we all swarmed round and hugged her and plucked snacks from the bags of food she'd brought. All the while Marlin wagged and yelped, crawling over the backseat and nudging us with her nose. We'd been saved – right when we were ready to stop the endless water trudge and nurse our injuries and our pride – the Vauxhall chariot had stormed in with ol' Mother Hen at the reins and her springer sidekick, riding shotgun. It was just what we needed, precisely when we needed it, and, with a few stoic words from Mum, we were off again with lifted spirits.

Mum met us again when we reached the bridge outside

Kirkby Stephen and clambered up the steep bank to finish for the day. In unison, we pulled on our padded jackets and scarves while Calum put plasters on his mashed blisters. After that, Mum drove us to our second rendezvous with Dad and we said goodbye and thanked her for saving us. Then Dad took us to our new campsite, where we rolled up to the lawn, all crammed into his Beetle, with the Swim the Eden banner stuck to the rear-view window. As we unpacked the boot, the landowner came over from a crowded picnic table, wearing a mischievous grin. He told us he'd misread the sign and mistaken us for a group of wetsuit-clad *swingers*. Feeling much happier, but still not in the mood for swinging, we put up our tents and wrapped ourselves in the steam and water of a warm shower. After that we finally wandered into town and found the local pub, like all respectable athletes.

During that first day on the Eden the sense of having returned home was ever-present and particularly calming. For me, it was enhanced by the cathartic feeling of being active. I found that I was able to relax simply because I wasn't stuck indoors, being lazy. Sure, those moments spent swimming were few and far between, yet still they woke me to the idea that you must escape from time to time, if only to see your freshly built cage from the outside, looking in. This steady realisation seemed to clear my head as well. In a way it felt as though the water was washing me clean and flushing my mind. With hindsight, I realise that I was starting to let go of my precious, manicured self. In fact, we were leaving everything behind. Down hillsides, into valleys, through forests and gorges – slowly the Eden was leading us to the sea. I couldn't stop thinking that this was something our species had done from time immemorial. It felt more real and true to me, as though I was locking into a version of the human experience that eclipsed my recent mechanical cycle of routine and rest. It might sound slightly hokey, but I felt closer to our primal origins.

I'm curious to look at what our physiology says about our development and our relationship with certain marine animals. For example, in the first sixth months of growth, human babies have a much more advanced diving reflex, which is a mammalian response evidenced by seals and other aquatic animals. During this period, if a baby is submerged underwater they will instinctively hold their breath, slowing their heart rate and conserving a supply of oxygen for their most vital organs. As we grow slightly older we begin to lose this ability, while also becoming more susceptible to drowning. It's this same conscious control of our breathing that allows us to speak. The only other animals that possess this same control are built for diving underwater.

Have you ever watched someone jumping from a high board and arcing into a faultless swan dive? Could you imagine an ungainly chimpanzee performing the same move? The precision of movement required in that moment is an example of our unusual physique and dexterity. Somehow, we have become this hairless, big-brained mammal, capable of feats that no other primate could accomplish. We are also the only primate with a subcutaneous layer of fat. Other land-dwelling mammals have deposits of fat held inside the body wall, which cushion and protect their vital organs; we, on the other hand, like whales or seals, have this layer of blubber pressed under our skin. Make no mistake, this is human *blubber*.

The more I read evidence like this and the more I experience the water for myself, the more vividly I can picture our ancestor – the aquatic ape. Now, it doesn't strike me as odd that our relatives combed prehistoric coastlines and rivers, hunting and scavenging in the shallows. To me, it seems so much more believable that we found strength in the water, rather than going it alone on the sun-beaten savannah. Consequently, I think we are still married to the different waterways that surround us. We have been pre-programmed to relish and utilise water. From what I've read, it seems as though this programming is wired into the reptilian brain – the oldest region of the human brain – which incorporates both the brainstem and the cerebellum. Essentially, this particular region is an instinct factory, managing our unconscious bodily functions, from our breathing to our body temperature. The automatic processes of the reptilian brain are largely concerned with the primitive self. We're talking about territorial dominance and many other aspects of survival, churned out by this flinching, rapid-fire system. As part of our subconscious, this region struggles to separate reality from imagination. Think of those conjured projections you find in dreams . . . imagine, say, some shady figure appearing at the side of your bed. These projections are conjured up by the reptilian brain, which serves to present your conscious mind with hypothetical threats. This supports the idea that our survival instincts are embedded deep within us, since they can be traced to the oldest structures in the brain. However, what's most fascinating to me – someone whose forays into science are analogous to the random pecks of a magpie rootling through haystacks looking for shiny things – is the origin of these instincts we've acquired.

For some reason, perhaps simply for survival purposes, I think our reptilian brain preserves our proclivity for swimming. I believe this element now flows through our unconscious minds like a deep, subterranean river. After all, our earliest moments of being occurred within the womb. It makes sense then that the congenital sensation of being submerged would stay with us – in other words, we'd retain memories of that cushioned sanctuary, within the amniotic sac, where we lay furled, suspended in fluid. The formation of our infant mind was nurtured by this environment. That was where our brains began to develop. Then, rather rudely, we were expelled from our mums and thrust into a world of swastikas, socks and risk assessments . . . that is to say – we suddenly shot like a screaming bullet onto dry land and were forced to adapt.

Plan Your Route (Jack's Tip): In the water – deprived of your usual senses – your thoughts will surface in different ways. You'll also register minor fluctuations in your breathing pattern. Clear goals can help to counter anxiety and help you stay calm. So plan your route carefully before you enter the water. Is this going to be a point-to-point swim? How long are you staying in for? Listen to your body. If numb fingers or unsteady breathing instruct you to exit the water, then do so. It might also help to choose something like a cluster of trees to mark your exit point – a prominent natural feature to leave your things beside so you know exactly where you're headed.

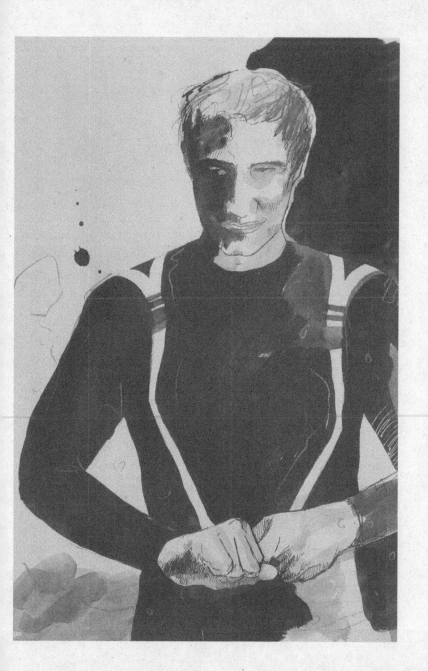

5

Water Therapy

Simply put, routine outdoor swimming can greatly improve your mental health. It's also fun, communal and stokes the kind of visceral good feeling you'll keep coming back to. All it takes is that first little step. Once you've braved the icy plunge and outlasted the rush of discomfort, you can find an innate love for the water and the freedom it gives you. Indeed, it's not often you get to enter an entirely new world, but once you do you'll be privy to a pure form of therapy, capable of lifting the yoke of anxiety and restlessness.

When folk say that swimming helps with depression, they aren't just offering some arbitrary solution for deep-rooted, complicated problems. Swimming really *can* help to prevent anxiety and stress. There is a scientific explanation for why this is possible – why so many of us discover a second home in the water. We need this element for many different reasons. When a baby leaves the womb, their bodily composition is 75 per cent water. Water is used throughout the body for various vital functions. It allows us to salivate, enables our cells to grow, multiply and survive, lubricates our joints, helps to deliver oxygen to our organs and acts as a shock absorber for the brain and spinal cord. As we grow older, the amount of water in our system reduces. By the time we reach adulthood, about 60 per cent of our body is water. So, in a sense, the strain of ageing becomes a gradual process of *drying up*.

There are other factors to consider as well. Those of us who regularly hit the junk food and dodge exercise will start to *dry up* more quickly. This is because fat tissue contains less water than lean tissue. One of the things routine swimming does for you is it allows you to build up a broader, more muscular physique, commonly referred to as the *swimmer's body*. And, as you gain this physique, your body will start to produce more water, which in turn will be used for all those vital processes carried out automatically inside you. Simply put, your body and mind will run more smoothly, and they will be better lubricated, just so long as you drink plenty of water (around four to six pints a day) and swim regularly.

Perhaps the most famous advocate of this kind of wild remedy was a little-known naturalist called Charles Darwin. During a period of prolonged writer's block, Darwin took up wild swimming and began to frequent Malvern Spa, hidden among the green hills of the West Midlands, where he underwent numerous cold-water therapy sessions. Supposedly, Darwin was so amazed by the results that he arranged to have huge volumes of water diverted from Malvern's natural spring to his own home, for use in his bath.

Important though he was, Darwin was just one among a great many other respected intellectuals who popularised cold-water therapy in the eighteenth and nineteenth centuries. In fact, it would be impossible to offer even a brief summation of the practice without mentioning Vincent Priessnitz. Today, Priessnitz is credited with the widespread revival of classical hydrotherapy. The story goes that he was run over by a cart and left crippled with several broken bones. Supposedly, his doctor wrapped his injuries in wet linen, which was cut into strips and drenched with cold spring water. Within a fortnight, Priessnitz was up and walking, like a mysterious revenant. Then, after he'd made a full recovery, he began work turning the family farmhouse into a water sanatorium, known today as the Water University and situated in Gräfenberg, which is part of Austrian Silesia, half hidden among the forested mountain peaks. When patients visited – as they often did – they were subjected to a spartan experience and given basic rooms with windows that were left open to the harsh mountain air. Every morning they would be woken at four and usually put through a breakfast ritual of being wrapped from neck to toe in wet linen. By the end of their therapy the patient would've endured a strict regime of mummifications, waterfall massages and mountain pool baptisms, interspersed with various healthy meals – mostly just wholemeal bread and strawberries.

While hydrotherapy was common among European intellectuals in the eighteenth and nineteenth centuries, it was also being embraced by countless others throughout China, India and Japan. However, most of the recorded proponents do refer to European resorts and luxury health spas, which doubled as medical institutions for sufferers of chronic illness. In most cases these places proved that water was replenishing weary bodies and soothing troubled minds. Over time, the subtle mystique and simple nature of this practice had attracted several eccentric Victorian practitioners, none of whom have been quite so celebrated as the founder of Darwin's clinic in Malvern, Dr James Manby Gully. During his career, Dr Gully put Malvern on the map and attracted a roster of famous patients, including (besides Darwin) Charles Dickens, Florence Nightingale and the English Poet Laureate, Alfred Tennyson. According to his own account, Tennyson visited the clinic after a nervous breakdown and later stated that his time there, spent roaming the scenic grounds and sampling the springs of Malvern Hills: 'half-cured, half-destroyed [him]'.

There have also been several prisons and asylums over the years that used flowing water to facilitate the gentle rehabilitation of inmates and patients alike. In Damascus, Syria, there is a mental institution that is one of the oldest in the world. Within this institution there are a number of rooms with thin partition walls, built around an open courtyard with a view of the sky overhead. At the centre of this yard there is a large fountain filling streams that bubble through carved stone channels, snaking outwards into each individual room. It was believed that the perpetual sound of running water would relax the patients and encourage them to be more cooperative. Still water is often seen as being impure in many Arabic and Islamic cultures, whereas flowing water is considered to be purifying. This was another key principle of the Syrian mental institution. According to records kept at the time, their use of running water had a very positive influence on many of their patients.

Further evidence of water treatment has also been found in the remains of the ancient Greek and Roman civilisations.

For example, we know the latter constructed towering aqueducts, sending ribbons of fresh water tumbling to pristine marble baths, reminiscent of modern-day spas. Slowly, the role of water in our societies evolved beyond its use for cleanliness and sustenance. We can now look back and find myriad references to the significance of this elixir, from trivial accounts of peasants bathing in rivers, to flourishes of fantasy, like Ponce de Leon's Fountain of Youth, which was thought to confer long-lost vitality.

In fact, the more you peer into the history of water, the more you realise how many influential figures have used it as a constant source of inspiration. Recently, I read that Lord Byron and Rupert Brooke both used to swim naked near the water meadows of Grantchester. Supposedly, Brooke would paddle his canoe up from King's College and bathe in the natural pools and river spots he knew. Sometimes he'd also wander down to the water late at night for a moonlit dip with his friends. Then they would camp around open fires, strumming guitars and singing together. I like to think that it was in these moments, hidden under the leafy shell of the forest, that he discovered the value of the English countryside, which he later lamented in his most famous poem, 'The Soldier':

> . . . *There shall be*
> *In that rich earth a richer dust concealed;*
> *A dust whom England bore, shaped, made aware,*
> *Gave, once, her flowers to love, her ways to roam,*
> *A body of England's, breathing English air,*
> *Washed by the rivers, blest by suns of home.*

Another writer who took lessons from the water was William Wordsworth, one of the Lake Poets who romanticised and roamed the Lake District. Wordsworth once wrote: 'the child is the father of the man'. After I read that line I became kind of hooked on it. For me, it was a reminder of the need to keep in touch with your kid-self. Whenever I go back to it I feel emboldened, itching to get outdoors and dive into a cold body of water somewhere. When I reconnect with that part of myself, I'm always reminded of a time when we were free to express ourselves without limitation, although, I wonder – doesn't it go back much further than that?

As I mentioned before, it's likely that the sport of wild swimming was enjoyed by our earliest ancestors. Therefore, when you jump into the water you are partaking in a primordial activity – one that our hirsute relatives seem to have pursued. If this is true, then it wouldn't be a stretch to say that wild swimming connects us to all the former species of the *Homo* genus – the same animals who developed an octave scale to play music, painted cave walls with beautiful ochre horses and decorated the graves of their loved ones. Let's dip our toes, then, into that congenital memory pool – let's take a second to imagine how they must've felt, swimming in those unspoilt prehistoric lakes and rivers.

It's quite a wonderful thought, isn't it? I'm sure that we can scarcely roam back far enough to realise how long this sport has been embedded in the human soul. What we do know, however, is that water came to flow continuously through the veins of our greatest civilisations, just as the Nile pumped life into the arid heart of Egypt. We also know that water has helped our psychological evolution, from the element-hardened Neanderthals, splashing through glacial rivers, to the wetsuit-clad workmen bouncing up and down the lidos of our modern cities.

Fortunately, we haven't yet lost touch with the waters of this blue planet. More and more hardy folk can be found waddling into the waves like wacky frogmen. Together, we are starting to rediscover the physiological and psychological benefits of swimming outdoors. This is the revolution in motion, ushering in an era of improved wellbeing. We now know that wild swimming is proven to strengthen the heart and lungs, while also offering a respite from the guttural growl and whistle of mechanical society. Even some of those partly immobilised by agonising back injuries can usually swim with little to no pain. The same is true for those with damaged joints and ligaments. So, one last question comes to mind: what are you waiting for? It's time to re-enter the natural world as equals. Time to see the leafy riverbanks and rugged coastlines sweeping by. Time to feel the rainfall on your cheek as you reach through the water. It's time for all those vagaries of sensation and wonder.

Swim the Eden Expedition, Day 2
Sunday 16 August 2015

I woke early the next morning and peered out of my tent to find coils of mist, like icy ghosts, roaming our campsite. I savoured those last few moments of warmth. Then I treated my fellow campers to the sight of our tent giving birth to a six-foot-three man-child, like Jim Carrey in that scene from *Ace Ventura*, squeezing through the rubbery sphincter of an animatronic rhino.

I found that the grass was still cold with dew, and that our wetsuits, which we'd draped over a nearby picnic table, had collected the moisture and were now heavy from the added weight. Still half asleep, I scanned the campsite and looked out over the surrounding trees, beyond the roving fields, to where the hills stood as markers for the way ahead. Then Calum crawled out from the tent behind me, bleary-eyed, but ready, he told me, for a much easier day in the deeper current.

Before long, Dad arrived and Robbie and I went with him to meet a woman from a local news station who wanted to interview us. Robbie and Calum had both been filmed for a swimming promo a few days earlier, but this was the first time I'd been in front of the camera. The reporter seemed in good spirits when we met her, which perhaps had something to do with the setting she was about to film. Together, we all walked up to the wall that edged the lay-by, hoping to get a better look. From the bridge, we could see right down into Stenkrith Gorge, over a series of steep, cascading waterfalls that snaked out of sight. The fast water roared as it crashed into a ragged gully, the mouth of which was shaded by a drooping canopy of leaves, with their myriad tips glistening in the morning light. The roar of the water was enough to convince us that we were finally going to get a chance to do some swimming.

Sucking in the fresh air, with the promise of a deep opening stretch, Robbie and I agreed that good things awaited us. The River Eden, our old childhood plaything, wouldn't let us down. Finally, she'd gathered her momentum and collected a powerful volume of water that would sweep us off the rocky bed and carry us downriver.

For some time, Robbie, the reporter and I talked about the previous day and the brief stint of canyoning, while waiting for James and Calum to arrive. When they turned up it was clear that no one wanted to delay. Dad helped us pour sachets of energy supplement into our water bottles and we stuffed everything we needed into the dry-bags – we didn't have James's kayak yet so we could only take what we could carry. Once we were all ready, with our cold wetsuits zipped up and our dry-bags tightly sealed, we followed a wooden stairway through the forest, down into the steep gorge. The view from the bottom was even more stunning than it was from above. The river funnelled over tall precipices and tumbled into black plunge pools shadowed by stacked outcrops of rock. These rocks stepped up over us and created a shaded seclusion that turned the water an inky black and made it look less than inviting. However, the fact it was deep was enough to keep our spirits up. We could also see the arc of the bridge far above us, half hidden by the canopy.

I took a moment as the other two pulled on their wetsuit shoes and cleaned their goggles. I listened to the wind as it breathed through the leaves and ran my fingers through clumps of sagging clubmoss, tracing the faces of the rocks above us, which were patched with white lichen and wrapped in tufty cinquefoil.

'Did you ever read Hunter S. Thompson's writing schedule?' Calum asked, dancing on his feet to warm up his body.

I nodded: 'It's nuts.'

'Up to midday he had about six hours of cocaine,' he went on, 'then in the evening he was onto the weed and acid.'

'All with gin and whisky,' I added.

'Every day.'

'Yeah, it's crazy.'

'He didn't start writing until about nine.' Calum grinned, plucking his goggles from a nearby rock. 'He was basically nocturnal.'

'I don't know why he couldn't just start without all that.'

'Well, he was just an insane, crazy, genius writer.'

'And he was also a gentleman,' I said. 'He had a wife – lived on a big country ranch.'

Around us leaves were falling through glittering clouds of tiny insects. The leaves pirouetted as they fell and then hit the water and rushed downriver. From where we were standing it did look beautiful and, the more I thought about it, the more I felt that this was the perfect place to start our second day on the Eden, replete with all the enclosed quietude of a natural sanctuary.

The little segment we did for local news involved an interview and several shots of us following each other through the narrow pools, over sloping cascades blanketed by moss. It gave us a chance to get used to the freezing water, and was also the first time we'd all swum for a camera together. When the filming was done, the reporter gave us the thumbs-up and Dad waved us off as we floated away under the trees to begin our second day on the Eden.

For some time, we were buoyed by a distinct sense of

escape. The bustle of the town receded behind the canopy and the overgrown banks began to enclose us. Suddenly our aching feet had found relief, kicking through the water as we groped the riverbed and crawled along with the current. Meanwhile James scrambled up and down the bank with his camera. Then he joined us in the water further downriver. At that point the pools turned to smooth chutes, shallow stretches and the occasional waist-deep swathe. For the most part we slid like penguins, slotted comfortably into the rocky creases that writhed across the riverbed. This was where the fabled Floaty God emerged incarnate for the first time. A moment earlier, I'd found the benefit of lying sprawled out with my butt cheeks clenched, my back slightly arched and my arms outstretched on either side of me. In this position, I managed to glide smoothly over knobbled stretches of shallow water – hence the fancy name that James decided to bestow upon me.

After that the commandments quickly followed, breathed into being with, I imagine, the same kind of heady enthusiasm that accompanies the start of any religion. Thou Shalt Not Covet Thy Neighbour's Float was the founding principle of our monotheistic cult, led by myself, assuming the role of the godhead. To my reclining delight, I became a rotund Swim-Buddha, who, through lack of training, had somehow pulled an inadvertent blinder and wound up warm enough to sit in the water during breaks, while the others – those well-built non-Buddhas – stood shuddering or dancing around in vain attempts to keep warm.

Anyway, the Floaty God gave his Sermon on the Mount

by way of water osmosis. Soon all four of us were lying on our backs, using our feet to feel for larger rocks as we floated onwards. Slowly I watched the clear sky turn to running water overhead. Then, as we continued down the Eden and approached midday, the journey grew increasingly pleasurable. Sometimes we were blessed with intermittent bends of deep water and we could swim through the reed-flanked corridors and lazily front-crawl without scraping our fingers on the rocks. It was such a great feeling to finally be doing what we'd trained for and to be in the water together, inching down the Eden, stroke after stroke. It was in those moments of escape that we found a calming rhythm, and time to relax, as well.

In fact, I still remember my thoughts quite distinctly. As I began to swim I started remembering my second year at uni. I was left just bumming around and being your average student. I was also smoking too much weed and letting go of too many things that deserved more care and attention. I distanced myself from my girlfriend and developed low self-esteem. I began to hunt for conspiracies, hunched in the darkness of a cluttered student den, prying strips of skin back from the inner organs of the world, or some such sanctimonious and ultimately inconsequential bullshit. I was hungry for vague information I didn't really understand. I wanted to know why there was thermite found in the foundations of the Twin Towers and the reason behind Tower Seven falling. I also wanted to know why JFK was assassinated so soon after giving *that* particular speech.

This behaviour went on for several months, until I'd pretty

much lost the will to stick up for myself and maintain my convictions. Once, I even remember sitting on the floor of Carlisle station, among the cigarette butts and chewing gum, since the only bench left was beside a gang of little teens and I was paranoid they'd harass me. I think that was one of my lowest points, but luckily a series of jarring experiences finally woke me up. The one that was perhaps the most significant involved this grumpy kid at a house party in Manchester. I remember he took a drink out of my hand and I flicked his hand away and took it back. The problem was I hated confrontation so much at this point that I didn't even bring my eyes up to meet his. Timid, I'd just stared down at the floor while he smirked and turned away. It was an insult that injured my pride. Stupidly, I kept thinking I could've throttled the life out of him – he was smaller than me, after all. The morning after that party I realised I was starting to dislike myself. I'd got lost following the old Lotus Eater's myth of hedonic bliss, and I was becoming an ego-maniac in the process.

In the end, I knew that something had to change, otherwise I'd wake up one day to find the kid who'd wanted to be a writer had been disappointed, irrevocably.

I thought a lot about those periods as I dug my strokes into the river, listening to the water rolling over my ears. I remembered how much Beth and my closest friends had helped to reveal what really mattered. I remembered Robbie taking me for a run on the beach and pushing me back into the gym. Now, I felt like I was cocooned in the present, and everything that was behind me was far away. I could let it go – let myself off. *You just got lazy . . . it's okay.* This was a chance to be better. Gone was that spoffish student who thought there was nothing more to life than going out or getting high. With each stroke, it felt like I was gripping more of the grit that once helped me at school, especially on the rugby pitch. I was also starting to feel useful again.

Soon the river widened and the current invited us onto rocky plateaus, over which the swirling water flowed slowly, speckled with whorls of froth. On either side of us the river-banks were crowded with beautiful, young trees and the canopy was thick and verdant. I realise now that wherever water flows there is always natural beauty found in abundance, whether it's the stepped rice paddies of Bali, Indonesia, or the lily-dotted lakes in the botanical gardens of Marrakesh, Morocco.

We stopped for lunch after an hour or so and sat in a circle on the bank, enjoying the shade from the trees. The sun was at its highest and the field and green windrows around us were warmed by a pleasant haze. Little colourful birds darted and skimmed over the river as it flowed slowly on our other flank. It was even warm enough for us to unzip our wetsuits and dry the insides.

As we soaked up the sun, James handed out a round of sandwiches and we leant back and ate them with murmurs of approval.

'The beard is looking good Rob,' Calum said eventually, breaking the silence.

'I'd grow a beard if I could,' said James.

'Why don't you?' I asked, through a mouthful of seeded crust.

'I couldn't have it if I went back on duty.'

'The army would make you shave it off?' I asked, slightly stunned.

'Yes – I could have a moustache, just not a beard.'

'Could you have the David Brent?'

'Goatee?'

'Yep.'

'Nope.'

It seemed odd to me and it must've confused Calum too, because he jumped in with another question: 'Do they let you have tattoos in the army?'

James paused and we all took a moment to digest the idea. Calum blinked: 'That's a stupid question, isn't it?'

We all started laughing.

'Sergeant,' I chirped, putting on a squeaky, high-pitched voice, 'can I have a tattoo?'

Later, Calum got onto the subject of what it was like being a sales manager. He explained how he'd been hired as someone who could socialise with clients, generally providing a grinning face for an office full of sheepish tech gurus. It didn't sound so bad, but then he started to reflect on his previous role as a sales drone. One day his mentor had called the sales team in before another day on the phones. Calum told us how he'd stood there, po-faced, in front of a high-intensity montage of rugby hits. All the while, his zealous sales mentor stood nodding along as the brutality unfolded, convinced of the link between his team smashing their targets and the players smashing each other. Calum went on to describe how the despondent sales team trudged back to their desks and slumped into the macho and jockish imposture of life as a seller – or, to put it another way, life as an ant under the leather-wrapped boot of Bill Hicks.

Every time we asked Calum – as we did then – what it was he was selling, his answer was always punctuated by several world-weary sighs. The short answer was he worked for money – and, man, was the money good; well deserved too, I should add. Job satisfaction didn't come into it though – not really. It sounded like a sure way to drive yourself crazy. Evidently the inane grind had taken its toll on him, hence his wild escape into Nettle Warrior, Tough Mudder, Iron Man, Celt Man and the general devotion he developed towards training and bodily torment.

The reason I stress that point is because it made it all the sweeter when we set off again, after lunch, and watched as Calum strode ahead of us and launched himself into a flamboyant water dance. Suddenly he was frolicking in the shallows, strutting and flicking his legs like a camp heron. He was free from the cage match of Blighty's business hub. He was a dainty butterfly unfurling from its stiff chrysalis. A man who'd been liberated, let loose from the predatory consumer hunt. For one day only – and for our amusement – he was a water-bound Louie Spence, wriggling and jiving like there was nothing better to do in life. He seemed to relish every step, softened by the fresh, padded shoes he had remembered to pack that morning. Then, occasionally, he'd hear us laughing and look back, egged-on, before his dance evolved into outrageous new territory, causing startled birds to disperse around him, bursting from the trees in fits of squawking disapproval.

There was no one else for miles around and for a long time our only company was the cows that peered over the banks and occasionally followed us, galloping dopily through the adjacent fields. It was clear that we were starting to make ground as well. The scenery grew increasingly wilder, until the tangled thickets and nettle patches encroached upon the river and sealed us in our own private waterway. All the while the Eden continued to repay us with secluded stretches of swimmable water, although for the most part we still wound up either wading or crawling over the rocks, at which point I'd often lie flat with my lips submerged and my eyes level with the water, glimpsing insects as they skimmed across the surface.

Later, the clouds cleared and the thickets peeled back and slowly uncovered the bucolic heart of the Eden Valley. We reached another stretch of deep water as the wind softened and the current slowed. Soon the banks were screened on both sides by wilting reeds and I felt their cool shadows as I moved through them, taking care to keep some strength behind my strokes, so as not to lose any heat. Carried by the current, I slowly swam out from the striped shade, until I was surrounded by a peaceful, grassy wold, warmed by the sun. Then the stone church of Great Musgrave came into view, alongside wide, open fields dotted with grazing sheep. Slowly the banks parted and the water became shallow enough for Calum to polish his fruity dance moves. This time we decided that he deserved a new name to match his energetic alter-ego, and thus he became . . . Lorenzo Falls.

Our second day closed as we rounded the next bend and approached the hilltop village of Sandford. We were still several miles shy of Appleby, but all in high spirits, having swum enough to protect our blisters and the odd twisted ankle. We decided to call it a day and pitch our tents on a green somewhere in Sandford. Grinning, our mum greeted us as we climbed up the bank and peeled off our cold wetsuits. She was followed by the frenzied, wagging whirlwind of Marlin.

Swim the Eden Expedition, Day 3
Monday 17 August 2015

The next day we were travelling further down the Eden with plenty of deep water ahead of us. I made a point of reminding myself to forget all our reasons for starting the swim, in favour of savouring the experience. I found it much easier to stay comfortable. I'd grown accustomed to waking up early because of work. The thing that did surprise me, though, was the surreal experience of wiping the sleep from my eyes, lifting the door of my tent and finding greenery on my doorstep.

Slowly, I climbed out onto the dewy grass and took a moment to stand and enjoy the hills, the fields and the fresh air. Then I wrapped myself in my warm Alpkit jacket and pulled my woollen balaclava up over my lips – those cold early hours could be unforgiving and I needed several layers to take them in my stride.

As soon as I was warm, I walked around the field while

the others untangled themselves from their sleeping bags. It didn't take more than a minute or so, but I compiled a mental list of everything I knew about the day ahead. Before long I got to thinking about a message we'd been sent the night before, courtesy of our cousins, Owen and Gareth. They'd managed to sort out a lift up north with Luke, which meant they'd be waiting for us at the end of the swim. I was excited to see them again, at the mouth of the Eden. We'd visited them from a young age and spent three holidays a year at their house, just outside of London. They're both similar ages to my brothers and me, and we were all into the same things growing up, so we became very close.

I remember how we'd always meet up after Christmas and gather our toys to see what games we could invent. It's funny, Gareth and Owen had this private water-pistol arms race that went on for years. Every time we arrived they'd have a new super-soaker and then a super-deluxe mega soaker, until I was half expecting them to go the full whack by commandeering a water cannon from the metropolitan riot squad.

I have myriad good memories from that time, many of which would've escaped me were it not for a handful of photographs that aptly sum up our childhood together. One image that springs to mind shows Robbie, Calum and me locked in an intense game of football while Gareth and Owen are busy throttling each other in the corner. Another – we joke that it's evidence of why Calum never became an artist – shows Calum drawing at a lone table while Robbie sits gleefully at an easel, attended by various family members.

Soon the sun peeked over the distant Pennines and peeled

the shade off the long, misty fields and farms that rolled away ahead of us, like our very own Hobbiton. I could hear the trill of birdsong, the guttural purr of a quadbike on some hidden country lane and the rattle of an off-road jeep as a yawning farmer headed off into his field. Having found no local landowners, we'd camped on the village green, nestled close to a large bush, which had shielded us from the nightly rain. There was also a single picnic bench nearby and our wetsuits were stretched across the seats, still wet and ominously cold.

Before Dad arrived, we packed the tents and gathered our things on the bench. While we were packing, several early risers pulled their jeeps onto the grass verge and asked how far we'd come and wished us luck. It seemed we were becoming local celebrities since our little stint on the news the previous morning. We'd been able to watch the coverage too – Calum had managed to find a few bars of signal before we went to bed and so we'd all huddled around his iPhone. It was surreal seeing our faces and hearing the reporter talking about our swim. We knew that we couldn't let it go to our heads though. Celebrity in Cumbria is not such a hard thing to come by. You could steal a chicken one afternoon and overnight you'd be the talk of the entire county, lauded by the *Herald* as the mysterious chicken bandit.

So, the morning came and the cold passed as the sun came up and announced the dawn of our Z-list fame. Among the folk who wished us luck there was also one farmer who offered us his outhouse. This meant we had a chance to sit on an actual toilet and avoid squatting in the bushes, like the ape-men we were fast becoming. Mind you, ape-men or not, we were still getting a version of the VIP treatment. In fact, when we got down to the bridge it only improved, since a cameraman and another reporter were there waiting for us.

The cameraman quickly attached a GoPro to my head, which I held in place using the strap of one of my two swim caps. After that the three of us waded out into the Eden until we were waist-deep. Standing with the cold current rushing against my legs, I looked down and held my Speedo goggles dangling from my fingers. The goggles had picked up a few scratches after I'd been bundled into rocks and dragged across the riverbed the previous day. I spat into the lenses and rubbed some water over the insides to clean the grease and mist. My brothers were waiting on either side of me, swinging their arms and psyching themselves up for the early plunge. The first one was always the hardest, partly because your mind was still swathed in the warm sleeping bag you'd just abandoned. Now it seemed like it was taking us longer and longer to dunk our heads into the icy river. There was only one thing for it: it's like when you jump from a rocky outcrop into water; eventually you just have to count yourself down and say: '*Fuck it.*'

Once we were in the water the cold soon faded and the morning swim became slow and peaceful. Dreary clouds loomed over us and the river bore us on a snaking path between walled fields flanked by sparse huddles of trees. A pattern was starting to emerge in the way we tackled each day. We were also finding our roles as the swim unfolded. Undoubtedly, I was the kid of the group, the first one to ask for a food stop, but also a calming influence as the relaxed Floaty God. Calum was the frontrunner, responsible for guiding us down the river. James was the documentarian, who also made a point of staying off camera and out of interviews. He ensured, through his own volition, that the swim remained just about the three of us. In fact, his relentless good conduct gave testimony to his job, as a captain in the British Army who'd seen one tour already in Afghanistan and witnessed first-hand the drudgery and foul play of modern warfare. He later told us how his duty had led him into the position of relaying coordinates to drone operators. I remember I'd spoken to him a month or so earlier, when he explained how he wanted to do something to help people in the future – something more training-orientated, perhaps. Then, finally, there was Robbie, ever the unstoppable turtle, ploughing through the water like a stocky tugboat. He never complained, but instead acted like a perpetual motor, churning water at the back and propelling us all forward.

Soon the forest gave way to shrubs and the banks began to rise up on both sides. Occasionally I noticed sloping trees jutting out over the tall grass, spotted with pale clumps of lichen. Then we passed under the arch of a tall railway bridge – the very same one, in fact, that I'd travelled over a few days earlier. I remember how I'd looked down, seen the river and thought how wonderful it was going to be to swim the full length of it. Now here I was, paddling through the shallow water and talking to my brothers about a whole range of things, but mostly just about how good it felt to be in the Eden.

*A few days into our River Eden swim, still smiling
and enjoying the leafy surroundings*

As the day went on we pressed forward at a slow pace and edged between swathes of low-lying farmland, through stretches of open water, flanked by overgrown banks that hummed and clicked with insect life. At one point, I remember rounding a corner and seeing a red stone bridge that arced between the distant treetops. There was a lone old woman standing on the bridge, hunched over the wall. I had no idea how long she'd been waiting for us, but her presence gave me a sudden surge of inspiration. Then we passed under the bridge's shadow and she began to clap, before leaning over the wall and shouting out pointers for the obstacles ahead. Floating on, we quickly thanked her and rolled over onto our backs and waved as we were swept away with the current.

When we rounded the next bend, I began to think about how close the country community can be, especially when it came to something a little mad. *Nowt so queer as folk* was one of the more popular maxims that did the rounds in our local pubs and never failed to draw a wistful murmur from the elderly fixtures who stooped over the bars. Madness was a quality Cumbrians were drawn to – wildness too, which seemed to be a mark of a life well spent, far from neat, big-city sensibilities.

The first place where we stopped and got out of the water that day was Appleby. Its nearness was heralded by a series of stone houses and secret gardens that tapered down to the water's edge. Then wide-open lawns came into view and a small crowd appeared, spread along the bank, many of whom already knew about the swim and wished us luck. Eventually we climbed out of the water and headed to where Mum was waiting, close to the local swimming pool and gym. I remember Robbie treading water while Calum picked him up and waded into the shallows, carrying him cradled like a baby. Then Robbie put on a child's voice and looked up at Calum with big, doe eyes.

'My hero,' he crooned.

We didn't take long for lunch because the cold was starting to make us all shiver. We had just enough time to dive into the food bags Mum had brought, take a photo with the local lifeguards and meet a young boy who'd just finished his swimming lesson. Then the cold and the miles ahead beckoned us back into the water – it was midday and we still had a long way to travel. We wasted no time in paddling out into deeper water and diving under once we reached it. Then folk waved from the banks as we swung around a fast-flowing arm of the river. When we began to swim again I slowed my stroke and with each breath I took a second to take in our surroundings. I saw shaded greenhouses, cluttered lawns, dirt paths and dog-walkers, all sweeping by in a foliage-wrapped flurry of little country images. Eventually, I looked back at the last few houses in Appleby and felt a pang of gladness, still somewhat overwhelmed by the welcome we'd received.

As we drifted out of town the sunlight began to spread across the bank, revealing a row of caravans and trailers, positioned close to the river. The low light, windless air and undisturbed water seemed to combine in creating an encompassing sense of calm, such as you tend to associate with those finer moments in life, when everything slows down and your mind relaxes and your senses clear, before the ebb of clarity crowds your head again with garrulous thoughts. In that fleeting moment, the still reflection of the campsite was held on the water's surface, rippling ahead of us. And we swam through this smooth, sunlight mirror, one after another. Between each stroke, we could then turn our heads and steal further glimpses of cluttered, fenceless gardens and low-lit rooms, framed between the trees.

The rest of the day passed without many incidents. We walked a short distance along the bank to avoid the fetid outflow of a sewage facility. Apart from that, though, we were mostly just swimming downriver at a slow pace. We'd keep turning our heads away from a world of airy birdsong and rushing water, then sliding under, among the rolling sonorities of the cold, green underworld. We repeated this over and over, with each third stroke, until the rhythmic action of *one, two, three, breathe* lulled us into a state of calm detachment. At that point the cold became a soothing embrace and the act of swimming was transformed into an escape of sorts. I couldn't say from what exactly, but at least in the sense of feeling as though both mind and body were connected and similarly engaged in this primal activity, which is far older than ourselves.

In a way, it seemed like we were being rewarded with several miles of uninterrupted swimming. However, I did start to fear for this dramatic yarn I'm spinning here. I needed something exciting to happen. A rogue goose erupting from the reeds and attacking us, perhaps. Or maybe an appearance from the dreaded pike. Luckily, these vain hopes were eventually disrupted by an eccentric farmer called Elizabeth Warburton. She first revealed herself with a cheery flourish as she sprinted out of her stately farmhouse and bounded down her garden, towards the river. It was Robbie who first caught sight of her, while he was splayed on his front, being tugged along by the current in turtle position. She called cheerily to us and waved from the water's edge. We exchanged confused glances and waded within earshot, at which point Elizabeth beckoned us over and confessed to having waited several hours for us. For what, you might ask? Surely not just to glimpse the Hudsons and their goonish grins? No, of course not. Elizabeth, as she proceeded to explain, had been waiting for a chance to offer us samples of their organic milk.

Slightly confused, we staggered up the bank, introduced ourselves and accepted the rather generous, if a little unexpected, offer. Then her friendly kids, two daughters and son, came down the long sloping lawn with a tray of glasses and a pitcher of fresh milk. They poured each of us a full glass, fresh from the udder, and Calum gestured to Robbie's look of flushed delight, explaining that he was in the habit of knocking back whole pints of milk whenever he exercised.

After a few more glasses we bounded back into the Eden, where we were treated to the odd sensation of swilling milk in our stomachs as we swam. As it happened, we only had about an hour left in the water before the last embers of sunlight faded behind the hills. After that, ominous shadows clutched the icy river and the yoke of night loomed over the treetops.

Done for the day, we stopped at a bridge several miles shy of Boldon and agreed to make up the extra mile or so in the morning, if only to escape the prospect of swimming in the dark. The place where we got out was isolated and there were no buildings in sight, save for a lone farmhouse encircled by a ring of crops. Exhausted, we trudged over the hump of the bridge, and Dad, who'd arrived an hour or so earlier, snapped a picture of us with the Pennines in the background. It was a significant moment for us since those were the same hills we used to see from our house in Langwathby, which meant we were close to home. I remember how we took the bus back from school every day, approaching the Pennines down a long road, rolling past the cricket and football fields and then over the green military bridge, with the grey Eden rushing below us. Those rugged hills were getting much closer now. We could even make out the white dot of a spherical hilltop building we called the Golf Ball.

That night we would, to our relief, be staying with Scott and Lissie Stevens in Temple Sowerby. Back at their cosy house we ate steaming, meaty pies with gravy and stroked their dogs as they nuzzled our legs. By the time we'd mopped the plates clean, our stomachs were bulging and making the low, appeased sounds of dreaming beasts. Feeling deeply satisfied, I thanked our hosts, retired to bed and buried my head in the thick pillows.

Make It Social (Cal's Tip): You'll be surprised how many people respond to odd adventures. Share your wild swimming exploits. This can range from telling the local swimming club to spreading the word through local press and beyond. You'll be amazed at the positive responses you'll often recieve from the outdoors community. For Swim the Eden we had locals who offered up their gardens for lunch stops – elderly couples brought us hot mugs of coffee at the end of the day and one man even vowed to come swim with us, accompanied by his award-winning Cumbrian cheese. All these little gestures go a long way to making your adventure truly memorable and a hell of a lot more fun.

6

No More Kings

Mum once said that if there isn't a heaven for her dog then there isn't a heaven for her either. If there *is* a heaven, and if it really is all it's cracked up to be, then I assume the gate walls will be prowled by lazy cats, and elephants will lead you down sunlit avenues, while armies of hamsters scurry around your feet, digging through the cotton-wool clouds. In fact, there probably wouldn't be many humans there at all. After all, who are we to deserve such innocent and modest company? No animal has ever shown such wanton destruction, within its own species, as we have. No other animal has survived, despite the degeneration of its own natural habitat, in such a way as us. We are unique in the extent to which we've upset the symbiotic balance of the animal kingdom. In fact, it almost makes sense for us to divinely ordain ourselves with the crowning privilege of being *human*. It shouldn't come as a surprise that many of us don't feel like we're an animal.

Despite our general disregard for other animals, there is a great wealth of ingenuity and sophistication to be found in the animal kingdom. I've always dreamt of knowing how much of this experience we share with other intelligent animals, like dogs, dolphins or any of the great apes. I remember that, when I was nineteen, I went with two friends to visit the orangutans of Tanjung Puting, in Indonesia. We were riding a houseboat down a stretch of coffee-coloured river, flanked by walls of jungle foliage. Suddenly we saw this older, grey-faced orangutan among the trees. She was clutching her baby at her side and standing upright, with her free hand clutching the trunk beside her. She watched us as we passed and didn't move, nor adjust her position, as you might expect. Excited, I scuttled to the side of the boat and fumbled with my camera bag. She didn't even turn her head to register me. At once it seemed apparent that I was in the presence of a more sophisticated being. In fact, the name orangutan is derived from a mixture of Malay and Indonesian that roughly translates to *person of the forest*. The way she looked at us then – I had no doubt that she was taking us outsiders in, as an indigenous person would, and she didn't look at all impressed.

While there is a considerable amount of scientific evidence, most of the convictions I have come from first-hand experience. I choose to trust my instincts and believe that emotion is not just a human asset. I think if you look into the eyes of any animal – really look, *closely* – it's likely you'll sense the movement of their emotions. You might see the scintilla of thoughts forming and changing. However, the question of whether their minds operate like ours is still very tricky. The brain is an organ more complex than any other structure in the known universe. The fluid, oceanic immensity within us is endlessly chaotic and confusing. Just think – there are one hundred billion neurons in the human brain, each of which is connected to another ten thousand, equalling a total of approximately one hundred trillion nerve connections. It's no wonder that our inner workings baffle the most advanced instruments of modern science.

That being said, neuroscientists have recently collated results from animal brain scans. These scans reveal distinct similarities shared between the dog and human brain, namely in the region called the caudate nucleus. Located between the brain-stem and the cortex, this region is responsible for recognising and anticipating enjoyment. In dogs it can be stimulated using (unsurprisingly) food or by having an owner suddenly walk into the room. Often it can be difficult to separate different cognitive functions, like untangling a web of balled circuitry. Fortunately, the caudate nucleus is known for offering clear maps that track our enjoyment of any given activity. These maps can even be used to reveal our preferences for enter-tainment, including our own individual interpretation of beauty.

Activity within a dog's caudate nucleus will also increase if a gesture is used to signal food. The same is true when the external stimulus of a familiar smell is used. It might sound like a small scientific gain, given that the reactions of dogs seem so easy to read, but this does serve as scientific proof that their internal enjoyment is much the same as ours. In fact, from what we now know about the canine potential for positive emotion, their sentience is comparable to that of a human baby. By extension, the suffering experienced during the Chinese Yulin Dog Meat Festival, when caged dogs arrive in droves to be brutalised, skinned and butchered, involves as much direct torment as it would if the same acts were perpetrated on human babies.

Interestingly, studies have shown that animals possess the same brain circuits as humans. This is further evidence of a conscious experience involving selective perception and positive emotion. While birds might not strike you as the most intellectual bunch, their neurophysiology has evolved parallel to the evolution of our own consciousness. Take African grey parrots, for example – a species with emotional networks and cognitive abilities that are almost mammalian in their complexity. It's also worth noting that the neural patterns of sleeping mammals, particularly during periods of REM sleep, display tell-tale neurophysiological patterns indicating the passage of dreams. At MIT's Centre for Learning and Memory, scientists studied these firing patterns in rats. They found that rats dream in long sequences, and not only that, their dreams are even linked to waking experiences.

To a certain extent, Charles Darwin applied his theory of evolution to the development of consciousness, noting the intrinsic value of continuity in the cycle of adaptation. He realised that certain qualities remained manifest, even after they'd been passed between species, suggesting that consciousness is hereditary. Despite mountains of conclusive field research, it wasn't until July 2012 that the University of Cambridge finally released an official declaration on the matter. In this paper, the scientists stated that, lo and behold, God didn't sculpt the animal kingdom as a bovine buffet for humankind to pick at. Instead, they verified that non-human animals have neuroanatomical, neurochemical and neuro-physiological substrates of conscious states. They also recognised that other sentient beings are capable of intentional behaviour. This doesn't come as much of a surprise to anyone who's ever spent any time in the company of an animal. Just think about Jane Goodall and Birutė Galdikas, who have spent most of their respective lives alongside chimpanzees and orangutans. Do you think they were waiting with bated breath for this announcement? Of course they weren't. However, it should be mentioned that this was just a public statement, written to acknowledge the essential truth that animals feel and think, just like we do.

Many positive things could come from this acknowledgement. I'd hope that revelations about animal consciousness would lead to an increased interest in their welfare. This does seem to be the case in some parts of the world. There are, though, promising examples of nonhumans being welcomed into our formerly exclusive societies. For the first time in human history a female orangutan, housed in a zoo in Buenos Aires, received basic human rights courtesy of an Argentinian criminal appeals court. Andres Gil Dominguez, who was working for the Association of Professional Lawyers for Animal Rights, filed a writ of habeas corpus, claiming that Sandra the ape had been denied her freedom for twenty years. This was an unprecedented show of interspecies kindness. As a result of the historic ruling, Sandra was set free and granted her inalienable rights to life, liberty and freedom from injury. Then, in 2013, the Nonhuman Rights Project, which counts Jane Goodall as a member, launched three legal claims pertaining to four chimpanzees held in New York. This more recent case is still mired in a bureaucratic quagmire of appeals, but it does bode well for distressed captive animals that such precedents have been set.

When all is said and done, the only evidence of animal consciousness I ever needed was given to me first-hand. I've seen orangutans washing themselves with handfuls of soap, I've watched dolphins surfing better than I ever could and I've seen the happy, stoned expression a koala makes when it poops from a branch. To me, this is a clearer way of seeing emotion in animals. I wouldn't scan my own girlfriend and pry into her synapses to find out who she is, nor would I ever bother to do so with Marlin. Anyway, I think the important question isn't whether we can endow animals with humanity, but rather whether we can change that twee designation altogether. Maybe then, every member of our species might finally be able to declare that they are proud and rightful members of this kingdom after all.

Swim the Eden Expedition, Day 4
Tuesday 18 August 2015

Most mornings when we got up we'd unzip the tent, climb out through layers of dewy canvas and be faced at once by the morning cold. In a way, it started to take the edge off that inevitable plunge into the river. The thinking was simple: if you made it out of the tent you'd already taken a shot of discomfort, which meant you could take the water as well. That was what we'd all convinced ourselves of anyway. It's a little different, though, when you wake up in a warm bed, unspool yourself from the heavy blankets and get dressed in a heated room. Tackling the Eden becomes a much ruder experience under the latter set of circumstances. It's kind of like taking off a fur coat and wandering bleary-eyed into the arms of a snowman.

So when I got up that morning I was feeling slightly less enthused about the day ahead. The swim seemed a lot less appealing after sleeping all night in a cosy country house. Nevertheless, we took the short drive in Dad's car through the bucolic Cumbrian scenery, with the sun rising over the Pennines and the sleepy mist falling onto the fields, while the dew still rested on the grass. When we arrived at the bridge we decided to rush down into the river and make up for lost time. There was also no press that morning, which meant we could brave the cold without delay.

One after another we zipped up our sodden suits and stepped out into the shallow water. As always, we each paused and stood for a moment, ankle-deep, and shivered and laughed at each other. Slowly I wriggled my toes and felt the cold seeping through my boots. Then I steadied my breathing and stared at the churned rapids into which I was about to hurl myself.

Any second now: *Right. Okay. Three, two, one . . . Right.*

I hesitated, prolonging the dive and mulling over that moment of submersion, after which it's all okay, although up to that point each slow, pimple-inducing second becomes a test of willpower.

Just then, as I was making a meal of my entry, a large fish

suddenly leapt up through the water and slumped into a fantastic belly-flop. Turning quickly, I caught sight of the muddied scales as they hit the sunlit surface. Then the monster disappeared, leaving a large, spreading ring of ripples. From the size of the disturbance it looked to have been a good weight – an acrobatic grayling or trout, perhaps.

With that, I adjusted my swim cap and moved the strap from my upper lip to under my chin. Perhaps inspired by the fish, I decided to opt for the splayed, head-first approach as I dove out from my perch, into the rapids. I came up a metre or so downriver, found my feet and rose out of the water until the current was being bundled into my chest. I allowed the harsh immediacy of the cold to steal my breath for a second. Then I dove forward again, staying under this time, and I was propelled into the tug of the current. Quickly I turned my head to one side and saw two adjacent ribbons of bubbles. I had slipped into the twin wakes of Robbie and Calum. Excited, I dug my hand in for the first stroke and together we set off swimming down the murky river, between the trees.

The morning swim turned out to be quite relaxing and the cold soon subsided once we each found our rhythms and drifted off into a thoughtless respite, far from the common anxiety of having to maintain and uphold a self. Instead, the slow front crawl rocked our shoulders and lulled us into a deep state of calm. After a while you began to feel like you could go on swimming for days, snatching glimpses of the undulating banks, the tall grass and the pebbled shores as they edged by.

Wild swimmers often say that they use their sport as a form of meditation. Funnily enough, there are many similarities between the steps involved in swimming and those associated with the practice of yoga. In both disciplines, physical strain, rhythmic breathing and deep concentration are used to escape the clamour of your surface thoughts. In long-distance swimming, the idea of reaching a sweet state of thoughtlessness is essential to success. Really the only way to last in the water is to lead yourself first to a quiet, calm place inside your mind – somewhere no one else but you exists. In that place, you can escape the muscular ache and monotony of pulling your hands through the water and kicking as you swim.

Usually you would start your yoga lesson with various stretching postures, which are used to relieve physical tension. Similarly, as you begin to swim you experience the extension and relaxation of skeletal muscles, loosening any bodily tension. The next step in yoga would be to move on to gentle breathing exercises, slowly gaining greater awareness of your *prana*, which is the life-giving force behind each breath. Swimming involves a similar breathing exercise, performed almost unconsciously as you focus on fitting each sharp intake of air into the rhythm of your strokes. Next your yoga teacher might move onto *pratyahara* exercises, which involve the withdrawal of the senses, deflecting the outside world so that your sensory organs no longer stream information to your brain. This is followed finally by the stage of *dharana* – a practice of deep concentration, sometimes facilitated using a visual stimulus such as a candle flame. In the water your sense perception is reduced so that you can only glimpse what's in front of you. Also, you can only feel the water and hear your breathing, causing your brain to process less and less, while your mind sinks into silence. As you swim, your hands become the candle flame – the point of fixation used to train your focus – reaching out towards the peripheries of your vision. Often in cold water they are clear, pale and they almost seem to shine amid the bubbling flurries of water and flashes of gaping sky.

Given the similarities between these two disciplines, it's no wonder that long-distance swimmers often report moments of serene mindfulness, which allow them to swim for longer at a faster pace, without any intellectual restraints or jarring thought processes. By applying the teachings of yoga to swimming you can also learn to relax and improve your form, extending your reach and maximising the glide that follows each stroke. This is a great way to ease into that mindful state, until eventually it feels as though there is no water, no pool, no you – in fact, you can't feel anything.

There are several contemporary scientific studies that support this idea that swimming can be a form of meditation. These studies prove that routine swimming stimulates neurogenesis in the hippocampus, which is thought to be the centre of memory and emotion in our brains. Neurogenesis means *birth of neurons* and refers to the process by which new neurons are birthed from neural stem cells. This has significant implications when it comes to our ability to educate ourselves, retain memories and avoid depression. Conversely, the hippocampus wastes away under conditions of stress and anxiety, effectively constricting the brain. While there are certain drugs, like Prozac, that can combat this, there are also everyday activities like swimming that have been proven to elicit a similar response.

What this tells us is that all that open-water mind-expansion malarkey is verifiable. Swimming strengthens the hippocampus and improves our powers of learning and memory. Also, when you swim, you are engaging in a cross-patterning, bilateral movement. Just as crawling helps to advance the cognitive development of babies, swimming provides motor and sensory stimuli for the brain development of adults. Over time, the action of swimming increases the amount of information passed along the band of nerve fibres connecting the right and left hemispheres of the brain. This effectively facilitates an ongoing communication between the two, activating both hemispheres of the brain simultaneously. Not only does this lead to greater cognition and learning, but it also swirls the perfect cocktail of brain chemicals to do away with depression.

If you'd like to conduct your own empirical study, why not head for a swim and spend some time afterwards thinking about how it changed your mood? If you force yourself to stay in the water, at least for a few lengths, you'll usually find that you'll leave the water with an intense high. It's an endorphin hit that grooves through your body and soothes your mind. I get it whenever I'm walking home from a long swim. Suddenly my steps feel lighter and my whole body becomes more buoyant. You feel like you've accomplished something – that the air is a little fresher and the world a little more open than it was before.

There's another, perhaps more surprising, benefit to wild swimming that's worth considering: it has actually been shown to improve your sex life. There was a recent study, conducted by Czech researchers on cold-exposed humans, in which the objective was to discover whether cold-water immersion could improve the physiological status of an individual. Among other things, the researchers discovered that repetitive cold-water immersion actually raised sex hormone levels, increasing the production of testosterone and oestrogen in men and women. These hormones enhance the libido in both sexes and also improve your chances of fertility.

In addition, short exposure to cold water provides rejuvenation, exfoliating and cleansing of your skin, while also increasing your circulation. Suddenly you feel more alive and then, if you stay in for long enough, you start to relax and the cold disappears. Over time, if you swim regularly in cold water, it becomes much easier to let go of stress and anxieties – essentially you stop getting in the way of yourself.

Essential to this kind of meditative swimming is the ability to cultivate calm internal conditions. Everyone has their own pace and their own method of finding mindfulness in the water. I tend to think that the only way to reach this sweet spot is to learn to love what you're doing. I have these small rituals I use as triggers to get me into that condition, from packing my bag before I leave to rinsing my wetsuit in the shower when I'm home. I try to treat each swim as though it is a privilege and not a chore. I remind myself to be proud of being a swimmer – someone who identifies with other swimmers around the world – and to enjoy all the little details of this wonderful sport.

★　★　★

Later, we turned from crawl to breaststroke and kept our heads above the surface as we talked. I asked Robbie whether he felt different swimming here than he did in the lakes or pools of Berlin. He said he did and that it kind of felt like a pilgrimage to him.

'I feel very calm,' he said, smiling as his chin gently split the water like the bow of a ship. 'I think it's just doing this repetitive action, like a whirling dervish.'

'What's that?' I asked.

'It's a dance I saw in Istanbul where you spin and spin in continuous circles.'

'Remember those Hindu pilgrims we saw in India?' I tilted my cheek against the water and looked at Robbie: 'They lug big stones around for days,' I went on; 'take them up mountains to holy sites.' 'I remember the ones at Ranthambore,' Robbie said. 'They were measuring out the distance they'd come with their bodies. Every few steps they'd drop and lie flat with their lips to the ground.'

'Crazy,' I said. 'They could be world-class endurance athletes.'

After a while we stopped talking and switched back to the crawl. I spent some time in the greenish murk with my thoughts, but it wasn't long before my breathing stole my attention again. Then I focused on smoothing my strokes between each intermittent gulp of air. I could feel myself being carried along over the rocky palm of Mother Nature. It became very comfortable. On the river, you also experience the nuances and workings of that ancient organic gear train that we have tried so diligently to dismantle. You see fish scatter in the murk beneath your fingertips and you see ducks guiding their ducklings through the shallows, darting under roots that dip into the water like spindly fingers. It's a world of littler things – a fragile one indeed, but one that whirs and ticks nonetheless.

After a break we decided to walk a little way along the bank to avoid a quiet spot where two fishermen had cast their lines. Calum told us that the fishing community had been one of his chief concerns when he was planning the swim. He also said that the Angling Association had invested a lot of money in local salmon fishing, which was why the swim hadn't been officially recognised by them. They couldn't be seen to support us in case it upset the fishermen who paid for their private patches of the Eden. We didn't want to stray into the issue of ownership either. Also, we could understand why they might object to being interrupted by a motley crew of wetsuit-clad brothers, flopping suddenly into view and chasing away their prey, like inelegant eel-men. At the same time, we all kind of agreed on the policy that it's a river and essentially just a natural thoroughfare, no part of which should be owned by anyone, really. So, if we encountered any members of the clipboard army, we were just planning to float on by, perhaps whistling the 'Bare Necessities' tune as we bobbed downriver on our backs.

The first fishermen we met looked at us as though we were an apparition and then chuckled and waved. After that we saw others at regular intervals and opted to climb up onto the bank and walk around the edge of the field until we'd passed by. We did that several times, so as not to disturb their catch, and we were always rewarded with a pleasant exchange, which assuaged our initial concerns about the hostility we might receive. In fact, out of all the fishermen we met, there was only one who took issue with our appearance. I remember him standing in his waders with a sullen look on his face, like someone caught in the midst of a flood.

'Lovely day,' James said, smiling, as we walked by on the bank.

'It was until you showed up,' he grumbled, before turning back to his wilting line.

Further downriver we fought our way through a dense clump of trees and came upon this big, bald local who grinned at us as we edged down the steep wall of crumbled soil and snare-roots. He was standing in his waders, up to his knees, with his hands on his hips. Beside him a painted boat rested in a muddy furrow, moored to the bank. Leaves tumbled around us, plucked from the gleaming canopy, which shaded the secluded patch where we were standing. We talked to him only briefly, although in that short time he distilled a fine feeling and sweetened any sourness picked up from the previous fisherman we'd met. By all accounts this was the quintessential Cumbrian – a man in constant contact with nature, who had found a certain peace in isolation, to which he frequently returned.

'We could be in Northern America, or anywhere in the world,' he chuckled, gesturing to the slow current of the grey river and the calm quietude that moved with it. Then he offered us some advice for the approach to the Solway Firth and warned us about the currents and the mudflats. After that we parted in renewed good spirits and took to the river together at an easy pace.

We were all in agreement that this had been our best day so far. Slowly the Eden was getting under our skin and washing through our minds. There was this real sense of freedom we'd gained, being alone in nature, even just for that short space of time. We'd already seen Calum cutting loose with his new Louie Spence dance routine. You could tell that whatever it was we were looking for was finally close by. By now we'd spent four days riding the slow currents and wading in the shallows. All the while the river bore us with a steady, supple hand, while we were learning to float, roll and dive and relish its rhythms. Occasionally you'd hear yawps, cries and bursts of laughter from the others – in those moments it was clear to me that we'd become kids again.

Later, we paddled into a still pool shielded by a fallen tree draped in cobwebs and moss. I rested on my knees in the shallow water, pulled off my goggles and spat into the lenses. Robbie was sitting cross-legged in the shallows beside me.

'How are those goggles Jack?' he asked.

'They're not bad,' I said, lowering them again and inspecting the insides. 'Still misting up.'

'I've been using spit too,' Robbie offered.

'Saliva's good,' Calum said, stepping down from the bank. 'Just don't rub the lenses or you might remove the coating.'

Just then I noticed something large moving in the field over Robbie's shoulder. Panicked, I jumped up to find a motley gang of Clydesdale horses looming over the top of the bank. These were huge, strong Scottish draught horses, coloured with a gleaming mixture of black, chestnut and grey, with white markings and feathered legs like 1970s flares.

Robbie leant back in the water and lay looking up at them as they crowded the fence. Up close they were very impressive, their muscles and sinews jumping and twitching as they moved.

We stood for a while, watching them snorting and leaning over us. Eventually the subject drifted and we got to talking about other Goliaths, now extinct and all but lost to the depths of the Earth.

'Did you ever read that chapter in *Feral*?' Robbie said, almost as if he were talking to himself – or the horses.

'The one about the giant wombats?' Calum asked.

'Yeah.'

'What's that?' I asked, eyeing one of the more suspicious-looking horses that had what seemed like a limp moustache dangling from its muzzle.

'There's a chapter in *Feral* where he talks about all the Australian megafauna,' Robbie explained. 'Apparently, millions of years ago, they had these huge wombats that weighed the same as a rhino.'

'And seven-metre-long monitor lizards,' Calum added.

'Yeah?' I asked.

'Five-ton ground sloths.'

That last one rang a bell. I remembered seeing a CGI animation of one of those hulking, muscular mega-sloths. They called it megatherium. As a kid, I couldn't believe it – the thought that there once existed this giant relative of the little sleepy tree-dwellers that I knew of. 'Did you see that scene in *Walking with Beasts* with the giant ground sloth?' I asked.

They both nodded. Then Calum gestured to the river and the steep banks crowded with foliage.

'All of this would've been rainforest then,' he said. 'If we were doing this then, we'd probably be watching out for crocs and hippos.'

I thought for a moment and added: 'Not swans.'

We went on like that for a little bit before we eventually got back into the water. By that point the sun had burned a hole in the clouds and the light was shining directly onto our entry point, piercing the depths and revealing shoals of minnows.

'So, our genes are less diverse than those of most other species,' Calum went on, reaching over his shoulder and pulling his wetsuit zipper up by its cord. 'They think the only reason we survived was because we all clumped together in big tribes. That's how we made it through the Ice Age.'

'They found a cave in South Africa filled with human fossils,' Robbie agreed, 'so they reckon there was a tribe that sheltered there together.'

'Like it was an ark,' I offered.

With that we were all ready to go. Closing the strap against the nape of my neck, I leant back, outstretched my arms and gently kicked my feet up from the riverbed. The current took hold of me as I drifted out from the pool, and the next thing I knew I was floating downriver, watching the horses as they disappeared behind a screen of foliage.

Soon the Eden began to widen and the riverbed smoothed as cracks and crevices forked through the rock like veins. Peering through the greenish water I saw us sweep over a drop-off and was suddenly jolted by the abrupt change in depth. Occasionally the water would turn black like that, receding under the whip of my pale, wrinkled fingertips, like an abyssal hole leading down to the centre of the Earth. It did make for good swimming though, since we could extend our strokes without scraping our knuckles on the riverbed or slapping a large rock. Sometimes the current would also move up a gear, meaning I could switch into torpedo position, with my hands clamped at my side, safe in the knowledge that it was too deep for any rocks to jump out ahead of me. The scenery was beautiful too: tall pines now crowded the banks around even taller sandstone cliffs, traversed by branches and roots embedded in the rock like sinuous fossils. Then these reddish cliffs curved into a long wall, crowned with bushes, which cradled the bend of the Eden and guided us round to a deep, unspoilt stretch of water.

For some time we swam freely in a staggered formation, each enjoying the feeling of stretching our arms and fingertips and dragging them through the deep water at full extension.

One, two, three . . . breathe.

Those perpetual instructions soon faded and the body went on independently, picking up the vestiges of sensation, yet allowing the mind to wander inwards again to that distant place, which is a refuge for the laden heart, and the only paradise there is. Eventually we each looked up and were greeted by the jarring sight of a concrete bridge and a few passing cars. It was the first time we'd seen evidence of a town or city for several days. The sound of the engines surged into the sky and brought our relaxing swim to an end. As we neared, we changed our course slightly and headed between the dirty concrete struts, following a swan and six of her cygnets. First the birds floated down the rapids, bobbing with ease, but then they turned and seemed to wait for us on the other side of the bridge. Momma Swan looked like she was ready to take us on. Her tall, slender neck was bent back like a taut bowstring, ready to let loose that menacing orange beak – also, she had the queen on her side.

The thought of being pecked gave us reason to pause. Instead of following the swans we decided to wade over to the other struts and follow the rapids as close to the banks as we could. Luckily the swan decided to give us a free pass and we rode the current downriver and left her and her cygnets to their journey. We spent the rest of the afternoon with our heads in the water. The only time we switched from crawl to breaststroke was when we passed through a cluttered corridor of bungalows and allotments. Then we slowed our pace a little and waved at the odd local we found milling about their garden or sitting on benches overlooking the river. We also had to navigate several cascading weirs. One after another we stepped carefully down the barriers and then leapt out into the deep water at the bottom, savouring the plunge and the freedom to trail your limbs and spin and move in whichever way you wanted.

Before long we saw the grass banks disappear behind a verdant forest. Then the trees loomed over us and held their drooping, leafy branches close to the water. I took the opportunity to roll over onto my back to rest and drift and stare up through the bright leaves and shimmering sunlight. I could see that the rays were beginning to ebb and sink. It was a reminder that we were coming to the end of our eleven-mile day, which had been extended because we'd stopped short the previous day. Supposedly we had about two miles left, and the sun was already setting. At this point I could also feel my shoulders starting to ache and, for the first time, I realised I was going to need a second wind if I wanted to keep up with the others.

One, two, three . . . breathe.

Slowly we arced out from among the trees and were greeted by an overgrown meadow with a single, moss-covered alder, half hidden behind a web of crumpled limbs. I don't know if it was the sight of that beat-up old tree or the constant swimming, but I was starting to grow lethargic and grumpy in the water. The sunlight had started to fade and a light rain to drum on our quiet waterway, pattering on the still surface and puncturing the muddied reflection of the surrounding trees. I lifted my head and kept my eyes level with the river, breathing gently through half-mouthfuls of water. For a moment, I watched the leafy branches as they bowed under the weight of the rain and shaded the riverside. Then the overgrown banks enclosed us as we entered an unruly wild garden, coloured with the lavender heads of sand leeks and wrapped in tall, tentacled stems of wild garlic.

One, two, three . . . breathe.

Turning slightly, I kicked my feet and slid towards a thick raft of green algae, half submerged in the muddied shadows. Ending my crawl, I rolled over, planted my feet on the sandy riverbed and rocked on the current, peering up through towers of tufted sedge, their spidery fingers splayed across the sky. In this position I allowed myself a moment to relax, catch my breath and rest my shoulders. Then I slipped slowly underwater and pushed the air out through my nose. From behind my tinted goggles I could see the ripples as the rain hit the river, backlit by the filtered sunlight. There was something altogether soothing about the way the ripples interlinked, forming myriad circles that spread gently and faded, only to be replaced a moment later.

When I resurfaced I felt as though my mood had been lifted. Then I went on, this time swimming breaststroke, and inched into a deep channel flanked by open fields. James paddled a short distance ahead of us to scope out the next stretch of swimming and check for rapids. We followed his kayak around a long corner and came across a woman standing on the bank. She was dressed in a wetsuit, holding a swim cap and waving at us from among the tall grass, close to a little stone boathouse, beside which a jetty jutted out over the water.

I squinted through the rain and saw that it was our mum. 'Come on boys,' she cried, as we dug in, groped the deep water and approached the jetty.

It changed the rhythm of the swim having Mum along and it was great to share the experience with her. Before that moment I'd been growing increasingly tired and disgruntled, but now a new wave of energy ran through me, sparked by the sight of her cutting a path through the Eden, with the front crawl she'd perfected over the last year. She swam with us for a mile and led the group with ease. All the while Calum kept at her side and Robbie and I trailed a little behind them. When it was time for her to get out, we all hugged, and she thanked us and said that the experience was 'magic.'

After that we caught another gust of wind and dug in for a long stretch of crawl. I remember seeing Robbie's bubbling wake ahead of me and being reminded of the fact that we were close to Langwathby, our childhood home. Gritting my teeth, I put more strength behind each stroke and swerved slightly until I came up at his shoulder. The next thing I saw was Calum moving into position on Robbie's other flank. I matched my strokes with my brothers' and held their pace. Every time I came up to breathe I felt the light rain pricking my cheek. Then I'd roll back under, into the whipped, greenish murk, and I'd find the riverbed rushing beneath my fingertips, like another, cobbled river. I could see Robbie's reaching hands in the corner of my eye and through watching each swipe and learning his rhythm I began to reflect his movement. This was where our training kicked in – at the end of a long day we'd found ourselves side by side and burning with energy. The more we swam the more in tune we became, until our hands were cutting the water at the exact same time and, because I'd only learnt to breathe on my left side, I could watch them swimming beside me.

We swam like that for several minutes, the three Hudson brothers, and it gave me an overwhelming sense that I was in the right place – that what we were doing was, in some vague way, good.

In time we came to the final rapids before Langwathby,

which swept us downriver with surprising force. Between each gasp of air I peered through the incoming water and searched for signs of metal debris or sharp rocks that might slice suddenly through the murk and impale me. It was an uneasy case of trial and error and we received a fair amount of bruising in the process, bouncing like pinballs between the little boulders and clumps of what looked like water celery.

As I said before, there's a certain amount of glamour that surrounds the idea of adventure. I think it's an association that exists somewhat at odds with the reality of what these things actually entail. It's quite difficult to reconcile the glossy idea of adventuring with the memories I have of several dangerous drop-offs. For example, on the previous day, I'd squatted in a grotty concrete hole, doing my business under a bridge, like a troll rejected by society. That moment when we fumbled and bounced down the rapids was another instance in which reality peeked through the rose-tinted, media-friendly veil. However, I suppose you're probably not paying attention if you look good when you're in the thick of it.

Soon we were thrown out from the rapids into gentler, deeper water. We could just make out the fir trees that marked the edge of Lady's Walk, where we'd taken Marlin to run and dig many times over the years. The trees stood in a dense line and seemed to form a paling fence around the boundaries of our old roaming ground. They also reminded us that Langwathby was just around the bend. Then a forested hill came into view and we saw rows of rooftops and chimneys and the rest of our neighbourhood, with the rolling Pennines behind them. A year or so earlier we'd wandered to one of those houses when it was empty and still under construction. I remember how we'd climbed the scaffolding, sat beside the slated roof and smoked a joint with the country stars hanging over us and the moonlight spread across the hills. Now we'd left that village behind and we were entering a new stage of our lives — I guess that was why it felt like we were coming to say one last goodbye.

The closer we came to our garden the more we were reminded of home and the time we'd spent in Cumbria. First Iain's sister, Caroline, came down to the water's edge and wished us well. Then we rounded a long corner and saw Mum standing with Marlin on a pebble beach that formed part of Lady's Walk. After that we floated onto a shallow stretch, which for some sixteen years had been our most treasured playground. In the distance, we could see the green military bridge. We drifted towards it in a tight group, passing steep banks that led up to houses half hidden behind the huddled trees. We stopped for a moment when we came to the foot of our garden and sighted the roof of Wells Cottage, under which a new family was now living. I took that time to pick out all the things I remembered: the stepping stones that curled out from the reeds, the two trees that kept our hammock off the ground, and the gnarled bench that Mum had built, which had been reached by the river during the floods. The view from the top of the bank had always been a source of immeasurable comfort and pleasure. It was best enjoyed from Calum's room, I think — or Iain's and Mum's, which overlooked the long, furrowed fields of Lady's Walk and the football pitches behind them that produced whistles and calls on Saturday mornings. Oh, and then there was the forested beacon, which shaped the horizon and cut radiant slivers of light as the sun set each evening.

We didn't stay too long at our bank since the nostalgia seemed somewhat retrograde. It wasn't as heart-warming as I'd thought it might be, knowing that the garden was no longer ours. We were also very tired and the end was now in sight. Rolling back into the water, we edged with slow, weak strokes towards the small crowd that was waiting for us. I felt a wave of relief when we finally trudged up onto the sandy beach and tiered slabs of concrete, under the bridge. We greeted the locals who'd wandered down to see us and were handed hot coffee and protein muffins, courtesy of Luke's mum. We also met a woman called Ruth with her little son, Edward, who stared wide-eyed at us as we ate, shivered and hopped around, like the tribal acolytes of some obscene river cult. Meanwhile, Marlin sniffed around, licked our ankles and snatched any crumbs from the muffin that flitted to the ground.

Needless to say, it wasn't long before we were whisked away to our old local, the Shepherd's Inn, where Robbie and James ordered pints while still in their wetsuits. We soon followed them and commandeered the long table at the back of the pub, close to the open fire. Then more friends showed up and we all sat and drank together and heard stories and countless other memories that sounded distant, as though seen through the tunnelled scope of adulthood.

That night we stayed with Robbie's friend Lee, whose parents owned a beautiful house with a log cabin at the foot of a long field and track. We all huddled together inside the cabin, eating hot soup by lantern light and talking excitedly about the day ahead. We knew that this next stretch of the Eden, heading downriver from our old house in Langwathby, was going to be familiar to us. It would lead us through most of our favourite swimming spots and the lopsided stacks we used to jump off as kids. Now, for the first time since we'd climbed out from the source, we knew exactly where the river was taking us.

Remember The Duct Tape (Cal's Tip): Everything can be fixed with the mighty duct tape: broken kayak paddles, wetsuit tears, broken tent poles . . . We also found that nothing really heals in the water, so we used duct tape to bandage cuts and blisters and bind ankles and feet, and even my head!

7

Going Under

The next morning, Lee's parents, Danny and Liz, came to the cabin with their lurcher and brought us cups of tea. We stood and sipped our steaming drinks on the little terrace and talked and watched the sunlight rising over the fields. After a while it came up that Liz was an avid country music fan, at which point she decided to hurry off and change into her western outfit. When she came back we all posed together for a photo in front of the cabin. Then we took a few more photos of our surroundings and Calum updated our social media before Dad's Beetle rolled into view along the driveway.

Before we left, Liz decided to give us a little leaving show. She asked us to gather round and proceeded to lead the lurcher out into the field. We lined the stone wall and watched as she untied the dog's leash. Then, jolted by a short whistle, the lurcher suddenly bounded across the grass, like a greyhound leaving the slips, with its ears pulled back and every inch of its skeletal frame honed for the chase. I'd never seen a dog move so fast, especially not Marlin with her stubby little spaniel legs and baggy ears.

When we reached the Langwathby Bridge there was a small crowd of locals waiting for us, as well as a journalist and a photographer – the very same photographer, in fact, who'd visited our schools when we were kids. Of course, our memories had dimmed somewhat, but we still knew that his name was Fred and remembered his propensity to ask for embarrassing poses.

True to form, Fred had us crouched over in the river with our thumbs up and our teeth out. It was this photo that later ended up on the cover of the *Westmorland Herald* – a big deal for fish in a small pond like ours. Then we pulled on our goggles in unison, edged out from the shallows and dove deep into the pull of the current that tumbled under the bridge.

At this point we were used to our routine, so we waved goodbye to the onlookers and turned downriver without hesitation. I didn't break my crawl until we were halfway down the stretch, close to a pebbled causeway that slowed the current and forced us to stand. Then I looked over my shoulder and saw the distant military bridge, between the drooping trees, and thought about the likelihood of us ever returning to Langwathby. Suddenly it felt like another place that I wasn't inclined to revisit. A page of my life that I'd turned and, though I might re-track the words on that page someday, I'd now resolved that it was better not to turn back to it too often. With that, my eyes flitted onto the shallow path ahead and I pushed myself up through the water and limped after my brothers, feeling occasional stabs of pain in the ligaments of my right ankle.

An hour or so later we were walking around another shallow arm of the Eden when someone decided to bring up work again.

'What do you think you'll go into?' I asked Calum, referring to his plan to up sticks, travel to Australia and then find work in Sydney, at least until his natural restlessness got the better of him.

'I'll probably look for a sales job somewhere,' he said.

I began to moan. 'I thought you didn't wanna go back into sales?'

'I don't, but it's hard when the only experience you've got is in that area.'

Robbie stumbled within earshot and pulled off his swim cap. 'I think you'd be good doing something with fundraising,' he said, rubbing the back of his neck.

'Yeah, you don't realise how hard it is to switch jobs though,' Calum assured us. 'I'd have to go back in at the lowest level and work as an intern for years before I could earn anything like what I'm on now. It's expensive being in London.'

This was the dilemma that Calum had found himself in. By now he'd learnt that sales was a vapid game and, while the money was good, it didn't sit right with his childhood ambitions to be a vet, nor with his adolescent ambition of becoming a human rights lawyer. At the time, I was also working as a sales-orientated copywriter, so I thought, somewhat arrogantly, that I knew his side of the argument. Every so often I'd be waxing lyrical to try to hawk some luxury item. Then I'd suddenly hear the battle cry of Bill Hicks, the comedian, as he chomped his fangs into the Kill Yourself bit from one of his last stand-ups.

'Is anyone here in marketing or advertising?' he'd said, dressed to the nines in Johnny Cash black. 'Kill yourselves. I know you think: "Oh there's a joke coming . . ." There's no fucking joke coming: kill yourselves.'

Calum referenced Bill Hicks as much as any of us. I guessed that he felt the fierce urgency of his words, which is to say, you could tell that he was becoming increasingly conflicted. The sales industry was starting to get under his skin, so much so that he now felt the need to flee London and spend nine days in a river. Granted, the work did suit his innate confidence and the salary meant he could live, eat and travel well. When it came to justifying it to himself, however, he seemed to seek counsel from his inner nihilist, as well as from his fervent disdain for sanctimonious folk. He wasn't a saint himself, mind you, nor did he try to act like one. He loved to flout his own opinions and was somehow able to pirouette over minefields of contradictions and emerge unscathed, partly because he never took himself too seriously. At the same time, Calum is and always has been a very fearless man. He travelled alone from Istanbul to Cairo for his year out, where he almost died from heatstroke while wandering to the border of Saudi Arabia. He was also evacuated from Lebanon in an armoured car. I think there is a bit of madness girdled somewhere deep inside his mind – a wild spark that could easily transform him into a force of nature. When he was acting off-kilter we called him a sociopath, but he was much too empathetic and grounded for that to cause any insult.

After we crossed the shallows we were swept into a meandering current that carried us through a verdant patchwork of open fields. Cows loped in herds along the banks and sometimes came down to the water's edge and watched us passing by. It's always been odd to me that an animal of such uniquely bovine stupidity could also be so persistently curious. Needless to say, they followed us until the fields were enclosed by an electric fence, at which point we slipped away under the shadow of a tall railway bridge, behind which stood the wavy, ruffled contours of a hilltop forest.

Our next stop, around the corner, was Lacy's Caves – the closest swimming spot to Langwathby and the one we'd always cycled to in the summer. As we passed under the bridge I pulled my head back, yawped and listened to the echo as it resounded around the arch. Then we drifted into a wide expanse of sunlit water and at once the sandstone cliffs came into view and we heard the sound of several rushing waterfalls. It wasn't long before the increasing pull of the current forced us to stop swimming and straighten up. Treading water, we began trying to plant our feet on the riverbed to maintain an upright position. It was like walking without gravity and we kept stumbling forward and catching our legs on hidden boulders. We weren't sure whether the rain had continued overnight, but it seemed like the falls were much louder and the current much more powerful than we remembered.

We decided against riding the kayak down the tiers of rock and instead opted to walk up to the drop-off with it, before pushing it over the edge and watching it glide slowly down-river. Meanwhile, Robbie, Calum and I shimmied down a ramp of flattened moss, until our feet were hanging over a waterfall. Beside us there was a hole, set a little further back from the gushing tunnels of water, which someone had found many years ago, long before we started swimming there. This hole led directly down into the rock and turned at a right angle through an underwater arch that opened out into the water below us. We'd all been through it several times before, so I attached a GoPro to my head, lowered myself down into the hole and felt the bend of the arch with my feet. Taking a deep breath, I pushed myself down into a greenish flurry of coiling bubbles and rolled over and gripped the underside of the arch with both hands. As I turned through the hole I lifted my eyes up to the surface and saw the rays of sunlight beckoning me. With a sharp kick, I finally tore through the murk, burst out of the water and savoured the air as it rushed into my lungs.

Slowly I floated away on my back and noted all the little quirks I remembered from our surroundings. Another feature that made the caves so popular among the locals was a river-side stack we called The Tower. It didn't look like a tower at all – it was more of a shoddy pillar, built up with tiered rocks and a rusted pole that protruded from between two hunks of concrete. This pole also acted as a handle to help you climb up onto the jumping point. If that wasn't enough, there was even an old mine shaft that you could step back into and use as a run-up before throwing yourself from the precipice, far out over the slow-flowing river. It would've been rude to drift downriver and pass up the opportunity. This time it was Robbie who stepped up to take the plunge. We watched him from the rocks below as he sprinted from the mine shaft and leapt out under the trees, his arms wheeling like a fledgling trying to fly, before he dropped into the river, with the heavy plonk of a leaden stone.

After floating around and resting our shoulders for a while we climbed back up onto the rocks. We took a little longer for our first break that day and sat with our feet in the water, watching flecks of froth spinning by. Further downriver, we could just make out a row of sandstone caves, half hidden among the trees. Supposedly those caves had once housed several hermits who sought refuge in the winding chambers, the walls of which were now marked with the stone-scrawled tags of primal graffiti artists.

Soon we climbed back down into the river, pushed off and paddled along with the current, enclosed by the drooping branches. A little way downriver we passed the caves, which were hewn into the cliff-face. After that there was nothing much to report until we reached Lazonby. It was just a long, winding stretch of river, flanked by intermittent fields and forests. Occasionally, I saw white-breasted swallows bursting out from among the bulrushes. I watched them as they circled quickly over the water and rushed back into hiding, leaving us with nothing but a few faint notes of their song. For the most part, I just kept my head in the water and thought about lunch – that and the prospect of seeing my closest mates, Sandy and Dave, and my beautiful girlfriend Beth as well.

Meanwhile, Dave, Sandy and Beth had just met up with

Mum at Langwathby railway station. Later, Beth told me that Mum was being her usual excited and disarmingly friendly self. Before they set off she kept trying to get her tracker to work, waiting for the blip to appear, which would signal our whereabouts and confirm that we hadn't toppled over a waterfall or found ourselves lodged in an underwater hole somewhere. Eventually they decided just to expect our arrival at Lazonby and set off with the kayaks strapped to the roof of their car. They caught up as they drove through the country-side, while Marlin sat panting in the back, with her slobbering chops rested on the seat. Beth told me that Mum became ever more excited and chatty the nearer they came to the village. Her car had broken down the previous day, but she'd wasted no time in ringing around to ensure that it would be fixed for the following morning – the last thing she was going to do was miss out on the adventure.

Back in the river we were slowing to the pace of a swim-ming pygmy sloth. Luckily, we'd pretty much reached our lunch stop in Lazonby. The first sign of the village was a dirt path and several dog-walkers, half hidden behind a screen of trees. Just around the corner we saw Beth standing on the steps above a concrete jetty. A minute or so earlier she'd spotted three figures in the distance and called to the others, thinking they were us. However, a second glance revealed that she'd mistaken us for ducks – it's nice to know that your girlfriend can't tell you apart from poultry. I just hope this doesn't mean that one day I'll come home to find a duck lying on my side of the bed, wearing my dressing gown and drinking tea out of my shark mug.

As we drifted around the bend I peeled my goggles back and grinned at our little welcome party. Then I picked out Sandy's face from among the group. I hadn't seen him for several months but I'd known him for over eleven years at that point, having first been drawn to him on the school court because he had long hair and was a skateboarder. Behind him was Dave, sporting the world's most expressive eyebrows, and, at a considerably lower height, Beth – my anchor. I was very happy to see them all. After being on the river for so long it felt like a reunion. Then we all hugged and joked around before Beth spoiled us with containers of baked brownies, flapjacks and pasta.

When we'd finished, Dave and Sandy lugged their kayaks down to the water's edge and set them ready to be launched onto the current. Next we pulled off our coats, zipped our wetsuits back up and joined them on the concrete jetty. Finally, we thanked our parents for keeping us going and then leapt out into the cold Eden. At once we were bundled into a goggle-tinted flurry of sky and water, having been swept quickly down the churned rapids that carried us under the bridge.

Further downriver, Dave and Sandy decided to paddle a little way behind us. Then James joined them a moment later and planned a loose formation that would allow them to keep an eye on all three of us at once. For the most part they split up after that, taking it in turns to mind the middle, the front and the back. Sometimes I'd put a little more strength behind my strokes and cut in alongside one of their kayaks. Then I'd either hold on to their rope handle to be towed or I'd match their pace, following the stern underwater. In this way, I could use their path as a marker, which kept me heading in a straight line. It also meant that I could occasionally switch to breast-stroke and have a little chin-wag.

A short while later we came to the first in a series of thrashing rapids. Feeling somewhat over-zealous, we bulleted down them in torpedo position, keeping our hands outstretched and feeling our way between the rocks. I soon remembered that the rapids would become increasingly wild the further we travelled downriver. Sure enough, before long we were being rocked and bounced around like marbles in a drainpipe. It was a pretty bruising experience. The only thing that made it worthwhile was the thought of looking back once the river spat you out and seeing the kayakers preparing to take the same gauntlet.

I remember one time when I climbed out onto a rock padded with river weed and looked back at Sandy and Dave as they slid towards the mouth of the rapids.

'Go on Sandy,' I shouted, just before he rammed the nose of his kayak into a rock and turned sidelong into another. Pinned between these two rocks, he began to take on a kayak's worth of rushing water, before he eventually flipped and was barrelled between them and spewed into the torrent below. Each time this happened we'd have to heave the kayak to the bank and lift it from each end until it was drained. We did this several times and yet it never became a drag, simply because of the hilarious fail that always preceded it. It was also inevitable. James was the only one with a spray deck and so he could ride the cascades without taking on any water.

Sandy and Dave, on the other hand, seemed like they just couldn't help themselves. In fact, every time the kayak flipped and they went under, it was always followed by a sharp burst of laughter.

After the first few submersions we started taking bets on who'd be next to tip over. During one of these bets a couple of walkers stopped and saw us standing on the rocks, beside a fairly hairy stretch of rapids, dotted with ominous crops of boulders.

'We'll tell them you cheated,' they called through the trees, and we laughed it off, feeling none the worse for having avoided being pummelled by the rocks like human dough.

Further downriver, the rough rapids subsided and we began to feel the current pulling us into deeper tracts of water. I took that opportunity to turn myself upright and peer down past my feet, into the murky blackness, as though I was in the middle of a spacewalk, trudging over the depths of the Milky Way. At one point, we also found a rope swing hanging from a rusted pulley. We tried to climb the bank, pull it back under the trees and make it work, although the best we could get out of it were a few squeaky jerks before it shuddered to a halt.

For our last break of the day we waited until we were in what seemed to be the heart of the forest. It was a very peaceful hideout, enclosed by two tangled walls of large conifers and suffused with the serene calm of a holy place, like a monastery isolated in the mountains. As we ate and drank I sat cross-legged on a tier of rock that sloped into the water, and stayed in the river, wrapped in my blubber, while Robbie and Calum hopped and danced around in vain attempts to keep warm. The sun was now starting to sink behind the trees and the cold was becoming uncomfortable. I kept telling them that Armathwaite was just around the bend, but in truth this whole verdant arm of the river looked the same, with continuous flanks of sandstone cliffs and tall trees.

It was dusk by the time we eventually found Dad and Beth, on the outskirts of Armathwaite. We'd arranged to meet them at a secluded beach with deep clay-coloured sand. To our relief that's exactly where they were, standing in the shadow of a tall bouldering cliff dotted with chalk handprints – another rock we used to jump off as kids. Beth came down to meet me as I lumbered out of the water. She wiped the grime from my face and gave me a kiss that made me forget the cold. She also said she'd found Dad lost in a bush somewhere and they'd wound up flicking through her magazine together, filling out crosswords for a few hours before we showed up. I was so tired and relieved that I couldn't stop smiling. Finally, the endless bend of cold, forgotten river was almost done and soon we could get ourselves warm and dry again.

First, there was one final obstacle between us and the day's end. I remembered this particular cascade from the start of summer, when we'd last kayaked to this part of the Eden. By all accounts, it was the second biggest waterfall we'd faced.

Feeling somewhat anxious, I crouched on the rocks with Robbie and Calum and waited at the ready in case we needed to jump in. If anyone was expected to leap to their doom it was the qualified lifeguard. Never mind the fact that waterfall rescue wasn't really included on my certificate.

From our position, we could see the whole force of the river being funnelled through a rugged bottleneck, which ended with an abrupt drop into a thrashing whorl of rapids. This time, with the added rainwater, it was going to be even more ferocious. It was fine for us because we could simply climb down the rocks, where the water wasn't so fast-flowing, but for the kayakers it tempted some adrenaline-seeking behaviour.

Several slow seconds eased by. There was a house on the bank to our left and a civilised couple were sitting on their balcony, overlooking the river. I saw them both step up to the railing as Dave approached the cascade with increasing speed. Then we all watched him as he ploughed through the chop in a direct line, dropping over the first dip, swerving with the whipped current and gliding almost sidelong over the waterfall into the torrent below. None of us, including Dave, could quite believe he'd made it through.

By the time we reached the bridge we were all very tired and yet satisfied with how the day had gone. I was especially fond of that last little hurdle, handled with a grace that was uncharacteristic of Dave, who was usually as clumsy as myself. While my brothers and I collapsed on the bank the others kept on paddling and took the kayaks to our campsite at Drybeck Farm, which was situated beside the river. After we'd changed out of our wetsuits Calum jumped into Dad's car and Beth took Robbie and me to the farm, where we were staying. Funnily enough, the farm was owned by the man who Mum used to buy her Christmas turkeys from, and it was a well-hidden sanctuary, replete with North American yurts and colourful gypsy caravans. It also had a wooden compost toilet and, wait for it . . . an outhouse shower with hot running water.

Once the tents were up and we were all showered, we decided to head into the village for a pub dinner. The pub was crowded with folk from Armathwaite and the surrounding villages. It was the quintessential country hive, padded with hearty laughter and choral 'ayes' that gave the atmosphere a deep, steady rhythm. It also had low ceilings, long knotted tables, brazen bar rails and photographs on the walls of the recent floods. We could've been in Hobbiton, inside the Green Dragon with a motley crew of bumbling Hobbits.

Indeed, it seems evident that ours is a very private and often quite insular little island. Orwell once described us as a nation of flower-lovers – 'a nation of stamp collectors, pigeon-fanciers, amateur carpenters, coupon snippers, darts players, crossword puzzle fans'. I would agree that we do seem to be a quietly eccentric bunch with our fair share of hobby- ists – myself included. I imagine that at least one of the above pursuits would be in some way familiar to you, even if it isn't something you take part in directly. What's interesting, though, is that even our communal activities, like going to the pub or the theatre, support the fact that anonymity is a prized possession in British society. We might as well accept that we're a little more sheltered than some of our European neighbours. That is to say – we're more likely to build secret hideaways and take playground insults, like being called a gossip, as visceral attacks.

There was something altogether soothing about being back

in the bumbling countryside. We'd grown up drinking in rustic pubs like this one, which are softened by lyrical, often incomprehensible, dialects and warmed by muttering open fires. To me, it was the kind of temple you needed after spending several stagnant months stuck in the city. Of course, I could complain about the fact we're hemming ourselves in and no one's going outside any more, but at least in the world of wild swimming the tide has long been rolling back on itself. Recently, we've seen Brockwell Park Lido being reopened, we've seen King's Cross Pond drawing urbanites to its chilly water and (closer to my digs in Newcastle) we've also seen plans for the restoration of Tynemouth Outdoor Pool. I like to think it has something to do with the psychological benefits of jumping into cold lakes, lidos and rivers. I think more and more people are discovering how it feels to roam in and under open water. Many of us are finding those conditions in which the world expands, inviting you into a silent, alien atmosphere, where you can learn how it feels to fly and float weightless in the hands of the current.

In *Waterlog*, Roger Deakin noted that the body is mostly water and so the metamorphosis that occurs when we swim has a physiological basis. He also related this, as I mentioned earlier, to our time in the womb, when we were submerged in amniotic fluid and protected in a private, watery world. These were two observations that appealed to me, but I loved it most when he described different British beach scenes and described all the sand-castle building, dog chasing and wave jumping that takes place in those environments. He noticed how folk become instantly playful when they visit the beach.

Suddenly the everyday grit of neurosis and propriety is washed away, like all those tiny grains of sand swept out to sea.

It made me think about the importance of playing and not taking life too seriously. I was also reminded of something Robbie once told me about an artistic movement called Dadaism. Supposedly this movement began after the First World War. At first it seemed like an early branch of surrealism, defiantly critical of the accepted ideas that comprise the status quo. Admittedly, I didn't really get it. Why would you invite audiences into empty theatres and plaster canvases with nonsensical anti-art? Then Robbie explained how accepted, common ideas, like sensible society and imperialism, had led humanity into the abyss of the First World War. Over time I saw the heartache and tragedy behind the movement and it began to make more sense to me. Essentially, the status quo had been proven to be infinitely destructive, which created room for new and more outlandish ideas. If there isn't a right way to go or act, then we are truly free to define ourselves, right? Why not embrace nonsense and all those other subversive ideas that disrupt unchecked commonalities? Why not chase your dog across the beach and bury your friends in the sand? The act of playing is inherently subversive. It offers us an opportunity to swim against the current and search for calmer waters, regardless of what the status quo has already prescribed.

It's important and healthy to play – and what playground is better than the natural world? Just look around you . . . see all those animals locked in games together, from the dolphins that leap and dive, side by side, to gibbons chasing each other among the bending boughs of jungle trees. I often find myself envying these animals for the simplicity of their lives and the ease with which they enjoy their habitat. It certainly casts a sad shadow over our tombs of metal and concrete, and our unending acquisition of everything under the sun.

Soaking in the warm, rhythmic atmosphere, we chose a table at the back of the pub and ordered the kind of steaming fry-ups that English dreams are made of. Dave, Sandy, Beth and I all shared a corner bench and two seats, huddled around our ringed pints of ale and Thatcher's cider. After the first round, Sandy and I got to talking about one of our old rugby coaches, a gentle but colossal debt collector. He used to coach Calum as well; in fact it was Calum who told me about the time this coach was holding a training pad and a kid drove right into it and dislocated the coach's thumb. After wincing for the briefest moment, our coach gripped his thumb, rammed the joint back into place and then picked the pad back up, adopting a wide stance, ready for the next charge. Calum also told me about how our coach would drive his son, Ryan, through town and crank up the volume on a pop radio station and wind the windows down and sing in a loud, lurching voice to embarrass him.

'Did I tell you about his donkey?' Sandy asked.

I shook my head and replied in the negative, through a mouthful of gammon and egg.

'Apparently, he was meeting a group of gypsies at their campsite. I don't know much about it, but he said they had a donkey tied to a chain and it was in a really bad way.' Sandy leant forward, clasped his hands on the table and rested his fingers against his pint. 'So, he said to the gypsies: "I'll fight one of your guys – you choose whoever you want – and if I win I get ya donkey."'

I spoke to Calum later that night and brought up Sandy's story. He confirmed that for as long as he'd known Ryan, his family had owned several donkeys. We could only assume that our coach's prize had since been introduced to a mate and given birth to several foals. I think there's a certain sweetness to that story – one for the Disney bods, perhaps.

Occupy Your Mind (Rob's Tip): Something I did for these longer swims was prepare a quote I'd repeat over and over as I swam. A lot of time can be passed forming repetitive lists in your mind, so I'd choose a mantra and use it to calm my mind, gain confidence and concentrate on the moment. I found that I could better establish a rhythm if I repeated the phrase to myself. Here are two I alternated between while swimming for two and a half hours in the chilly Norwegian waters:

In the depths of winter, I found in me an invincible summer.
(Albert Camus, French/Algerian philosopher, writer and footballer)

Just keep swimming.
(Dory – a cartoon fish with limited mental faculties)

8

Planet City

I woke the same time as I usually did, just when the sun was peeling over the roof of our tent, revealing the drops of dew that dotted the outer cover. It was warm inside, among the bodies, bags and coats. For a while I lay inside my sleeping bag with my eyes open and my arm around Beth. She was only supposed to stay for the day, but in the end she'd opted to spend the night, which meant it was her, Dave and me all crammed into that small space. The warmth from our bodies was enough to bring out beads of sweat, while also worsening the idea of what was waiting for us when we went outside.

Soon I decided to bite the bullet. I lifted my weight onto the balls of my feet, slid into my padded coat and pulled on my balaclava. Then I crawled out into the open, stepped into my wetsuit and pulled it up to my waist. I could smell the urine that'd soaked into the rubber, although I guess I was used to it by now.

After checking the campsite to see if anyone else had stirred, I walked down to the river and stood behind the reeds, with my bare feet on the cold grass. Ahead of me the Eden flowed slowly by, shadowed on the other side by ranks of squat trees. For the first morning since we'd started it actually looked inviting, warmed by the naked sunlight and speckled with golden beads as the rays glanced over the ruffled surface.

I reminded myself that we were on the homeward stretch – so to speak. We'd already passed the halfway point and there was a certain solace to be found in the fact we'd got this far. A lot of folk, myself included, had doubted that I'd be fit enough to last the full ninety miles. Now I was convinced that I was going to make it and, what is more, that I was going to be able to keep enjoying it. In time, I also thought about Sandy, who we'd said goodbye to the night before, and my cousins, Owen and Gareth, who would soon be heading up north for their first visit to Langwathby, and staying with our friend Luke. We were going to have a reunion once we finished the swim – everyone who'd been on the India trip a few years earlier. Folk from both sides of the family had decided to travel up to the mouth of the river (Port Carlisle) as well. This meant we'd finally lumber out of the Eden towards a crowd of familiar faces. Also, it served to make the end of our swim just that little bit more appealing.

While I was watching the river the tents behind me began to rustle and shake, like baggy-skinned monsters. Slowly the faces of our little team appeared, one after another, poking between the zips and blinking, bleary-eyed in the fresh sunlight. We didn't waste any time in pulling everything we owned from the tents and collapsing them and packing them away. Then breakfast consisted of a few dewy biscuits, bananas and several large gulps of water. After that, we gathered all the supplies we needed and piled them on the grass, ready for Dad's arrival. The kayakers, Dave and James, were going to wait with their kayaks, since they'd paddled them down to Drybeck Farm the previous evening. Robbie, Calum and I, on the other hand, would be driven back to the bridge in Armathwaite. Unfortunately, we'd have to spend the first part of the morning swimming down to where we camped. It was a small psychological blow, but we tried not to think about it and instead busied ourselves filling the dry-bags with sports bars and glucose water.

In keeping with our expectations, going from the heated, comfortable car to the knobbled, icy Eden turned out to be a rude shock to the system. It took us a lot longer than usual to inch into the current and submerge ourselves. We wound up standing in the river together, waist-deep and all equally unwilling to take the plunge. Then Calum began to play air drums, hammering his way through a frantic solo to try to get his blood pumping. Meanwhile Robbie shivered and danced around with a mixture of Muay Thai stretches and Zoidberg crab moves. When that didn't work, they took to telling each other that they really wanted to dive in, perhaps hoping to trick their body into suddenly buckling and flopping under-water. All the while I watched them and laughed through chattering teeth. I preferred a more subdued approach myself – I guess it was the blubber that kept me calm. I usually tried to slow my breathing, while also keeping quiet, at least until I stopped shivering. When I felt relaxed enough I'd lower myself underwater, until the water spiked my neck and my chin was resting against the surface. At that point all I had to do was bow my head, relax my body and sink under. Finally, with a slight kick, I'd propel myself forward through the spiralling murk and into the supple hands of the current.

After all that fuss, the morning swim turned out to be quite pleasant and not at all as cold as we'd imagined. When we reached the campsite we found Dave and James sitting in their kayaks, along with Dad, who was standing on the bank in his trunks. It might've had something to do with Mum's brave show a few days earlier, but Dad saw us approaching and charged manfully down the bank into the shallows.

'*Anchalog*,' he shouted, before he threw out his arms and dove forward into the water.

In case you're wondering, 'Anchalog' is the Gaelic name of a mountain in Scotland, and a word he loved to shout when we were kids. We'd heard that battle cry countless times while wielding cardboard shields and sticks and having little medieval battles together. He'd used it most frequently in the phrase 'Anchalog Warrior', which was the cry he made before he sprang an ambush, ran at us and then mimicked a dramatic, flamboyant death as we hacked him down with our sticks, like a great spectacled ogre.

A moment later Dad resurfaced and began to paddle out in front us. We all swam along with him for a short stretch before he staggered out of the river, pink and shining, and disappeared in the direction of the warm campsite showers.

It was just the five of us after that, easing down the widening river. The two kayakers kept a steady pace at the back and occasionally stopped to record some film or take in our surroundings. Meanwhile, the three of us had found our rhythm and we kept a close formation at the centre of the river, where the water was deepest.

Over the first few days I'd quickly realised that the most demanding moments occurred during the early morning, when the sun sat half-dressed on the horizon and the blustery sky was that shade of Cumbrian grey that makes you want to stay inside, close to the fire. That being said, the river could also be an ally of sorts. It gave us a place to be and a way to go. In a way, I also liked being in the grip of something I couldn't control. Often I'd just lean back, outstretch my legs and float on the current. It became a ritual of sorts. In fact, it made me think of Douglas Adams and one of his better-named characters, Slartibartfast, who said that the only way to start enjoying life was to first hang the sense of it. In a way, the river helped to validate that idea. Whenever we found a deep tract of water, with a strong current eddying through it, all we had to do was relax, lean back and let the Eden take us to the sea.

Further downriver we came to a place where the banks narrowed and the trees gathered on either side. Slowing my crawl, I began to peer through my goggles, watching the riverbed inching closer to my fingertips. Soon a wide expanse of smooth rock rose through the murk and rolled like sand dunes beneath my strokes. Occasionally, I would extend my hand and run my fingers over the snaking troughs and rolling peaks. We went on like that for several minutes, drifting over those rugged dunes striped with tangled plumes of vegetation, before it became too shallow for us to swim. Then I stopped with my hands pressed against the rock and looked over at my brothers, lying like crocodiles in the current. Robbie told us he'd just seen a large eel coiled in a crevice. It was a reminder that we were heading deeper into the wild, especially when he added, 'I wonder if we could eat it.'

We stopped again on a pebble beach in the late afternoon and met a local swimmer, Becky, who'd arranged to join us for the last two miles. Her parents were there too, and they unrolled a picnic blanket and kindly served us tea and lemon cake. Across the river from us there was a stately home mounted on a cliff with various tunnels, chambers and winding staircases carved into the rock. It was quite a majestic view to occupy us as we ate. We could also see a sculptured fountain encircled by flowers, an unkempt hedge maze and the stately house itself, framed by the trees and cloaked in ivy and wisteria vines.

Unfortunately, as much as we might've wanted to linger and wait for the cake to digest, we had to press on. A moment later I was shuffling slowly down a shelf of sloping rock, widening my stance as the current tugged at my ankles. Feeling the cold, I took a moment before I dove forward and stood still for a while. Looking down, I noticed the sunlight had created a glowing patina on the surface of the water. I could see the minnows more clearly now. They were moving closer to my pale toes and supping the little bubbles that collected on my skin. The next thing I knew we were all back in the river, led on by the kayaks as we bobbed under a viaduct and dodged the tangled limbs of an uprooted tree. Then suddenly we were being bundled down tiers of cascading rapids. Even I, the Floaty God, had to abandon my technique when I was given another brief colonoscopy by a particularly protrusive rock. Letting out a plosive howl, I rolled over onto my front and outstretched my arms, fending off the rounded boulders as they jumped through the murk. It wasn't exactly the best introduction for Becky either. I imagine she wasn't expecting to be hurled down a river into an onslaught of rocks and drowned foliage.

For that reason, and for the sake of our battered arses, we were glad to find that the rapids didn't last too long. In fact, after the first mile the river became very calm and the water was deep enough for us to fully extend our strokes. Having found our rhythm, we then swam without interruption until sunset, when we came to a forest-cradled bend with a church spire in the distance, peeking over a wall of bright, broad-leafed willows. We knew that we were close to the end, so we stopped swimming and allowed ourselves a quiet moment to float past the church and inspect the verdant parish lawns and the well-kept graveyard. After several more twists and turns, we were finally greeted with the glorious sight of Warwick Bridge, connecting the banks ahead of us.

Another day was done.

Once we'd said goodbye to Becky we peeled our wetsuits off, pulled on warm jackets and rolled down balaclavas. We'd taken a bit of a beating that day and the evidence was manifest. I watched Robbie unwrap several layers of duct tape from around his feet, revealing a few raw, wet blisters that dotted his ankles and heels. Calum was now suffering from earache too, and it was getting much worse since we'd left the water. He pouted angrily, his jaw tensing as he tilted his head and rested his ear against his bunched scarf. He didn't talk much after that – the pain was such that he really couldn't think about anything else.

That night Calum went with Dad to the hospital and learnt that he'd picked up a parasitic hitchhiker from the river. This parasite had then burrowed inwards and infected his eardrum with a pus-filled boil that clogged the inside of his ear. The doctor also told him that in the next few days the boil would burst like a lanced spot and ooze . . . yeah, you get the picture.

It didn't take Calum long to put a more casual spin on what was clearly an infuriating situation. As his grimace faded he began to tell us that he wouldn't be able to channel his alter-ego, Lorenzo Falls, any more. He'd arrived at the conclusion that the parasite was actually a homophobe, killing his camp flamboyance.

'Right now,' he said, 'Lorenzo is chasing it down my ear canal like Gandalf and the Balrog.'

We all burst out laughing, no doubt enjoying the same image of ol' liberated Lorenzo hurtling down Calum's ear, with his sword held aloft.

Swim the Eden Expedition, Day 7
Friday 21 August 2015

Waking up the next morning, I took several minutes to adjust to the light and the reality of where I now was. My mind was still rifling through some of the images from a vivid dream I'd had. It all started with Steven Spielberg taking me underground in his metallic lift – as he does. Then I found myself in this bright, cavernous womb dappled with eerie light reflected from the pools around us. Standing in this womb was a strange entity, one that I soon pictured as a beautiful AI robot – no doubt picked up from the film *Ex Machina*. There was also an angular gateway to another universe, through which I could see the triangle from the *Dark Side of the Moon* album. I knew, for some reason, that the next stage would be to enter that gateway . . . but then suddenly I'd woken up.

Still half asleep, I zipped up my jacket, which I'd worn all night to keep warm, and climbed out of the tent into dim beams of clouded sunlight. It was the start of our seventh day on the Eden and I was beginning to feel the pall of our constant exertion, mainly because I had twisted my ankle and couldn't put any pressure on it at all. Outside I found our wetsuits hanging from a tall chain-link fence. I went to check them to see how grim our morning dress-up would be. Luckily it hadn't rained overnight and they'd avoided the dew, so they weren't too bad. Next, I went to find a new home for the feast we'd had the night before. The bartenders had kindly left the back door open so we could get into the pub and make use of their porcelain. It doesn't sound like much, but it saved me from having to squat in a tangled bush some-where, so I felt intensely indebted to them.

It wasn't long before everyone else was outside and milling around, trying to wake up and stay warm. By now we'd picked up our own shorthand, qualifying us as a regular expedition team. We took our tents down in quick succession, filled water bottles, added the powdered glucose, chose our food rations, pulled our wetsuits up to our waists and finally gathered the dry-bags together. Every one of us played a part in this process and did their bit to support the machine of our adventure. As a result, that machine kept whirring and striding out ahead of us, overleaping the countryside, like a giant tin man. Soon there was nothing left for us to do but follow its stomping footprints. You couldn't complain, and of course no one wanted to, because to do so would mean singling yourself out, and at that point we were all driven by a unanimous sense that we were one. It's the psychology of a unit, I guess, and it's pretty damn powerful. It also helped that we were close enough to want each other to succeed. When it came down to it, our bond would dissolve any sibling rivalry and niggling competition. Like a clearing mist, the shroud would peel back over a plethora of happy memories, revealing three kids who are lucky to have each other.

From the first moment I planted my foot into the icy current I knew we were in for a rough day. Calum was about to face a gruelling test of his mettle. Just from looking at him you could see that he was in considerable pain. In fact, the doctor had already advised him not to continue the swim. Defiant, Calum had already made up his mind. He gritted his teeth and wrapped several bands of duct tape around his head, securing a wadded bandage to protect his ear. I watched him as he walked across the bank and stepped into the shallows. Then he stood for a while, staring at the water with a look of grim resolve, his head bowed and his shoulders hunched forward slightly.

'The last thing you want to do when you've got earache,' he said, grimacing, 'is jump into a cold river.'

I didn't envy him having to suffer something as irritating as earache at that stage. Luckily, the morning swim was nothing worse than a pleasant distraction. We were edging through the last vestige of the forested hinterland, finding secret glades, which were so enclosed by trees and thickets that I suspected you could only reach them from the river. All the while, Calum swam breaststroke and kept a steady pace, while also holding his ear above the water. Every now and then he'd stop, swivelling on the current, with his hands in the water and his eyes closed. It was usually during those moments when the sun breached the scudding clouds, at which point I'd see him leaning back with the light on his face, no doubt relishing our respite. Other times he'd paddle alongside Robbie and me, occasionally handing us the whisky bottle. Just one gulp was enough to put fire in your stomach and spread some warmth to your extremities. I couldn't take too much on-board though, since whatever I swallowed was then swilled around in my stomach as I swam. It also didn't help that the taste reminded me of one of the most punishing drinking sessions I've ever had. I'll just say that it involved an hour-long wrestling match between Robbie and me, an atomic wedgie, a bitten bicep and a stomach-churning Christmas morning.

As we approached midday the trees began to disappear. Then the sloping hills gave way to vast flatlands split by tributaries that snaked out from the main stem of the Eden. This helped to create shallow stretches of smooth pebbles, over which we usually walked, taking a moment to consider our surroundings. Overhead the sky seemed to have grown, dimmed with a grey covering of rainclouds. We could also see a pale glow that arced over the crest of the horizon, although mostly the sun failed to pierce the drear, which kept the water at a low temperature.

Soon we rounded a sharp corner and disturbed a flock of seagulls that erupted suddenly into the sky. I watched them flying as they broke formation and became a mass of speckled white dots that faded into the clouds. To me, their caws signalled the nearness of the coast and reminded me how close we were to the end of our swim. These were our last few days and, in a way, it felt like we had reached our final obstacle – not a waterfall or a steep canyon, but a series of desolate and remote vistas, unlike anything we'd seen so far.

Up to that point we'd been swimming among the rolling hills, walled fields and squat forests of the Eden Valley. In hindsight, it had all been rather idyllic, but now we were surrounded by far-reaching plains dotted with pylons, like the husks of skeletal machines left rooted in the earth. We could also feel the city, Carlisle, creeping closer, as though the buildings themselves had brought the onset of some sinister ailment that affected not only our moods, but also the scenery around us. Over time, this new feeling got under our skin. When the water shallowed again we found that our moods had suddenly taken a turn for the worse. For what felt like hours we were bent over, wading slowly through the water, in an agonising trudge. All the while the overcast sky ruled over us, huge and dreary, inviting the old pathetic fallacy that is so commonly applied to English weather.

As I tramped, I kept sight of Calum out of the corner of my eye. I could see him leaning forward and grimacing as he stumbled down into waist-deep water. His eyes were hard and fixed on the dirty current. Then he clamped his teeth together and began to mutter angrily, as though he was reciting a defiant mantra, or perhaps repeating the words of some old stoic, like Hemingway – the same ones, I imagined, that Robbie had scrawled on the back of that portrait he gave Calum last Christmas: *Man is not made for defeat.*

It was just the kind of thing you needed to tell yourself when your spirits took a nosedive, as ours had. Then the merciful river decided to give us a break and we were finally able to swim again. Suddenly our legs lifted behind us and our hands groped the depths as we each slipped underwater, like slow-moving submarines. All of us were starting to suffer from the constant exertion, which meant our strokes had become slow and lazy. I tried to relax my shoulders to relieve the ache, but doing so caused me to repeatedly veer off towards the bank. It was slow going for almost an hour – not to mention the fact that Calum had to keep his head out of the water and was still being reduced to breaststroke.

All the while the treeless scenery seemed to roll by, unchanged, until we drifted onto a long stretch with a concrete dual-carriageway far ahead of us. The fleeting growl and rumble of passing cars hit our ears like an abrupt alarm. All at once the signal had sounded and we knew we were leaving the countryside – at least for now.

As we neared the bridge we noticed one of the cars suddenly flash its lights, slow and then move over onto the hard shoulder. Next, we saw the window being wound down as a hand was thrust out that began to wave at us. We rolled over onto our backs and peered at whoever it was who seemed to know us. It wasn't until we'd drifted a little closer that we recognised the car and realised it was Mum in the driver's seat. Funnily enough, she'd been crossing at that exact moment and was keeping an eye out for us.

Further downriver, the banks narrowed and became crowded with trees again. We could tell by the height of the sun that we were getting close to Carlisle. It was just as well, since the only thing keeping me warm was the little whisky I had left in my system. Sure enough, evidence of the city limits soon emerged on either side of the river. Through the trees, we caught glimpses of suburban houses and parks where dog-walkers wandered and threw sticks across the grass. Then we came to a series of metal bridges and bobbed along on the thrashing current and dodged rocks as we lost control of our momentum. The second bridge we reached was lined with onlookers and among them we sighted Iain's other sister, Anne, having heard her calling to us as we approached. We tried to wave but the ferocity of the current had us spinning and rolling in every direction. In fact, to her it must've looked like we were taking a beating.

Finally, the deep rapids rolled high like waves and bundled us towards a sandstone bridge, much larger than the others. We tried to use the current as a slingshot, turning hard towards the bank and swimming quickly to avoid the middle struts of the bridge. It wasn't too difficult to find that last thrust of strength now that the end was in sight. Once we'd climbed out of the water we pulled both kayaks up onto the sand and pushed them into a bushy thicket so they would be hidden from view. It was then that a disarming, middle-aged fella rushed over and introduced himself as Mark Thurston. He was one of the swimmers Calum had asked to join us for the last two days, until we reached Port Carlisle. He was older than Robbie and James – a tall, athletic and friendly family man, who'd been keen to come along, giving up his weekend to accompany a team of strangers on the last leg of their adventure. What's more, you could tell how excited he was and his energy was immediately infectious – just when we needed a dose of something positive.

After ripping off layers of duct-tape bandaging, we limped up the bank and re-joined civilisation by way of a concrete path that edged a busy road. Dad had left his red chariot in a nearby car park, which was situated beside the Sands Leisure Centre. It was one of the areas of Carlisle that they'd invested a lot of money in, which meant it had nice open expanses of grass and clean paved pathways. It wasn't long before we'd packed the car, collected our towels and piled into the Leisure Centre, hoping to use some of their hot water. Then James played some music through his phone and we traipsed dirt and river-stink into the shower, before disappearing into our own private cocoons of warm, spattering water. The feeling of washing yourself clean and putting on dry trousers and a padded jacket was hard to beat.

Start Off Easy (Rob's Tip): *As with anything, it's best to start and learn through doing. However, if you're entirely new to wild swimming, it might be wise to research your surrounding area – scout out rivers and lakes and think about local waters you've noticed before. It's great to find an idyllic, perhaps more isolated, body of calm water for your first dip. That way you can allow yourself time to acclimatise to the temperature in relaxed conditions. Once you've done all your research and located your personal haven, it's simply a case of breathing deep, taking your time and soaking it all in.*

9

Borne Back . . .

When I was a teenager I remember being told that there are 'certain hoops you have to jump through in life'. I think that to a certain extent this is surely true. The only problem is if you jump through too many you wind up performing in the circus. By that I mean you end up being a pawn on a chessboard with an orange king who brags about sexual assault. Then you end up doing what you're told too often, while also forgetting to challenge powerful idiots. Let's just take a minute and consider our options. It's never too late to look around and find inspiration in wild places. Indeed, there are myriad different tribes and communities on this Earth, and each one is unique and intimately complex.

Take the Bajau sea gypsies of Borneo, for example. You might've seen this population in an episode of *Human Planet*. They're a group of seafaring nomads who live on the lukewarm Bajau Sea in makeshift stilted houses. Their lives unfold, nestled in the rugged cradles of the vast Coral Triangle, which is almost half the size of the United States. By day the Bajau canoe to deep water and dive down over the surrounding reef. They hunt using handmade spear guns, nets and lines, and earn their local reputation as masters of free diving. Sometimes they swim as deep as twenty metres, at which point they can use negative buoyancy to walk along the reef, like naked astronauts slinking over the surface of the moon. They search for fish, urchins, pearls and sea cucumbers and stay down for several minutes on a single breath. This was a previously unimaginable feat, yet the Bajau have developed superhuman aquatic abilities through years of living on the ocean. The children also show signs of improved vision underwater, having adapted to their shimmering, liquid world. If you were to spend a day on the reef, among the Bajau, you'd likely see mothers, lathered in sunscreen made from guava leaves and tapioca, bathing their babies in the shallow water. You'd also see children splashing and playing below the houses and men paddling upright in dugout canoes, weaving between the struts and ladders, laden with woven baskets.

At night, the Bajau sleep together in small rooms on boarding or bamboo. I imagine they must see the moonlight bouncing from the water and rippling against their ceilings – they must feel the little lives of the reef fluttering busily beneath them. To me it seems like a paradise of sorts. I sometimes feel that if we filled their shoes, even just for a day, we would be connected to a magic we seldom experience. If we travelled with them for a year, moving seasonally and following their ancestral pathways along the forested coasts of Borneo, I think we would be changed irrevocably. However, life for the Bajau isn't quite as romantic as you might want it be.

Make no mistake – they are outsiders stricken by poverty and continually forced to compromise their subsistence lifestyle. Dynamite, cyanide fishing and compressor diving, which involves divers holding tubes in their mouths as they swim down to the seabed, are now commonplace. Yet that dream of paradise still exists, and for the most part the Bajau can survive in harmony with the reef, although every day their way of life is threatened by large fishing industries, as well as by our collective acidification of the water through the burning of fossil fuels. This is not just hokey nostalgia for a simpler time. It is stark evidence of how our everyday demands affect those with less destructive ambitions.

It is now estimated that we have killed 90 per cent of the large fish in the ocean. If tribes like the Bajau, who've adapted to reach every morsel and grain in the marine food web, are struggling to survive, what does that say about our impact on the world? Many of us, including myself, would like to live closer to nature, but we lack the tenacity to abandon the benefits of being in the city. Certain realities (or hoops) must be taken into account. If you want to earn money, it's probably not wise to build a cabin in the woods and embrace the isolation. It is true that the wild is daunting and unpredictable, whereas the alternative is safe, structured and scattered with comfortable places to sit. However, the point I'm trying to stress is that all the years of mechanised expansion, since the Industrial Revolution, have led us to a critical point in our evolution. It seems like we've almost disconnected from the natural world altogether. Our civilisations are now bloated and overcrowded due to overpopulation. Never have we been more in need of a psychological exodus. Never has it seemed more essential for us to understand our place in the animal kingdom. After all, we are older than all the cities and civilisations we've built, fostered by love immemorial, and inextricably bound to all life on Earth.

Swim the Eden Expedition, Day 8
Saturday 22 August 2015

Rising that morning, with two days of our Eden swim to go, I noticed I was feeling increasingly at home. Mind you, it was going to be a tough day, although we were prepared for it, and I don't just mean that in the context of the swim. Learning to fall, learning how to take a knock – this was something that was beaten into us over the course of a decade or so, through skating (rollerblading). I guess you'd say it's one of those extreme sports that quickly turn kids into aspiring stuntmen. For example, there was one occasion when a friend of ours attempted to roll down the slated roof of the local church. He went so fast that his boot-cuffs sparked when he hit the car park, and he crumpled quickly into a rolling ball of twisted limbs. To be more specific, the form of skating that Robbie, myself and a few others were involved in was called aggressive inline. It was a high-octane strain that evolved out of the colourful style of skating often seen on Californian beachfronts, when your average skater used to spin and dance like an extra in a Will Smith rap video. Aggressive inline, on the other hand, grew up on the streets and was distinguishable by the fact that we skated faster, fell harder and incorporated grabs, spins and grinds into our repertoire.

Over time, the cumbersome breaks disappeared, the wheels shrank and fattened, and the boots grew larger, fitted with grind-plates and wrap-around cuffs. Unfortunately, inline never achieved the kind of underground status that skateboarding has. The skateboarders were once outcasts, seen, stereotypically, as sporting long, lank hair, piercings and beat-up flannel shirts. Now, at least in America, they're embraced like the jocks, while the culture has achieved the same kind of mainstream status as surfing or snowboarding. And yet aggressive inline remains unseen. It struggles on beneath the underground – a subculture that most of the other subcultures rejected, which is part of the reason we loved it so much. We were unique. We were doing ridiculous-sounding tricks like *fakie-alleyoop pornstars* and *topside fishbrains*. Essentially, we had our own language and a skill so underexposed that few others could get their heads around it. To us, this wasn't just some flippant hipster affectation; it was real and it required focus, athleticism and nerve.

The group of skaters I grew up with became very close. Mostly I was surrounded by skateboarders, but in the context of our smaller scene there was no animosity whatsoever – at least not after a few years, during the heyday of aggressive inline, when it earned its rightful place alongside the other X-Game sports. It was then, when the road rolled smoothly beneath our wheels, that we began the monumental construction of Langwathby Skate Park.

One of the kids in our group had his own shed and was

an aspiring joiner, despite only being about eleven years old. Another of our mates had a dad who was a builder and so we used to pillage supplies from the construction sites where he was working. Together, we learnt how to attach coping, bend the wood into a concave and nail it all together so it wouldn't break when we rolled down it. We used an old, sturdy school desk and built a fun box with a rail attached. Then we also built two shoddy quarter pipes, and before long kids were travelling from all over Cumbria to have a go on our creations.

Throughout the following summer, at the height of our parks success, we skated from nine in the morning to nine at night. I was about ten, or eleven, at the time. I don't really suffer from too much nostalgia, so if I was given the choice I wouldn't conform to that old cliché of giving it all up just to go back. That being said, I do think about that time a lot and I know summers like that played a significant part in shaping the way in which my brothers and I wanted to spend our lives, not least because we spent so much time outdoors.

It should be said that we weren't doing anyone any harm either. Nevertheless, that didn't stop the clipboard army from eventually descending on our skate park and sapping every bit of fun they could from our arrangement. Beforehand we'd been to several council meetings to try to keep our patch of concrete, beside the unused tennis courts and behind the village hall. Nonetheless – despite the efforts of a kindly, lanky old lady called Nancy, who befriended us all (a bunch of disreputable hoodies) and helped fight alongside our parents to beat the Man – the park was closed to comply with safety standards. As it turned out, the culprit was a single house, adjacent to our park, where a red-faced, ginger guy, who we nicknamed Big Man, was filing noise complaint after noise complaint and putting endless pressure on the council.

Just like that, we had to dismantle and move the best thing we'd ever built. So, what did we do with all that wood and welded railing? We built the longest grind-box we could and put it at the edge of the road, right in front of the village hall. The sun came out for one glorious day and we waxed the rail and had one of the best sessions I've ever had. Then we went away to see our dad for two weeks and when we came back, it was gone – the police had forced our mates to break the grind-box into pieces. That was pretty much the end of skating for most of us. Soon after that, I turned instead to rugby, and the baggy jeans and sagging skate-tees became striped tracksuits and Canterbury hoodies.

Looking back, I realise now that these early experiences helped to cultivate in us a lasting sense of wildness. They also woke us to the fact that hardship is an integral component of the learning process. My rugby coach, Mr Ellery, a lumbering Cypriot/Welshman, taught me that. He was one of my kindest mentors at school. He used to tell our team that uncomfortable situations were character building. That was how he got us to enjoy being out in the mud or taking a beating from a better team. It was something that always stayed with me, perhaps because it applied to skating too. Through learning that I could fall, hurt myself and then still want to carry on, I realised that pain was sometimes just an undesirable aspect of something worthwhile. You couldn't do anything about it, unless you wanted to bubble-wrap everyone's studded boots, or stick to grinding curbs all your life.

In hindsight, the risk is the reward, along with the knowledge that, having taken it, you conquered an inhibition. Indeed, one of the first things you had to do in skating, before a trick, was completely empty your mind. There's a high level of mindfulness involved in the process of executing a grind, twisting your feet in the perfect way, at the right speed, so that your grind-plates lock onto the rail and your centre of gravity remains fixed. Fear cannot exist in that fleeting moment. Every time it flickered into your mind, you'd fall. That's why so many skaters used to scrawl little declarations on tricky ledges, or onto the steps under steep handrails. You'd often see someone's name marked in chalk, or sprayed there, saying how they'd conquered the obstacle, and, with it, their fear. Then sometimes you'd see the date there as well, or it would simply read: fuck you.

We didn't waste any time that morning. Instead we dismantled the tents, filled our water bottles and packed the dry-bags in record time. Partly it had to do with the fact we were scheduled to meet Mark and another swimmer, Mike, who would be joining us for the day. But also I think we were starting to anticipate the end of our swim. Tomorrow we would arrive at Port Carlisle and we would become the first people ever to have swum the whole ninety miles of the River Eden from source to mouth. I thought a lot about what it meant as we drove towards Carlisle, past furrowed fields and rolling green hills. Occasionally we would snake through humble English villages that reminded us of our childhood roaming grounds. Then we'd see bucolic pubs with increasingly obscure names and unkempt greens with goalposts and lonesome trees to mark the pitch. It all reminded me of how important it is to remember where you come from. Nothing we do is disconnected. You're the same kid who used to run faster, climb higher and laugh louder. That's why it's so important to keep doing things that remind you of who you were – and are. In the end, I think I swim for the same reason I used to stand on big rocks and look down into valleys, or climb into higgledy trees, or seek out secret caves and coves. I want to view nature from all angles – to learn its secrets and find out what lurks around every corner. To me the waters of our world are just another cabinet of curiosities and one can only marvel at the sheer abundance of beauty therein.

Anyway, it felt like the start of a good day and we were already in high spirits. We found Mike, Mark and their families at a graffiti-covered underpass, near to the bridge where we'd stopped the day before. It didn't take long for us to become accustomed to each other. They were both keen swimmers and noticeably eager to get into the river. It was clear that they loved the wild outdoors as well. In fact, Mike was a cameraman who'd worked on various wildlife projects. He'd also just returned from a holiday spent kayaking around the outer isles of Scotland. By chance he'd heard about the swim while he was away and it happened to coincide with the return journey, so he'd decided to drop in and keep us company.

Soon we were all standing in the chalky gravel at the river's edge, wearing the matching red caps of the Outdoor Swimming Society. Then we shook hands, stretched quickly and walked out from under the bridge in a group, with Mark at the front and myself at the back. We headed towards our two trusted kayakers, sat wheeling in slow circles, and then edged into the middle of the river, until the churned tract of rapids tugged at our waists. It was much easier to dive into the cold when there were five of us doing it. It seemed like we were sharing the shock somewhat. In fact, having Mike and Mark there gave us a fresh reminder of how special it was to be doing the swim. So, with renewed gusto, I shot underwater, arced up slightly through the greenish murk and pulled my head back through the surface, releasing a heady gasp that flushed my body of any discomfort, like a tonic. Then I turned over onto my back, outstretched my arms and floated over a soft patch of river weed. I looked over my shoulder at Mark and saw him waving to his little daughter, who was standing with her mum on the bridge, peering over the wall. She seemed slightly distressed, probably due to the fact she was watching her daddy being swept downriver like a hunk of driftwood.

'She wants to come with us,' Mark joked as he turned onto his front and surveyed the way ahead.

At first we were carried by the strong currents that funnelled under the bridge. There was nothing for us to do but bob along, kicking our legs, until eventually the force eased and the surface stilled. By then we were all facing downriver, some of us with our heads submerged, watching the riverbed rushing beneath us, others with their heads up, so that they could chat and take in the scenery. Then, as if stirred by some soundless starter gun, we all suddenly dipped underwater, dug our first strokes in and pulled ourselves forward into a burst of fast front crawl. After that it took several minutes before we all found our rhythm, slowed to a steady pace and bunched into a tight group. At that point Dave decided to crack open the whisky again. Taking intermittent sips for himself, he assumed the role of floating bartender and delivered the bottle to anyone who wanted it. I didn't take on too much, for the same reason I'd watched my limits yesterday, but I drank until there was enough in my system to warm my blood.

By the time Dave had been around the group, we were coming to a quiet bend, enclosed by a forest. The river had grown much wider, yet on either side the banks were hidden behind dense walls of verdant foliage. On several occasions, we saw large willow trees, dipping their limp, tendril leaves into the water. We'd come to a secluded arm of Eden with a peaceful atmosphere soothed by the sound of running water. At once we could feel that the city had receded far behind us, just as yesterday we'd felt its approach through the change in environment. That was also the moment when we were reunited with the swan and her three cygnets – the same ones we'd met at the bridge a few days earlier. Unfortunately, we'd just rounded a sharp corner, concealed by trees, which meant that we inadvertently ambushed them. As a result, the swan mother panicked and took flight in our direction, its huge white wings beating the surface, creating ripples from the reverberations, while also emitting the loud, warbling sounds of a helicopter. It looked so massive from underneath that I half expected it to swoop down and pluck one of us from the river between its webbed orange feet. With the swan having flown upriver the cygnets then darted towards the bank and hid under a tangle of overhanging roots and leaves. We passed on the other side, so as not to disturb them, and made sure to look back to oversee the family reunion.

After thwarting that helicopter attack from Apocalypse Swan, we were ready for anything. It just so happened that there was only one other obstacle to face that day, which Calum had already anticipated. We came to it several minutes later – a short section of blocked-off railway bridge, encircled by orange safety fencing, which split the river like a dam. Dotted around the construction site were several workmen in orange overalls, some of whom were milling among the supports, while others worked on the scaffolding that hugged the structure. Apparently, they were using a vibration machine to ram steel piles into the riverbed, while also adding caps of pointed concrete and reinforced steel to strengthen the foundations. The idea was that they would deflect any dredged-up debris, which was becoming increasingly frequent ever since the severe floods of that last decade.

When the builders saw us they gathered at their Portakabin, waved us over and directed us to a set of makeshift concrete steps. One of them was wearing an unzipped wetsuit and he jumped in and helped us out of the water, one after another. They greeted all of us with warmth and immediately started asking how we'd fared, and cracking jokes. We stopped for a photo with the foreman and a young lad with a huge grin and a hard hat, who they'd nicknamed Tin Tin (I suspected he was the more adventurous one who'd made the arrangements for our arrival). After a few photos, the workmen proceeded to lead us down a special causeway they'd made. Without it we wouldn't have been able to carry the kayaks through the construction site and into the water on the other side. They really had gone out of their way to accommodate us and there was always someone to help at every turn. It was one of those moments of unsuspected kindness that do a lot to improve how you feel about folk. Needless to say, we went on after that with private smiles and a much greater feeling of camaraderie.

By now we had grown very used to travelling on our private waterway, drifting through swathes of gentle forest that seemed to tower over us, grand and silent as a cathedral. We floated in a group for a while and savoured the break, but it wasn't long before we left the forest behind and drifted onto an arm of the river so still it actually felt like the water was flowing back against us. All at once we were moving at the swimming equivalent of a trudge. Each of us sank our heads, dug hard with our strokes and edged towards the wide, naked horizon. And that was that – we spent the rest of the day winding slowly though open countryside, with mudflats emerging where the pebble banks had been and raucous songs provided by flocks of seagulls passing overhead. The only rest we took was when it began to rain and myriad raindrops pattered on the surface, striking the water and spitting little explosions that were wonderful to watch, especially when your eyes were level with the water. I also noticed flashes of white petals belonging to crowfoot flowers and sometimes even the floating yellow of a buttercup. The subtle beauty served as a reminder of what we'd sought by entering the wild. I dare say there's no better thing to be doing when it rains than wild swimming. Just as before, I would sometimes dive underwater, turn over and look up at the sunlit surface through my goggles. The rain had turned the murky water into a clear, pointillist painting, and on that lucid, upturned canvas I could see countless ripples spreading and interlinking, like the chinks in a shirt of chainmail.

I couldn't get enough of it – I kept diving under, spinning and repeating the same motion, if only to have that moment, before I surfaced, when my body lifted with the gentle buoyancy from my air-filled lungs, and I could try to absorb the minutiae, keeping in mind just how rare this view was and how lucky I was to see it.

Soon the quiet patter of droplets falling on the water faded and the rainfall retreated into blustery clouds, which in turn began to dissipate. Taking advantage of the change in weather, James decided to paddle over to the bank and test the drone he'd been carrying on his kayak. We were hoping that he would get some fly-by footage of us from a bird's eye view. He stood on the bank with the chunky remote in his hands and asked us to gather in the middle of the Eden. Then he started the four rotors and lifted the drone steadily upwards, until it hovered at head height with its blue eye blinking. He told us to keep swimming and focus our attention downriver while he guided the drone into a strafing dive behind us. Glancing over my shoulder, I saw the little silver craft as it tilted forward and cut a direct path towards us. It looked like a dipping spitfire and when I turned to swim I imagined parallel rows of bullets hitting the water behind me.

James did a few more fly-overs before he packed up his new toy and clambered back into his kayak. It was steady going after that – there wasn't much to see or do except continue digging in with our strokes and digging deeper into our energy reserves. We reached Rockcliffe by the time the clouds had cleared. It was the last point of civilisation before Port Carlisle – a rugged little civil parish and village, situated on a squashy peninsula fringed by squelching bogs and grassy marshland. It was also pinned between the wide River Esk and our Eden, which joined together further downriver and promised a day of strong currents on the morrow.

With mutual sighs of relief we finally stumbled out of the river and climbed a sloping bank that led us into a newly cut field. The first thing we saw, when we mounted the bank, was a cheery gaggle of country folk gathered around a hovercraft. It was quite surreal; in fact it made me think of the American Deep South – somewhere like Louisiana, perhaps, where the alligator trappers roam the watery swamps in various ludicrous floating contraptions. The group turned out to be a family and, as it happened, we'd bumped into them when they were taking the craft out for its first test drive.

Beth and Mum arrived while they were starting the engine and we had enough time to eat before the craft suddenly lurched forward. Then, standing at a safe distance, we all watched in awe as the wild driver gunned it down the bank and hurtled over the water. At first it worked perfectly and he skimmed effortlessly across the river, with wilting wings of water flopping in his wake. He then rocketed across the mudflats on the other side, turned and headed back without so much as a jolt. Unfortunately, the craft fell at the last hurdle, releasing guttural coughs and splutters as it left the river, recoiled from another slope and slid back down into the water. The driver tried several times to throttle the engine and force the craft up the bank, but its immense bulk kept slipping, and after several attempts it didn't look like it was going to budge. In the end, we didn't get a chance to see whether he made it because we had to get to our waiting cars and change into warm clothes.

The next objective, once we were warm and dry, was to find somewhere close to the river to spend the night. Encouraged by past success, we tried the local pub and were permitted to pitch our tents behind the gravel car park, close to the back entrance. It wasn't exactly an ideal spot, crammed in beside a skip overflowing with chunks of wood and plaster and a rundown house with a beat-up facade, although then again, it was also the last night of our adventure and it seemed fitting that it should cause us some discomfort.

It was a very good night and a kind of swansong session to celebrate how far we'd come. I felt very close to James, and of course to Dave as well, after so much time spent doing something that felt both worthwhile and unusual. It had been a heartfelt privilege to stray so far off the beaten track with them – to have done something together that had never been done before, and, moreover, to have done it with Robbie and Calum as well.

Make It Personal (Cal's Tip): Adventure is personal — embark on a journey you have a personal connection with and it will be so much more rewarding. Pick a river you grew up with, for example. What's the closest or longest river in your region? And don't be afraid to tread new ground! Most of the world's rivers haven't been swum. Martin Strel has ticked off some of the big ones, but there are thousands out there waiting to be attempted . . .

10

'Life's About Folk'

Swim the Eden Expedition, Day 9 (final day)
Sunday 23 August 2015

Shortly after we'd set out from the source of the Eden we'd started talking about daily awards that we could hand out within the group. In the end, we only came up with two. The first was the Rainbow Trout Award, reserved for the campest and most flamboyant swimmer. There hadn't been much of a fight for that one. Despite the efforts of a particularly stubborn parasite, Calum and his alter-ego Lorenzo had now been named the undefeated rainbow champion. The second and final accolade was the Brown Trout Award – a double-edged honour bestowed upon anyone who suffered the . . . well, you can probably guess what had to happen for you to win the *Brown* Trout. Honestly, I don't mean to be vulgar; the only reason I've brought it up is because on that final morning it was I who earned this unwanted commendation. In the early hours of the morning, I could be seen skulking among the trees like a shy Sasquatch. Then the moonlight became my torch as I stumbled over loose branches and groped my way through the cold night. I must admit it was quite an ordeal, although what happened in those woods shall stay between myself and the potential residents of a nearby house, which, upon looking up, I noticed was far too close for comfort.

Most of us were already awake by the time the sun began to rise. For a while I stood in silence at the edge of the car park and divided my attention between our camp and the river, which was partly visible through a line of trees. Slowly the dew that dotted our tents began to slide down the covers and sunlight lifted over the mist-laden fields below us and slowly warmed the serene parish of Rockcliffe. I had the feeling that it was going to be another good swim. We were only going to be in the water for half a day and we'd timed it so that we'd be following the tide out, catching the outflowing current like surfers hitting the sweet arc of a wave. Also, there was a hot shower, a bed and dry, clean clothes waiting at the end of it. I'd thought a lot about relaxing in our house in Newcastle and not having to change into my cold, urine-soaked wetsuit. It's funny how much you wind up craving something so ordinary when you're deprived of it – not even for a long time, just nine days of being mildly feral.

When we were all up and out of our tents we found out that Calum's infected ear swelling had burst during the night. He told us that he'd woken up to find his cheek sticking to his pillow, which didn't sound like good news, although you could tell by his smile that it was. Fortunately, Beth brought a little feminine grace to the group and encouraged less in-depth talk about our bowel movements and leaking ears. Somehow, she also managed to look glamorous despite our situation. James pointed out that it was nice to have someone there who didn't look like a dishevelled troll fresh from nine days spent sleeping under a railway bridge. She wasn't just a pretty face, though; she also managed to effortlessly fold up our tent, as though it were a simple exercise in origami, while I fumbled around with the bag of bent pegs and kept getting stung by the nettles.

The drive down to the river was accompanied by fleeting glimpses of sleepy Rockcliffe, subdued by the sunlit mist. It looked far more beautiful at that time of day. There was also room in Beth's car for us to stretch out, while the air-conditioning fanned us with gusts of cool air and The Cranberries yodelled through the speakers. Before long I was overcome by a sense of calm and I closed my eyes and turned towards the glowing window, with my head propped against the headrest.

We're almost there, I thought.

By now the whole expedition was starting to feel very pleasant indeed – to the point that I almost felt guilty for us nabbing a world record, especially when there were folk who happily covered their faces with washing pegs or tumbled over waterfalls in wooden barrels. By comparison our swim was a light stroll through an album of fond memories. Mind you, it really had been an unforgettable experience. You felt every day on the river and somehow it seemed important. Even the grand mechanics of time were starting to move like the water, ebbing and flowing without disruption from sign-posts or diversions. As the sun set at dusk we'd eat, and then shortly after we'd eaten we'd pitch our tents. When there was no light to see by we'd be in our sleeping bags, until the morning, which was always heralded by the rising sun. Generally speaking, time belongs to the city and, furthermore, our silly linear everyday has little to no meaning in the greater scientific realm. Like the self, time is a strictly human construct; one that can be shed, like a breastplate of uncomfortable steel.

Come to think of it, I remember a rugby tour we'd spent in South Africa when I was fifteen. We met this buxom matriarch called Aunt Sheila, who worked in a café in one of the large townships that bestrewed the outer limits of Cape Town.

'In England your watches speak to you,' Aunt Sheila had said, having decided to entertain/accost us while our food was being prepared. 'They say, now is when you eat, or, now is when you get up to work – you are owned by the time.'

The wisdom of Aunt Sheila wasn't something you could take lightly. Her words and her presence commanded the room. She belonged to a world of poverty and hardship – a world where kids used condoms as catapults and where broken glass bottles littered the football pitches. As a teenager, I took it as gospel when she told us that time was a burden. Her perspective stayed with me and sank deep into my subconscious. Perhaps she was right to say that we, in the developed world, are commonly enslaved by our routines. I'm not sure – I just know that it was refreshing to wake up at dawn and sleep shortly after the sun went down, without having to check your watch throughout the day. It was one of the many unexpected privileges that the swim afforded us.

Feeling content, we drove to the end of a narrow lane, from which you could see the Eden, and then walked across the field in a group. Mark and his dad joined us at the verge and we talked for a while, standing among clumps of stout hogweed, before we eventually zipped up our wetsuits and ascended the bank.

For some reason the water seemed much warmer that morning, perhaps due to the sunlight that was beating down on us, or maybe to the knowledge that we wouldn't be doing the same thing again tomorrow. Nevertheless, I took my time and sat for a moment in the shallows, with both arms submerged from the elbows down. I looked at the tears scattered over my new Speedo wetsuit, particularly the split on the crook of my right arm. Then I glanced down at my pale, wrinkled hands. The jagged scar that ran over my palm and up my ring finger had turned a pale shade of purple. It was very distinct. I could even see the little stacked lines where the stitches had been. In fact, I might as well tell you the story behind it . . .

A year earlier, Beth and I had been on holiday in the Dominican Republic. We were staying in a chalet in Samana, close to the beach, and one hot night we got back from dinner eager to find cold water and a place to collapse. As we stumbled into our room, slightly dazed and dehydrated, Beth turned the fan up to full speed. Then I came in behind her and threw my arms up, about to pull my sweaty t-shirt over my head, but not before my right hand hit one of the rusted fan blades, which hacked a chunk out of my palm and slit my finger. Beth was sprayed with a spatter of blood and plaster, like in a bad slasher movie. Then I was clutching my wrist, staring at the torn flesh and padded muscle of my palm, trying not to lose my shit.

Just like that we went from undressing for bed to both riding on the back of a moped down a rough dirt trail. Instead of a goodnight kiss, I received several injections administered directly through the open wound, as well as twenty stitches and a hefty hospital bill – it's safe to say that it wasn't my finest moment.

Over a year later the hand was still slightly stiff and I could feel a faint ache as I pulled it back through the water and edged into the middle of the river, where the others were waiting. Once we were all ready, we decided to set off swimming in a close group, relishing the sunlight and the feeling of being carried by the outgoing tide. At first Mike's girlfriend, Michele, had seemed anxious about joining us, but that quickly changed once she got into the water. I'm sure she felt the same communal warmth we all felt. After all, this wasn't a day for grumpiness, grit or grimacing. Our nine-day companion, the glorious Eden, was delivering us to its mouth with a gentle hand – the same one we'd felt that first day we arrived at our new house in Langwathby, hurried down the bank and waded out from among the reeds.

No sooner had the River Esk joined the Eden than a strong current was sweeping us downriver. There was no longer any use in swimming. Instead, we tightened our goggles, dipped our heads underwater and assumed the roles of launched torpedoes. We tried several times to stand up and walk back against the current, but it was impossible to keep your footing on the shifting riverbed, and we kept slipping and tumbling back with the outgoing force of the tide. When we weren't in torpedo mode, or fighting the current, we mostly spent that morning taking in the strange world we'd just entered. Occasionally, I'd look over at the mudbanks and see crumbled slices of earth half stacked, like the disassembled tiers of a chocolate cake. It was very quiet out there, as well, and the naked scenery offered bleak vistas reminiscent of an apocalyptic world. No matter where I looked there was always a reminder that the river was changing. The water was now reddish brown and very choppy, with shimmering waves that jostled me from side to side. I also saw how the rounded banks slumped onto sandy beaches cluttered with rocks, and noticed a belching fringe of mud that followed the water's edge. Meanwhile, the sky seemed much larger than before and the Eden too had grown in width, so much so that I could no longer see the bank on the furthest side.

Soon it became apparent that we'd reached a delta, intersected with thin ribbons of mud, like veins snaking through the water. It was clear that the mouth was close, so we rode the current over to the bank and decided to stop for an early lunch. I was very interested to see where we were, so I followed Mark over several piled slabs of broken earth and climbed up from the bank, into a vast field. Far from being a great spectacle, the land was quite empty – eerily so. There was nothing to see save a few lonesome sheep and a few tall pylons in the distance. Also, as if to add to the strangeness of

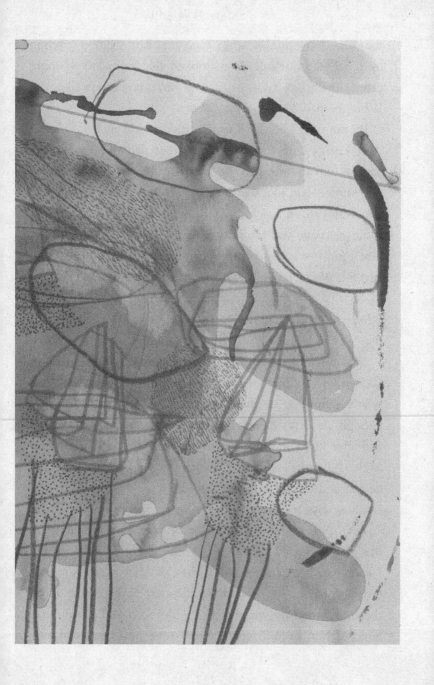

the scene, I saw this big, spiky gang of pollard willows standing by a fallen stonewall. They looked like bouncers keeping guard, ready to swat or stomp any trespassers, like the Whomping Willow in *Harry Potter*.

By the time I got back to the bank the others had dragged their kayaks onto the shore and unfastened the dry-bags to pass around the group. One after another we each dug into our supplies and plucked out handfuls of caramel energy bars, which was all we had left. Mind you, nobody seemed to mind at all; everyone was too busy laughing and joking about how much fun it was to swim at super-speed with the outflowing current. We were all in agreement that this was shaping up to be a very easy and enjoyable day. And then, while the others went on talking, Dave, Calum and I walked over to the river and stepped onto the soft mud that edged the water.

'If you stamp on it you can turn it into quicksand,' Calum said, and no sooner had the words left his lips than Dave was wildly stamping on the sloppy mud like a madman. Sure enough his heavy stomps began to soften the mud underfoot and after just a few seconds he was already buried up to his ankles. Nonetheless, he kept on stamping and gradually sinking deeper and deeper. It wasn't until he was waist-deep, and still laughing hysterically, that I finally grabbed him under his armpits and tried to yank him loose. The only problem was that he wouldn't budge at all. While he continued to laugh I suddenly began to panic. I already knew that Dave was prone to having near-death experiences. He'd told me about the time when he was surfing in Morocco and a wave had bundled him onto a reef. Another time he'd been climbing in France when a storm suddenly hit. Now I understood why he and the reaper were on such friendly terms.

Planting my feet on the mud, I clamped my arms across his chest and leant back with all my weight. It took a bit of leverage, but after a few attempts I did manage to jerk him backwards and drag him out from the sticky death-puddle he'd created.

Once he'd washed the mud off, Dave went and fetched his kayak and we all headed back out onto the river. It was relatively plain sailing after that little scare. We all slipped back into our earlier routine of torpedoing and occasionally wading upriver, against the current. At one point, I launched a lumbering charge towards Robbie, leapt onto his shoulders and tried to tackle him into the water. It was like trying to fell a great Canadian Redwood – the bastard just wouldn't go down. One of the other pastimes we picked up, albeit one quite similar to torpedoing, was called underwater sky-diving. The name might be an oxymoron, but the activity itself was pure, unadulterated fun. All you had to do was sink a foot or so underwater and allow your body to be taken by the current. A moment later you'd be gliding over the furrowed riverbed. Then, if you turned your hand slightly, you could change your course and swerve and swoop, like a skydiver riding the wind.

Further downriver we spotted Mum and Beth waving to us from a field above the bank. With some difficulty we grouped together again and swam hard towards the shallows. As soon as we could stand we all began to trudge with our legs spread far apart to counteract the force from the water.

We knew that Beth wanted to join us for the last stretch, so we went up to help her with the sea kayak they'd brought.

Once the kayaks were all in position, the rest of us piled into the water and dove into the current, which carried us like a conveyor belt and swept us downriver. With that we were ready for the last half-mile. Most of us decided to put our goggles on and swim with the tide, if only to make it feel like a final sprint. Beth and Dave, on the other hand, busied themselves with makeshift surfing. I could see them standing shakily on their kayaks each time I came up to breathe.

It felt good to be able to wind down and enjoy the river as we rode it to the sea. I took the opportunity to rest my shoulders with slow, lazy strokes, yet at the same time I was travelling at a sprinter's pace. The only problem was that my large skate shoes were weighing my feet down and making it hard to kick. After a while I swam over to Dave and threw the shoes onto his kayak to get rid of the extra weight. Immediately I felt lighter and more able to propel myself forward, with the cold water wrapped around my bare feet. I had no idea that this was soon going to come back to bite me.

Suddenly we came to a long, wide turn and slid into a channel close to the bank, where the current was surprisingly strong. As we swung around the bend we caught sight of another figure standing on the bank. This time it was Dad. He waved and called to us as we sped by. By now we could also see the outline of Port Carlisle, framed by the faint offing. The moment the channel spat us out we made a beeline towards it. All the swimmers switched to front crawl, including Calum, who was still wearing the duct-tape bandage over his ear. As we swam we naturally bunched into a tight formation and kept the pace that the Eden chose for us. The river was now so mighty that we had to fight to overpower the current. I really couldn't believe the strength of it, especially having stood on the trickle that bubbled out from the source, nine days ago.

As we neared the port, Robbie, Calum and I held back and the others disappeared into the distance. It wasn't something we'd talked about, but now that it came to it we did rather like the idea of the three of us arriving together, and alone. To kill a few minutes, we pushed ourselves upright and began to move with slow, leaping strides. It was then that my bare foot landed on something hard and slimy that recoiled and writhed beneath my feet. I jumped back and let out an anguished cry. Whatever they were – eels or flatfish – we'd strayed into their territory and disturbed them where they slept. It was instant chaos. We kept standing on their slippery bodies, causing them to erupt from the mud and slap our ankles with their tails. I couldn't hide how repulsed I was by the feeling. It almost felt like I'd fallen at the final hurdle, but then I heard a familiar battle cry that served as a distraction.

Confused, I turned to the bank just in time to see two pink bodies sprinting down the shingle beach. With matching splashes they both crashed into the water and came up gasping and swimming hard across the current. As they neared, we shielded our eyes from the sun, squinted and tried to see who it was . . .

'All right, Craig!' Robbie shouted with sudden delight.

Craig was an old family friend and former school mate of Robbie's. For many years, he'd treated our house like a second home, where he came to read books and occasionally ambush me for surprise wrestling matches. He was close to our mum and had known and loved Grandma Wild as well. He was joined by a friend of his who'd been up for the early morning dip. When they reached us we all trod water and hugged in the middle of the river. It was a circle of wide grins and pale, shivering faces.

After we floated away, I rolled over and looked back at the two distant figures we'd just been talking to. I could see them rushing towards the pile of clothes they'd left strewn on the shore. It was great – it made me realise how supportive some folk can be, especially when you're doing something that encourages a little madness. Then I thought about the builders who'd pulled us out of the water and helped us down their causeway. I also thought about the lone old woman who'd been waiting for us on the bridge. They were the ones who really stayed in my mind. After all, there was no reason for them to show up for us, other than kindness and a distant yet important sort of solidarity. It seemed surreal that such generosity could come from us selfishly wanting to swim a river together. I guess even seemingly stupid or painful things can create new and beautiful ground. Like Mum and Dad, for example. If their marriage hadn't ended it's likely we would've never left Yorkshire. I'd be an entirely different person now. No one could say if I'd be better or worse off, but I certainly wouldn't know folk like Beth or Dave. I would

never have been to Ullswater, nor would I have met Sandy
– that kid with floppy ginger hair who used to skateboard
and weave across the rugby pitch. This was something I
thought about from time to time and it never failed to make
me realise how infinitely effective our choices are.

The sun was at its highest point by the time we reached
Port Carlisle. We couldn't see the village, but the old harbour
looked like it was ripped straight from Tolkien's sketchbook.
The crumbled breakwater was mounted on a crag dotted
with tufts of tall grass. We paddled around the wall and saw
our Uncle Mike standing on the promontory. When he caught
sight of us he hopped down the rocks and started clapping.
Overcome by a swell of relief, I crawled into the shallows
and pushed myself up out of the water. Then I looked over
at my brothers as they stood and grinned at me. Quickly I
went and hugged them both and we reminded each other
that it was over.

Approaching the beach, I pulled my swim cap off and ran
a free hand through my damp, matted hair. It felt very surreal
when I finally stepped out of the water, hobbled over several
sharp rocks and jumped onto the slope of soft sand. Then I
looked up and saw our welcome party gathered along the
grass verge. My smile suddenly opened into a toothy grin.
Standing on the stone wall, at the edge of the grass, were our
cousins Gareth and Owen. They were joined by Luke, who
they'd been staying with, and their mate Joe. They'd all travelled up from London together to show their support. My
other cousins Katie and Judith were also standing further back
with Uncle Mike and Aunty Fiona and, of course, Mum and

Dad were there too, without whom the whole thing would've been impossible. Even Lee's parents, who'd put us up on that day when we swam to Langwathby, turned up suddenly in their car, mounted the kerb and asked how it'd been.

All in all, it was a warm ending to a great adventure. The last thing we did was pose for a photo in front of a signpost with 'Swim the Eden' written on one of the signs. Then it was over – we'd swum the River Eden. All ninety miles of it. There was nothing left for us to do but make our way to the Hope and Anchor pub, where the ales were calling.

That last day was one we shared with our close family and friends. It reminded me how important it is to have support and to appreciate the debt we owe to those who inspire us. The idea that we belong to a certain place, time or self is, I think, an illusion. None of these things are immovable fixtures. Even civilisation itself is a relatively new and delicate construct. Ultimately, our species is older than cities, towns, villages and camps. In fact, the atoms we are made of – first formed under incalculable pressure in the Big Bang – were once part of distant dying stars. You share these birthing grounds with all the matter that surrounds you. In this way, you are related to the water and the grass and the trees. You are connected to your surroundings like separate limbs of the same tree.

Our different bloodlines are like twigs snaking in various directions. No matter how much we might grow apart, we are always attached. The ego would have us believe that we go it alone and become the heroes of our own stories, but in the end, we are all attached. Our parents bring us into this world and endow us with a part to play. We borrow the love that's manifest in us. Then someday this love releases its hold and we depart. After that, the strange energy goes on without us, spinning life into a cycle, holding planets in the night sky and urging the blood through the veins of our descendants. I think that's what keeps this ride running, and company is what makes it all worthwhile.

'Life's about folk,' as Grandma Wild's brother (my great-uncle) once told me.

Over time I've been able to look back at our adventure from a distance. In doing so, I think I've gained a slightly clearer idea of what it meant to me. It was wonderful to escape to that river – it was not just we three brothers, but a fellowship of sorts, with all Tolkien's minor characters accounted for. From Gríma Wormtongue (that lone fisherman who'd snarled at our arrival) to the gangs of grinning Hobbits (every other Cumbrian we'd met along the way). Whenever I look back I'm always filled with gratitude. I remember how Dave provided an uplifting presence, full of *joie de vivre*, and whisky too, most of the time. Then I think about James and how he'd stuck with us every stroke of the way. And, of course, there was Mum, Dad, Beth, Sandy . . . so many good-hearted individuals who'd put down what they were doing and travelled to the Eden for an adventure. More than anything, I'd loved this time we'd all shared together and the memories we'd accumulated. Occasionally, they whisked me back to our home in Langwathby and those cosy, firelit rooms that were so often packed with guests.

Throughout our teenage years, Mum had always kept an

open-door policy, which meant our friends were pretty much welcome anytime. Now my memories of home are crowded with the milling and bustle of happy guests. They're also coloured with the conversational nuances of all our different friends crossing paths. Mum often joked about setting up a hostel and building a few extra rooms. It was certainly true that our house, like all good homes, was built to be shared

On Christmas Eve, we'd usually bring our friends back, after drinking at the pub. Then we'd sit, half drunk, by the open fire nursing stubby glasses of mulled wine. When the rest of the house was asleep, we'd sneak around behind the wood-shed and get stoned together under the piercing winter stars. There was one Christmas when Rob's ex-girlfriend, Ekin, visited from Turkey. We introduced her to several traditions, like the building of gingerbread houses and the dressing of the tree, using baubles, tinsel and a red-breasted robin, instead of any biblical angels or stars. She was also privy to the less common tradition of drinking too much and wrestling in the living room – a relatively short affair that year, which ended rather abruptly, after Rob gave me another atomic wedgie.

Of course, while winter was merry and wonderfully distinct, it had never competed with the heady buzz of summer. When those languid days stretched out, like cats unpeeled from the morning shade, we'd all take turns hosting barbecues and assembling starlit drinking circles in the conservatory. Suddenly the garden became a cluttered base for launching kayak and swimming trips downriver. Meanwhile, the trees reclaimed their green fineries and the dozy bees appeared again, bumbling among the flowers. In those fleeting months, the odd downpour notwithstanding, our quiet Eden Valley earned her grand name, and life was very sweet indeed.

Now it was time for us to say goodbye to all that. Our Eden swim had allowed us to cut loose and drift back to our upbringing in the country. We might've wanted it to go on, but reality beckoned.

Late that night, after we'd driven back from Port Carlisle, Beth and I arrived at our little flat in Newcastle. As soon as we were home I stripped off and hurried into the bathroom. I was ready to disappear for a while and melt in a warm shower. First, I took a moment to savour where I was. There's a feeling you get when you look in the mirror after you've done something you're proud of. You feel reinforced. Your eyes look more familiar, or, at least, they behold you in a way that seems more knowing than before. *You met the challenge. You pushed yourself and you did something that you'll remember for the rest of your life.* You'll tell your nieces, nephews and kids about what you did. They'll pretend to listen, in that vague, adult-has-a-story kind of way, while you chew their ear off and beam with a flittering spark of pride.

These were the thoughts I had while the shower was still running. I was standing on a little heap of dirty clothes as the steam coiled over my shoulders and reminded me of the reward I had waiting for me. This would be my equivalent of a Formula One driver shaking a bottle of champagne, or a boxer dancing a victory lap around the ring. This shower was about to make up for all those cold, dewy mornings, urine-soaked dress-ups, ankle-twisting stumbles and endless stretches of crawl. And yet, before I turned towards the shower, I closed my eyes and rested my hands on the rim of the sink. Leaning forward, I listened to the ceiling fan humming as it swallowed the wreathing steam. The sound lulled me into a state of relief, until slowly I began to slide back into my mind, pulled into the rip of all those recent memories. Then I remembered what Grandma Martin had said about her sailing adventures: 'It was good that we did that.'

Looking back, I realise that there were many reasons for us to jump into the Eden and the Corryvreckan. The fact they were both thrilling swims is one that I keep coming back to. Swimming – like travel, films or books – has been a constant source of pleasure in all three of our lives. As kids, we used to take trips to Spain and stay at our grandpa's villa, close to the coast and the rippling sprawl of Malaga. I remember how we gave our grandpa the role of a Roman emperor and stood him on the villa balcony, holding out his thumb, ready to appease the invisible stands of baying, blood-thirsty attendees. Then we performed these dramatic executions on each other, usually with me as the victim, getting kicked backwards off the poolside and back-flipping into the water, like the hapless messenger who gets booted down the well in *300*. Other times, we'd take our inflatable crocodile, Snappy, down to the coast and Robbie would throw a noose around his waist and swim ahead, tugging Calum and me out to sea, until we were bobbing freely beyond the waves.

As kids, we were always drawn to the salty, siren call of the ocean. That's partly why we were so happy when we moved to Cumbria. Suddenly we discovered these huge bodies of water on our doorstep, scattered across the Lake District. They were like little, contained oceans, only you didn't have to worry about being swept out by the tide or pulled down from below by the shark from *Jaws*. Soon, each one became a wellspring of fun and creativity. So many of our fondest memories took place in their waters. I don't know if it's just because you're smaller, younger or more appreciative of brief adult-free forays into nature, but there's something special about being with your friends at that age, immersed in the boundless outdoors.

Nevertheless, as we grew older, we began to drift away from the natural world. Slowly we adopted the lives we swore we'd never lead. We became those suited square-framed figures you see crammed into office blocks. One after another we wound up working in cities, lugging around those lovely burdens that hang on to the coat-tails of adulthood. Mind you, despite our change in lifestyles, we never strayed too far from the water. We might've left the forests and hills behind, but the water wouldn't let us go. Each of us continued combing British shorelines, swimming in the shallow coastal waters. In summer, we'd rush back to the lakes and rivers of our childhood. We even invented a tradition of jumping into a barrel of icy water every Christmas. Basically, we did anything we could to escape the sensory barrages and physical restrictions of dry land. In doing so, we kept hold of that part of our childhood. We also found new ways of turning life upside down and having fun. One of these new discoveries – the one that really stays with me – was scuba diving.

If you haven't got around to earning your PADI licence, I

highly recommend you do. I'll never forget that first open-water dive after we'd been released from the swimming pool. At the time I was travelling in Indonesia. We were all wearing those long, clumsy fins as we waddled out together from the black pebbled beach of Tulamben. Then I watched the furrowed cone of Rinjani volcano disappearing as I held my respirator and lowered myself underwater. At once I was hit by the surreal jolt of being able to breathe under the ocean's surface. It gave me a sharp dose of adrenaline and took some getting used to. Once we'd steadied our breathing, the dive master led us on through darting trevally shoals as we followed the sloping seabed down several metres, into the gloom. By the end of the dive we were gliding slowly through the sepulchral, disintegrating rooms of a sunken Second World War ship. I watched, wide-eyed, as Sandy pointed to the shadows of big sweetlips moving through beams of surface light, which cut like arrows through the rusted portholes. Later that same holiday we took a dive boat out to a cradle of tall white bluffs and dove down over a bright coral garden, where we watched manta rays soaring in every direction, like elegant, alien spaceships.

For me, the water got under my skin at an early age and ever since then I've been unable to go for long periods without it. I know the same is also true for Robbie and Calum. We've spent our lives looking for secret spots to swim together. It's been going on since before we even used the term 'wild swimming', whether it was thermal waters spilling over travertine tiers in Pamukkale, Turkey, or icy plunge pools under Himalayan waterfalls in India. At a push, I could offer you several more reasons why we swim, although, honestly, it's difficult to explain the strong effect that water has on your mind and body. I guess all I would say, finally, is that swimming gives us an excuse for a reunion. Often swimming is viewed as a solitary pursuit and, true enough, it's difficult to hold a conversation with someone unless you're inching along with your head above the water. If you don't mind the occasional silences though, it's a wonderful way to share time with the folk you love. That's what we took away from our nine days in the Eden. Our swim was an excuse for us to start playing again, and, when the long shadows called us, to swim along together in formation, joined in the rhythm of each extended stroke and each intermittent breath.

Shortly after we swam the Eden, Robbie took his return flight to Berlin, Calum started work again in London and I settled back into Newcastle, where I was welcomed by an immediate sense of withdrawal. After nine days in each other's company, swimming down our childhood river, the adventure had ended rather suddenly.

In the months that followed there were numerous signs that we'd spread ripples in the wider swimming community. Early the following year we were delighted to hear that the Swimming Trust, in partnership with Cumbria ASA, had started a bursary scheme to help Cumbrian swimming teachers gain ASA Level 2 qualifications. This scheme was supported by the money we'd raised through our Eden swim. It was a wonderful reminder that our adventure had been worthwhile. It was during this time that we also heard news of a young swimmer called Karl, who we remembered from school. Inspired to hurl himself into the water, Karl had embarked upon his own River Eden challenge, which was far more meritorious than our own.

Upon hearing news of this challenge, Calum decided to travel up to Cumbria to help Karl on his personal journey . . .

CALUM: I immediately knew that I had to meet Karl and be a part of his swim. I was inspired by what he'd set out to do and I was keen to join him in the water. At the time, I was making preparations for our swims across the Norwegian maelstroms, and I knew I could help Karl and that he, in turn, would motivate me as well. I also remembered Karl from school. He grew up in the same area of Cumbria as Robbie, Jack and me and we all went to the same school, Ullswater Community College. I was amazed that he was partway through an attempt to swim ninety miles – the exact length of the River Eden – raising money for Eden Mencap along the way.

Now, ninety miles is a great test for any swimmer, as we'd found out the previous year, but the challenge was far greater for Karl, who suffers from cerebral palsy and epilepsy, as well as having a learning disability. Without the true use of his legs, Karl was forced to swim using only his arms. Nevertheless, he had set out to complete the full ninety miles, over the course of a year, travelling up and down an indoor pool in the nearby town of Penrith. Every week he would swim a mile or two, gradually building towards his overall goal. However, like the rest of us, Karl had grown tired of his indoor confines and longed to complete a symbolic section of his swim in the river itself. Without a moment's hesitation, I agreed to help him by being in the water on the day. No sooner had I decided to take part than I was hurtling up north on the train, headed to the River Eden and the sleepy village of Langwathby, where we grew up.

The plan was to accompany Karl down a 300-metre section of the river, which flowed past our old house. We would start at a small sandy beach and finish at the military bridge, before the river arced out of sight. These two points would provide safe entry and exit areas. During the swim, Karl would also be supported by his care workers Julia and Paul, who'd both agreed to don their wetsuits and join us in the water.

When I met Karl at the sandy beach I could sense his excitement, which was immediately infectious. He looked me dead in the eye and smiled.

'Let's just go,' he said.

As it happened, this became a sort of catchphrase for Karl. I could tell he was growing impatient with the build-up and he simply wanted to get on with it and leap into the river. I could also feel a certain tension that came from the care workers, friends and family, who were nervously gathered around us. Of course, there were plenty of health and safety concerns, risks and dangers, in light of Karl's disabilities. And yet Karl never allowed these disabilities to stop him or hold him back. I felt that we didn't have the right to hold him back either.

As we waded slowly into the shallows I expected Karl to make a steady start to the swim, but the next thing I knew he'd leapt out into the water and was careering downriver with increasing speed. It was clear from then on that this was his swim and we were simply there to paddle in his wake. A short while later, I pulled up beside Karl, while Paul was on his right and Julia was watching from

behind. In this formation we swam and bobbed down the gentle
Eden. Then Karl looked at me again and said, in true, understated
Cumbrian fashion: 'This is good like, eh?'

To me that summed the swim up perfectly. Of course I agreed
– there is something inherently good about breaking free and enjoying
the natural world, on its own terms. Karl was now hooked on the
moment and I could sense that this one was going to stick with him.

Just then, Karl swerved into a submerged boulder, rolled over and
was unexpectedly pulled underwater. Cold currents thrashed around
him and froth-speckled water bubbled up on either side. At once Paul
grabbed Karl's arm, hauled him away from the rock and led him
back into the river's deep, central channel. When he came up for air
it was apparent that Karl was neither afraid nor fazed by the sudden
disruption. In fact, he seemed exhilarated. Chuckling together, we
went on swimming and Karl kept a strong pace, until we approached
the bridge and drifted into our end point for the day. Before we
pulled into the shallow bay, I moved back to let Karl finish the swim
on his own. Excited, he paddled under the shadow of the bridge,
while his friends, family and the local newspaper photographer, Fred,
rushed down to the water and gave him a true hero's welcome.

As I swam up alongside Karl, he turned to me and nodded.

'Let's do it again.' He grinned.

That was as good a moment as any I've had in the water. A lot
is said about heroes these days, but in my eyes Karl is a real hero
and his own ninety-mile Eden swim, which he completed on 17 January
2017, was a huge source of inspiration for me. I always look to those
around me to gain strength for impending adversity. Karl probably
won't know this, but I don't think I could have made it across the
Arctic maelstroms without having experienced the joy and defiance

with which he handled his own challenge. There is a level of cowardice embedded in the act of telling someone that they can't do something – that somehow you've determined they're not capable or strong enough. After swimming alongside Karl and recognising the wild sparks in his eyes as he tackled the Eden's boulder-strewn currents, I realised that bravery is contagious. Also, it would be folly to tell someone like Karl that he was incapable of a swim like that – he would have a field day when he proved you wrong.

It was a wonderful feeling to learn that we'd made a difference – even if it was only a small one. Together we decided that we were going to go on and attempt more expeditions as the Wild Swimming Brothers. We all felt as though we'd been given an opportunity to change not only our own lives, but also the lives of others. We'd also had a taste of that visceral rush you get from joining your family to overcome adversity. It's a story we're all familiar with. If you're close to someone in your family – a sibling or parent, perhaps – then you'll understand the strength that comes from this bond.

We were soon entertaining the idea of another big swim. We hit our various social media channels and began to ask friends and family for suggestions. Then an edited photo emerged of the three of us standing in front of the Nile in Egypt. Another friend told us we should attempt the Congo River. These were both interesting proposals, although both involved an unhealthy number of man-eating crocodiles. Instead, Calum started looking at a list of the seven most powerful maelstroms in the world. These included the French Pass in New Zealand; the Skookumchuck Narrows and the

Old Sow, both in Canada; and the Naruto Whirlpools in Japan. There was also the Corryvreckan in Scotland, which we'd already swum, and two more in Norway, called the Moskstraumen and Saltstraumen. The latter sat rather ominously at the top of the list.

We'd already agreed that we wanted to travel further afield to attempt a swim that was both exciting and unique. We'd also been mulling over possible encounters with big wildlife, having already missed out on seeing basking sharks in the Corryvreckan. The more we talked about it the more we realised how irresistible Norway was. Something about it just snagged our interest and gripped our imaginations.

Several months passed before Calum came back to us with his fully formed plan. We were going to attempt to cross the Moskstraumen (the largest) and the Saltstraumen (the most powerful) maelstroms, swirling beyond the outer reaches of Norway's many-fingered coastline. I remember watching Calum through Skype as he whipped out different documents, maps and books and chattered excitedly. He told us how the Moskstraumen was mentioned in Jules Verne's *Twenty Thousand Leagues Under the Sea*, in which it swallowed Captain Nemo's submarine, the *Nebuchadnezzar*. It took him almost five minutes to convince us that we weren't going to die and that it wasn't a totally insane idea. That isn't to say there weren't a few prevailing concerns, namely the pods of orcas that patrol the cold-water reefs around the Lofoten Islands. Also, we had to confront the fact that, as far as we knew, neither of these two swims had ever been attempted before. There was no blueprint for how to do it or where to start.

We were about to enter unknown waters, with little else besides each other.

Looking on the brighter side, we were also going to be swimming over some of the most fragile ecosystems on this fair blue planet – the last bastions of biodiversity, still holding the colourful intricacies of diminished life. At the time, it just so happened that environmentalists were fighting against plans for oil drilling in the region. It seemed like an ideal time to draw attention to those clear waters, which once divided Norway's open pastures and sculpted its spiked mountains.

Next, we discussed the logistics, looked at images that belonged in epic Viking legends and finally agreed that we were all willing to give it a go. The first swim would be a quick sprint across the Saltstraumen, which is less than half a kilometre wide, although it also happens to possess the strongest currents in the world, funnelling four hundred million cubic metres of seawater into a three-kilometre strait. Our second swim, across the Mosktraumen, would be an eight-kilometre point-to-point crawl between the islands of Vaeroy and Mosken. Frankly, they both sounded terrifying, and we knew at once that this was going to be a huge under-taking for us. Not only would we have to brave the Arctic water and the unpredictable tidal currents, but we'd also have to stomach the possibility of seeing huge orcas and lion's mane jellyfish. It was a lot to take in, especially considering the Corryvreckan had been one of the hardest swims I'd ever done – a punishing thought when I realised the Mosktraumen was about four times the distance.

Before we hung up, Calum talked us through the recent

press he'd arranged and gave us a list of the sponsors he'd been talking to. Then he announced what he wanted to call this next adventure: *Into the Maelstrom*. This was the symbolic bugle call to spur us all into action. With that the conversation ended and I was left to sip my lukewarm tea, reminding myself over and over exactly what I'd just agreed to.

The following morning, we each packed our bags and headed out to our first solo training sessions. Robbie walked to a pristine Olympic pool in Berlin, Calum cycled to the pale blue embrace of Brockwell Lido, in London, and Beth and I drove to a tarn hidden among the hills of Northumberland. After our hiatus that first plunge into cold water was a shock to the system. Luckily you do grow used to the touch of that icy masseur. In fact, you begin to yearn for it.

I think one of the reasons swimming is so addictive has to do with the fact it offers so many different physical and psychological benefits. Being an aerobic exercise, swimming is of course good for your heart and brain health. The repeated motion of your strokes improves the blood flow to your central and posterior cerebral arteries. It also helps to repair damaged brain cells and influences your body on a molecular and behavioural level, causing neurotransmitters to release stress-reducing hormones. As a result, swimmers tend to notice improvements to their memory, clarity and focus.

Over time we became accustomed to cold morning showers and hours spent inching up and down narrow pools. Then, in what seemed like no time at all, August suddenly pounced upon us. The next thing I knew, I was sitting in a shuddering aeroplane seat and thundering up a bare runway, glimpsing tilted flashes of buildings and trees as they whipped by in a frantic blur. All I could do was clench my armrest and focus on the strings playing faintly through my headphones. A moment later, we were tearing upwards through the crests of scudding clouds, at which point I felt the familiar weight of a knot in the pit of my stomach – a stark reminder of the wild task ahead.

Keep The Momentum (Rob's Tip): Fear will sometimes muddy your motivations. At times you might even lose sight of why you swim outdoors at all – why didn't you choose a more comfortable, warmer hobby? It's likely you've heard this before, but if you keep wrestling the butterflies, getting past those jittery moments, you'll begin to associate your nerves with that sense of achievement they lead to. If a swim feels like a battle one day that's natural too. Small victories – effort and time put in – build purpose and bring clarity. Always remember that adventure is completely personal. Only you will know – in your heart of hearts – whether you're truly getting out of your comfort zone. And that's where the real fun begins . . .

11

Into the Maelstrom

One of the most interesting things I read, in my research for this book, was an insight into Native American and European relations from George Monbiot's *Feral*. In this book, Monbiot quoted a letter written by Benjamin Franklin, in 1753, to an English botanist. Franklin explained that Native Americans who were welcomed into European society and introduced to more prim and 'civilised' customs would invariably, almost immediately, re-join their kin and return to a comparatively primitive way of life the moment they were given the chance. Conversely, white Europeans who were taken prisoner and held in the custody of Native Americans, exposed to their ways and customs, would usually elope back to their former captors after being rescued or freed for a ransom. Franklin noted the newfound disgust some of these liberated prisoners had for their former culture. It was enough to send them running back to the woods or plains and to the lifestyle of their supposed enemy. Widespread assimilation with the indigenous peoples was rife throughout the colonisation of the New World.

Perhaps even more surprisingly, there are accounts of European children being kidnapped and raised by Native Americans. During peacetime, when the Europeans came to collect these stolen kids, many of them would refuse to leave, sometimes even ignoring the pleas of their own parents. What this reveals to me is the mysterious wealth and value of such communities, so many of which have now disappeared from the Earth. Those indigenous populations that *have* survived are now hounded by the smog-wrapped tendrils of our expansive industrial world. If human expansion continues to trample Mother Nature, along with those who've built their lives in her employ, then detachment, destitution and confinement are inevitable for the many, not the few. I believe that under such conditions our civilisations would surely wither and die, in much the same way that a reef is killed by coral bleaching. A monoculture would form and we would see that same gradual process of whitewashing and disintegration.

When coral is bleached, due to pollution or a rise in water temperature, the algae, which is coral's primary food source, becomes stressed and leaves the coral's tissue. Soon the diversity of the reef diminishes and the blooms of vivid colour grow pale as the garden fades to an ashen shade and slowly dies. Take a second to consider what it is we're losing here. We're talking about a colourful living organism wrapped in myriad species of plant and marine life – a distant relative of jellyfish and sea anemones, in fact – capable of forming colonies and creating reefs so massive that astronauts can actually see them from space. It's difficult not to feel uprooted when you realise what's at stake. So much of what makes our home so wonderful to inhabit is being lost. A recent international study revealed that a third of our planet's coral is now perilously close to extinction. That's not even to mention the number of ancient species we've already lost.

I wonder what would happen if one after another we could hop into the DeLorean time machine and travel back to see those prehistoric reefs that once unravelled across the seabed. Would it change our minds to see how those organisms thrived? Take the spongy reefs of the Ordovician period (which began roughly five hundred million years ago), for example. These sprawling underwater gardens were once home to a rich variety of little invertebrates, called bryozoans, with feathered arms and tentacles. Picture these curious animals pinned to the reef, busily filter-feeding among blooms of waving sea lilies. This is just one example of the organic industries we're disrupting. After all, the bryozoans were gardeners of sorts. Over time they evolved to secrete their external calcic skeletons, creating the framework for towering (at least from their perspective) coral structures. Today, thousands of different species of bryozoans have died out. Those reefs, which were once so vivacious and marvellous in their functioning complexity, are fast becoming pale graveyards – dying limbs on the Tree of Life. If we were to lose our sense of wildness, our sense of community with the rest of the animal kingdom, I think the same thing would happen to us.

Fortunately, the instinctive will to understand the natural world is still strong in our species. We are yet to be urbanised and tamed entirely. There are many far-flung places on this planet where sheltered tribes enjoy relative isolation and independence. As far as I was concerned, Norway was one such place, comparable to the Scottish Highlands in that regard. I knew the great mountains and fjords would be good for the soul, but I had no idea how good, nor was I ready for the impact of leaving them behind.

After the short flight into the Arctic Circle, we spent our first few days in Bodø, where we were mainly confined to the harbour. Aside from swimming the Saltstraumen, we'd mostly taken it easy and stuck to our urban foothold. I'd grown used to idealising places before I arrived, so I didn't let the buildings and crowds dull my dreams of an escape. Also, I knew that we would soon be taking a ferry beyond the clenched fingers of the mainland and the scattered islets thereafter. I reminded myself that it was only a few days until we'd reach our second base on the Lofoten Islands, which would double as a launching point for our swim across the Moskstraumen. This was something we'd been waiting for with a mixture of excitement and uneasy anticipation. Over the course of the previous year this single name, which belonged to the largest maelstrom in the world, had both compelled and haunted us in equal measure. In fact, even Calum, who was prone to hiding his fear like a cat elegantly kicking dirt over its poop, confessed to having suffered a few sleepless nights . . .

CALUM: *One of my main concerns, when I started planning our* Into the Maelstrom *expedition, was the likelihood of us encountering orcas during our swim across the Moskstraumen. I'd read that there were around 600 orcas roaming the Lofoten Islands and feeding in the surrounding waters. This meant there was a real possibility of them making an appearance. Now, this was more of a psychological challenge than a physical threat. There are no recorded fatalities in the wild from orcas. There is only one recorded non-fatal attack on a human in California and the only recorded deaths have been from orcas kept in captivity. This makes a lot of sense to me – if I'd been kept in a tank my entire life and forced to perform for other people's entertainment, I don't think I'd be to blame for my behaviour. The documentary* Blackfish *has done a lot to bring the plight of orcas to the public's attention and we knew that if we saw these majestic animals we would be extremely lucky. After all, the chance to encounter such beautiful creatures in their natural habitat was a privilege and we were there to raise awareness about the threats posed by oil drilling in their home.*

However, no matter how sensible you are, no matter how many statistics you tell yourself, even if you know they don't have a history of attacking humans, it does very little to quell the fear in your mind. Over time, images of these huge predators began to stir up something that is known as Apex Predator Fear. This is a deep, innate fear – the same fear you get walking through a dark forest late at night. It is a primal reminder that we too can be prey and that we're not at the top of the food chain when we're deprived of our beloved modern tools. The fact that we'd be in the water, out of our depth, would only add to this fear. When you're swimming in deep water you feel as though you are suspended over the seemingly bottomless depths. Sometimes, it's difficult not to picture the large, beady eyes of leviathans lurking in the deep, carefully watching you as you creep slowly overhead. At times like that you start to feel incredibly vulnerable. You experience this intense helplessness – a reminder that anything below you could, if it wanted to, rise up quickly and snatch you from below. You wouldn't even see it coming.

I knew this irrational fear could potentially paralyse us during the Moskstraumen swim. Each of us had different ways of coping with this threat. Robbie told me he'd banned himself from watching any videos of orcas hunting, especially those ones from Planet Earth, when they breach the water and fling seals into the air. I, on the other hand, wanted to tackle my irrational fear head on. Eager to steady my nerves, I decided to change my desktop background to a photograph of a pod of orcas swimming through the sea in Norway. My colleagues must have thought I was a bit mad, but I wanted to force myself to meet and confront my fear every day.

One other technique I used, as we neared the day of our flight, involved a gradual process of creative visualisation. At the beginning, when I was alone, I would imagine myself as a ball of energy. Then I would focus deep inside myself, imagining a great strength emanating from within. In the early stages of research and preparation I had cultivated this energy myself. To build upon it, I would fantasise over and over again about completing the challenge. These fantasies came to me in all kinds of environments, whether I was cycling home or taking the train to work or even just sitting at my desk. Usually they would involve me confronting things that I'm afraid of. For the Norwegian swims, especially the Moskstraumen, I was terrified about the presence of orcas, the unpredictability of the weather and the unknown power of the currents and whirlpools. Of course, I was scared that I might be responsible for the deaths of my brothers as well. I couldn't bear the thought of picking up the phone and hearing my mum sobbing, her desolate voice piercing my ears as she wailed at me: 'I told you not to go, I told you not to take your brothers!'

Under the steadily increasing pressure, I created crazy scenarios that began with the three of us swimming through the ocean as rolling waves crashed around us and the sunlight poured over our backs. To my right I'd see my big brother Robbie and to my left I'd see my little brother Jack. Then, suddenly, I'd imagine this huge black shape appearing beneath us. All at once a colossal shadow would emerge from the depths as an adult bull orca began to surface. In the midst of the disarray, I pictured myself turning to my brothers and shouting: 'The orcas are with us, don't be afraid, they've come to swim with us. Onwards, onwards and into the maelstrom.'

With that we'd all charge forward and together we'd crash fearlessly across the ocean, while a pod of orcas emerged beside us, their six-foot-long dorsal fins arcing through the water as we all carved a path through the currents. Finally, the three of us would land on the rocks and the maelstrom would go on raging behind us as forks of lightning blistered the grey sky. These were the kind of fantasies that inspired me. I would picture these scenarios over and over again, until an upsurge of adrenaline coursed through my veins and surged into my heart.

Meanwhile, day by day, I began to draw more and more energy from the people around me. I gathered positive inspiration from my friends and family who told me they believed in me. I kept messages of good luck left for us by strangers on our social media channels. All the while I reminded myself not to underestimate the power that words of encouragement can have. Every small spark of positive energy has a part to play. In your darkest moments, these sparks burn through the doubt and fear and drive you onwards. And yet, even greater than all the positive comments, and the ones I crave the most, are the negative ones. I relish them. I take in everything the naysayers say. I remember their questions: 'Why on earth would you want to do that? It's not possible, you'll drown . . .'

Go on, *I think,* please tell me I can't do it – tell me it's not possible . . .

Admittedly, I'd started out in that small crowd of folk who thought Calum was on some mad, suicidal rampage around the world. I just couldn't see the three of us accomplishing something so dangerous and outlandish. However, our swim across the Saltstraumen had changed my mind slightly. Now the Moskstraumen was only a day away and it seemed almost appealing, like it would be a source of liberation, or something. In the end, all the wildness we'd been craving was waiting there in that untested system of whirlpools, which rolls and spins over the ragged spearhead of the Lofoten Islands. In the depths of this maelstrom, mighty currents thrash over deep ridges that run like sinews between the islands of Moskenesoya and Vaeroy. To say these waters are unknown is no overstatement. There was nothing for us to read save a few current charts and a little advice from those locals who take tourists out to see it. In lieu of any consid-- erable research, we turned to Edgar Allan Poe and Jules Verne, who included this roaring phenomenon in their writing. Sadly, they both described a destructive force, capable of turning a submarine into a cloud of metal flakes in an enormous, spinning fishbowl.

If you looked at everything I'd done up to that point, imagining my life as a linear path, then this was something of a detour – an odd phase, you might say. Picture a kid suddenly leaping off an intended path and storming through an entangled thicket, chased by the reasonable cries of their befuddled parents. Why would anyone do such a thing? You're bound to get scratched. You might even get lost. Why wouldn't you just stick to the path? Well, these are a few of the logical adult concerns, but what about the kid's point of view? Maybe the path was long and tiring. Maybe the kid spotted the glint of something behind the thicket. Who are we to say we know where we're headed?

One thing I could trust was my longing to see, more than anything else, the Lofoten Islands themselves. Ever since I first Googled that green archipelago, I'd known that the islands would be our introduction to life at the heart of Norway, replete with an abundance of rare wildlife. With any luck, we were about to spend the next few days with a few of the 3,682 threatened species that roam the area. It was unlikely that we'd see the critically endangered grey wolf or arctic fox, but we did have a chance of bumping into orcas – preferably when we were out of the water. I knew it would be risky to do so, but I secretly hoped we'd sight a few polar bears as well. Maybe we'd spot one as it floated down from Svalbard on a raft of sea ice, or, even better, one of the great, antlered elks, known locally as *skogens konge*, which means king of the forest.

As for the humans – I imagined these islands would hold a way of life much wilder and more intimate than the one we'd grown used to. While we were there, we'd arranged to set up our second base in a fishing village called Reine. It was here that I expected to find those wilder tribes, cocooned in isolation. I hoped that we would experience something of their private quietude. Then perhaps we might be privy to the hushed notes of their timeless music – the thunder of water cascading down narrow falls or the screech of eagles skimming the forested slopes.

By all accounts, the Lofoten Islands seemed both ancient and majestic, still bearing the graves of great glaciers, which have transformed the mountains into monuments of the Ice Age. We'd heard that one look at the surrounding peaks, twisted and bent like old trees, or at the clear waters, jumping with halibut, cod and salmon, would be enough to wash the city from our bones.

Into the Maelstrom Expedition, Day 2
(Arriving at the Lofoten Islands)
Tuesday 23 August 2016

With considerable effort, I wrenched the latch down with both hands and heaved the watertight door open. The moment I stepped out onto the deck my jacket began to flutter and the cold bit into my cheeks. I squinted through the wind and saw the distant mountains of the Lofoten Islands. I'd never seen anything like it before. It looked like the last stop before the oceans swept over the boundary of the Earth, tumbling out of our atmosphere, into the starry abyss below. I could see tall granite escarpments that lined the offing, some of them crowned with pointed peaks, many of which diverged at different angles, sloping upwards like jagged shark fins. This was going to be the base for our final swim – a place I'd seen only through the pictures from Calum's recce mission in July. Now the vista, in its entirety, was stretching eastwards all the way to the faint fingers of the mainland. And we were there – seven ragtag adventurers brought together by a mutual love of the outdoors. Again, I was suddenly hit by the realisation that this was exactly where I belonged. It was the same feeling I'd had on the Eden when we were swimming towards Langwathby.

Slowly the mountains drew closer, their sheer faces rising through a thin shroud of mist. Then I could make out colourful houses clustered at the feet of the steep slopes. It was obvious that there weren't many people living on these islands. I guessed that the harbour was likely to be the most densely populated area in the region. Yet, by the looks of things, it wasn't much more than a ramshackle village, serving as a reminder that this was indeed a gateway to the wild.

A moment later Robbie was standing beside me with his hood pulled tight around his face. I glanced over and caught him grinning – he later told me that he'd been listening to a black metal band called Burzum. Then a gust of spray blasted against the railing as the ferry ploughed through an oncoming wave. I untangled my headphones and pulled them up carefully under my zipped jacket, unwilling to offer an inch of skin to the harsh cold. Taking out my iPhone, I scrolled down to the Icelandic post-rock band, Sigur Rós, and chose a thread of songs from their album *Valtari*. I'd never heard it before, but I was suddenly immersed in the otherworldly chords and vocals. I spun the volume up a few notches and felt myself being engulfed by the thrashing of violins, keyboards and drums. Then I was swept into the current of the famous bowed guitars and carried along by the falsetto howl of Jónsi Birgisson. It was the perfect music for the inbound wilderness – pure and untouched. I listened to Jónsi's cries as each chorus reached higher and higher. When he reached the crescendo, it sounded like he was standing on the crest of a mountain, pouring his voice into the valley below. At that point, my shoulders lifted, pimples appeared on my skin and tears formed in my wind-beaten eyes.

Suddenly it felt as though I was close to the magic that once made this country so irresistible to me. My drifting mind began to gather memories of Norwegian folklore, which baffled and thrilled me as a kid. In fact, despite all the things I've forgotten from my time at school, I still keep a shelf in my mind for Norse mythology. The idea of celestial warriors battling each other seems to set young minds alight. Even before the impact of *Marvel* comics, you'd have to head very deep into the British outback before you'd find a kid who wasn't familiar with the hammer-wielding son of Odin, Thor – or, for that matter, Odin himself, the one-eyed all-father.

There were other gods too, of course, although their names and powers are often forgotten. One of my new favourites, since I'd returned to the subject, was the mountain-dwelling jötunn and goddess, Skaði, who possessed a penchant for both hunting and skiing. Then there was the hirsute seafarer, Njörðr, who could harness the amorphous forces of water and fire. Another favourite was a primordial giant, Ymir, who was the first ancestor of the jötunn and the first being to ever enter our universe, having gained life from the ice-encrusted Élivágar rivers. It was supposed that the Earth was then created using shreds of Ymir's flesh.

Interestingly, Norse mythology went so far as to mention different celestial bodies within the cosmos – a total of Nine Worlds positioned around the tree of existence, which they call Yggdrasil. Much like the Greek pantheon, different elements of cosmology were given their own incarnated deity. In this way, the interplay between the elements was conveyed, in as much as the various, warring gods were depicted as being inextricably bound to one another. In fact, when they clashed, the almighty, unnatural impact led to the apocalypse, Ragnarok, which caused the sun to turn a shade of ashen black, while the stars were all dismantled and the abyss rose smiling from below, like an ancient monster once spurned by the light. Next came the age of darkness, brought about after the gods and their enemies had done battle and left the ether in flames. Then, like the phoenix unfurling from its ashes, the world was reborn and the battle-scarred, surviving gods were left to oversee a fertile new beginning and the rise of Ask and Embla, the first humans.

An hour or so later we reached the coastal shallows of the Lofoten Islands. Our ferry seemed to shrink as we slid into a little harbour and slipped under the shadows of the crags above us. Slowly we entered a cove, having passed between two rocky outcrops, which seemed to close together like a gate behind us. As we drifted closer to the docks, I began to search our surroundings, finding little evidence of civilisation, save for a few small collections of colourful cabins and longhouses nestled close to the shore. Every home, it seemed, was dwarfed by the imposing scenery around it. In keeping with the typically wild Norwegian aesthetic, the trees and foliage had been allowed to sprawl untamed in every direction, until they encroached upon the boundaries of the town, as though they'd crept into the streets, curtailing the tiers of metal, glass and wood.

With a sonorous blast of its horn the ferry slowed and turned sidelong, redirecting its huge nose with all the haste of a glacier. I began to spot unused cars left like ornaments in cracked driveways. Some of these cars had even been disassembled, their ragged, rusted parts strewn over nearby lawns. I also sighted seabirds keeping watch over rows of rickety drying racks. At the same time, it suddenly became apparent that there were more buildings and industrial units than I'd first thought. This was a town of sorts – albeit one that lacked the more common features you might expect. There were no buildings larger than the longhouses: no churches, halls or schools. Most of the houses were painted red and half hidden under sloped grey roofs. Then there were a few quaint piling houses near the water, with thin struts that pierced the glassy shallows like reeds standing in a pond. The atmosphere was serene and unspoilt by manmade ugliness. This was our introduction to the Lofoten Islands. It was everything we'd hoped it would be.

Finally, the ferry eased in alongside the dock, muscling up to a line of painted fishing boats wrapped in wooden boarding. After we'd picked up our things and disembarked, we took the first bus out to Reine. We travelled on a single road that

wound uphill, splitting fields and trees, while never straying far from the coastline. It was an overwhelmingly scenic drive, until we made an abrupt turn and began to head through the mountain, at which point we were thrown into the eerie gloom of a long tunnel lined with lights. When we emerged on the other side, sunlight poured against the windows and swept up the aisles. The bus banked slightly, following a long bend that hugged the slopes. It was then that Reine came into view – a sprawled-out fishing village cradled by a horse-shoe of tall, serrated mountains.

We reached the local wharf a minute or so later and decided to pile up our bags on a nearby lawn before we went for lunch. The atmosphere was both serene and welcoming, softened by the sounds of lapping waves and cawing gulls. For a while there was no one there except ourselves, a few Lycra-clad cyclists and several other tourists, who we'd just arrived with. When the locals eventually started to appear, they did so without changing the atmosphere. Instead, it seemed like everyone had agreed to a bargain of peace, subdued by the natural hush that seemed to seep down from the mountains, like an unseen mist tumbling from the snow-patched peaks.

The first thing we had to do was meet Theresa and Lars. They were the tour guides of Aqua Lofoten who'd kindly agreed to get us across the Moskstraumen. We weren't sure where they lived but it just so happened that as we were leaving the harbour, two blond-haired Norwegian boys wandered out ahead of us and, unconsciously, we began to follow them. One was riding on a bike while the other, smaller boy, ran alongside him. It took me a while to realise they were actually our guides, leading us up the road, towards Theresa and Lars' house.

When we reached the garden, the taller boy jumped off his bike and ran through an open door, into a cluttered basement/office crammed with maritime paraphernalia. Before we went inside, I noticed colourful children's toys strewn on the lawn around two huge, bow-shaped bones lined with the teeth sockets of a great predator. Theresa later told us that this was the jaw of a sperm whale they'd found washed up on the beach.

Inside the office, we were hemmed in by corridors of thick winter wetsuits and display cabinets stacked with old maps and mouldy treasures. At one point, I turned a corner and came face to face with this crazy, pale denizen of the deep, spinning gently from a wire attached to the ceiling. It looked like an angler fish, with its thin, gaping mouth and sharp teeth. Then we found Theresa sitting with her laptop behind a glass-topped desk. We all introduced ourselves and crowded around her, displacing and jangling various metallic ornaments, like a gang of clumsy trolls.

It wasn't long until she and Calum were discussing the logistics of our upcoming maelstrom swim.

'This is a good place to finish,' said Theresa, trailing her finger over a large map coloured with the scattered green archipelago of Lofoten. 'There are some abandoned fishing villages here. Then the maelstrom starts here at the lighthouse.'

We bunched together and leant over the desk in unison.

'Low tide is in the morning around eight,' she went on, adjusting her chair and turning to her laptop. 'High tide:

five-thirty. If you're in the water from eight to twelve, you see? Then the current is going from high tide to low tide. Remember, it takes half an hour to get there if you're already on the boat.'

After several more minutes the details of our plan were all set. The following morning we would be leaving at seven to make it to the maelstrom between high and low tide. We would be swimming eight kilometres to the tip of Moksen, spending up to three hours in the Arctic water. All we had to do now was trust that Theresa, who made her living taking tourists to the maelstrom, knew the currents well enough to keep us safe. We would also have to be open to surprises, especially the big, mammalian variety. After all, part of the charm of the swim was the fact that no one had ever attempted it before, which meant we didn't know what to expect. It seemed like Theresa was warming to the idea. When Calum first consulted her about the swim she'd seemed reticent, perhaps unconvinced of our willingness to see it through. One of the reasons, she later revealed, was that she often received unusual requests regarding the Moskstraumen. She was used to mad parties asking to dive in the maelstrom and swim against the currents. Possibly, then, she never actually expected us to go through with it.

Outside, we stood and waited in the garden while James and Dave chose thick wetsuits for the swim. They wanted to do some filming in the water and Theresa had kindly allowed them to raid her kit stores. Naturally, they both opted for the neoprene equivalent of plated armour.

'I just wanna go now,' Calum said, his arms folded and his tired eyes half closed.

I nodded and watched as he turned his attention to the cloudless sky and squinted through the sunlight. 'I think it is lighter here,' he said.

Apparently, he was still nursing his dream of unending daylight. Back home, when we were packing our kit, he'd messaged each of us insisting that we needed eye masks to sleep at night. We were expecting the sun to be burning through the curtains. Now, after five consecutive sunsets, it seemed clear that we were too late to enjoy the spectacle of the Midnight Sun.

Sure enough, Calum's hopes were again thwarted as the azure slowly dimmed and the mountains slid under a sepulchral gloom. At dusk we were all holed up in our cosy, rustic hideaway. It was a quaint building located opposite an art gallery overlooking the harbour. From our squat kitchen, you could see the pointed mountains curving down to the water's edge. These mountains, which were unlike any I'd seen before, snaked into the darkness and created a long valley enclosing a deep, glassy fjord. At the end of the valley we could just make out a sandy beach, which marked the opposite side of the island.

Later, we all went out together, stood by the art gallery and stared over the starlit harbour. Imposing though it was, the vista also helped to keep us calm. There was this surreal stillness that settled over the scenery. The water, the trees, even the sky was frozen. It was as though everything was encased under a patina of ice. For a minute or so no one spoke. Instead, we took a moment for ourselves. First, I watched the surface of the fjord, speckled with the reflected stars. Then I turned my attention to clusters of warm, golden lights, clinging to the mountain slopes. I began to think about the folk who lived among those clusters. I wondered about their routines and the way in which the wild had entered and shaped their lives. I knew that in the sunless months they were privy to the multi-coloured fireworks of the aurora borealis. Many years ago, it was believed that these northern lights were the trails left by human souls as they were plucked from the Earth. The gods would then lift these souls into the ether, leaving willowy beams scrawled across the darkness, like white sparklers on Guy Fawkes Night. I'd heard other ghostly stories too – one was about a headless fisherman called the draugr, who roamed the shallows, clothed in seaweed, and drowned his hapless victims in the waters. It was said that on a still night you could even hear them screaming.

A half-hour or so later, everyone was wrapped up in their bunk beds, although most of us were still awake because the atmosphere was noticeably tense and quiet. Lying there, I could feel the walls sagging with the weight of what we were about to do. I was trapped and I felt confined – claustrophobic, even. At the time I wasn't really aware of how scared Robbie and Calum were because they hid it from me. It wasn't until afterwards that I discovered quite how unanimous that unease and discomfort was . . .

ROBBIE: *In preparation for our swim across the Moskstraumen I decided to write a note containing all of my concerns and fears. I called it: 'Swimming the Moskstraumen – A List of My Fears and How to Overcome Them.' Here are a few of the things I included:*

Fear #1 – The Cold

Take time. Acclimatise properly. All training swims will be done WITHOUT a wetsuit. Six months of cold showers (don't cheat, Robbie!). Enjoy the cold if you can.

Fear #2 – Negative Thought Processes

Keep it simple. Get in the water. Do not stop until you reach the other side. Everything you think during the swim is irrelevant. Focus on each stroke, focus on your breathing, focus on the end point... You do not have the luxury of choosing to get out of the water. The support crew will decide if I need to leave the water.

Fear #3 – The Deep Water

Be logical. You are a land-dwelling primate. Your parasympathetic nervous system is evolutionarily wired to remind you that the ocean is vast and dark and scary. It is full of things that are much bigger than you, hungrier and better adapted to be there. Know that this will happen – you will feel this fear. Greet the feeling with a big smile and keep on swimming. Focus on what you can control – your stroke, breathing and mentality.

Fear #4 – Wildlife

It's likely we'll meet a lot of jellyfish and possibly even an orca

pod. Sight carefully between strokes and avoid jellyfish blooms.
If we meet orcas — try not to look like a seal!

Fear #5 – The Currents

The Moskstraumen has never been swum before. The currents
are strong and unpredictable. We may be swept in different
directions and the swim could be a lot longer than 7.5km. Train
for a swim that is 10km. Expect to be swimming that distance.
Plan for the worst and don't stress out if you are swept off
course. Simply adjust and stick together as much as possible.

Final note to self: Don't be soft. Enjoy the experience. More
people have walked on the moon than swum across the
Moskstraumen. This will be an experience to remember.
    Line for the swim . . . keep repeating this one while swim-
ming, time it with your stroke and breathing, and weave it into
the physical action of moving through the water. It's an Albert
Camus quote that will help with the cold: 'In the midst of
winter I found in me an invincible summer.'

Peering into the cold darkness of my mind, I turned my
thoughts to the Moskstraumen swim and slowly began to
unpack my fears. For a while, I lay with my eyes closed and
spent time with each thought as it revealed itself. Despite the
nerves, I could still relax and think clearly, perhaps owing to
the fact I had Dave sleeping in the bed beside mine and Beth
in the bunk above me. The low murmur of their breathing
was very reassuring. The sound accompanied me as I slowly

drifted inwards, sinking through thoughts and memories, like a free diver delving into deep, dark water. Eventually, I reached the seabed, where the darkness was most severe and silence enveloped me. All I could think of then was how lucky I was to be in the Lofoten Islands.

Very few folk get to experience the wild nature of such places – on their own terms. Not to mention the fact that Norway, much like the rest of the world, is currently under threat. As you read this, the natural wealth of this beautiful country is being stolen by climate change. The loss of sea ice has withered the hunting grounds of starved polar bears, and migratory birds now arrive earlier each year. There is evidence everywhere of change and almost all of it can be linked directly to us. Take the increase in numbers of mackerel and red deer, for example. This might not sound so bad, but it helps to reveal the abnormal impact we are having on the natural world. We have created a chink in the food chain. Our generation may not have to fight in any world wars, but we will be partly responsible for stalling the damage we're doing to this world. The argument regarding Lofoten oil is just one example of the conflict at hand.

On one side, lobbyists argue that Lofoten would be a cheap option because the islands are so close to the mainland. However, drilling was prohibited in 2006 due to a call for sustainable use of the Barents and Norwegian Seas. That means approximately 1.3 billion barrels of oil have been left untapped in Lofoten, Vesteralen and Senja. In short, it's a big ol' sum of money. Meanwhile, Norway's sovereign wealth fund, Norges Banke, continues to explore the future potential of oil and gas, which is still coveted by Europe, in the hope of stimulating the economy. This means that drilling in Lofoten is still on the cards and, unless environmentalist pressure continues, the islands will likely be offered up to waiting companies.

It is true that a lot of Norway's wealth has come from petroleum and other fossil fuels. In turn, this wealth has enabled the government to create a successful welfare state, and there's nothing controversial about that, right? Well, consider the fact that between the years 1966 and 2014 Norway drilled around 5,085 oil wells, mostly in the North Sea. Recently, the Norwegian government offered coveted drilling licences to companies that are now being allowed access to unexplored areas of the Barents Sea. Supposedly, the next logical step is drilling in the pristine Lofoten Islands, among some of the most productive ecosystems in the world. The Norwegian energy minister remarked that we will soon be experiencing 'a new chapter in the history of Norwegian petroleum'. That means more oil drills will appear along the Norwegian shelf, in areas of shallow water cleared of ice floes because of the Gulf Stream currents. Some environmentalists have expressed concerns regarding the events of 2010 when the BP-leased Deepwater Horizon oil platform exploded in the Gulf of Mexico. During this event, around 4.9 million gallons of oil were released into the surrounding waters and eleven workers were killed. If such an event were to occur near to the Lofoten Islands it could cause irrevocable damage to the fragile Norwegian ecosystem, scarring coral reefs and contaminating clear waters roamed by myriad different animals, including basking sharks, porpoises, narwhals, sperm whales and orcas. Perhaps more pertinently, if Norway were to continue delving into the Arctic, in search of oil and natural gas, it would mean that they would be unable to commit to the universal promise they agreed to at the COP21 climate-change conference in Paris, which was to limit the rise in temperature to 1.5 degrees above pre-industrial levels. Of course, as a Brit sticking my big nose into Norwegian business, there's only so much I can say without passing unwarranted judgement. Nevertheless, it did seem to be a very worthy cause for our swims, particularly the one across the Mokstraumen, when we would be seeing first-hand what kind of natural beauty was at stake.

Into the Maelstrom Expedition, Day 3 (Mokstraumen) Wednesday 24 August, 2016

- *Point-to-point eight-kilometre swim.*
- *Islands in the middle used to signal lunch stop and assess swimmers' conditions.*
- *Entry point is at the tip of Lofotodden.*
- *Exit point is Mosken – swimmers to reach land and then swim back to the boat for extraction.*

I woke up quickly the following morning. The first thing I heard was the rustle of kit bags and the creak of old floorboards as someone moved through the corridor outside. For a moment, I stared at the wooden slats and gripped the sheets. It was six-thirty. We were supposed to be meeting Theresa at seven.

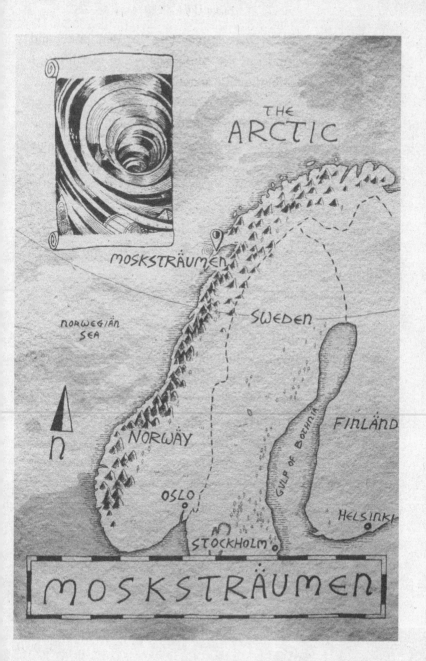

THE
ARCTIC

MOSKSTRÄUMEN

NORWEGIAN
SEA

SWEDEN

FINLAND

NORWAY

GULF OF BOTHNIA

OSLO

HELSINKI

STOCKHOLM

MOSKSTRÄUMEN

If all went to plan, we'd be leaping into the Arctic water and starting our swim across the Moskstraumen in two hours. I stopped myself from thinking about the cold. Instead, I pulled my bunched sheets tight around my shoulders, rolled out of the bottom bunk and stepped into my wetsuit. I'd prepared everything I needed the night before. As I yanked the neoprene up to my waist, Dave rolled over in the bed adjacent to mine.

'Good morning,' I said, as I caught his bleary eye.

The atmosphere was so tense that it almost sounded ominous. Then Beth poked her head out from between a pillow sandwich and peered down from the top bunk. I reached up and kissed her forehead.

'Morning Sausage.'

'Good morning,' she yawned.

While they both wrestled with their sheets, I began to fold and pack my things. Gathering my senses, I made a mental list of everything I had: swim float, goggles, swim cap, gloves . . . When I was sure it was all there I went out and wandered through the apartment to see who else was up. It wasn't long before every member of our team revealed themselves, yawning and wiping the crusts from their eyes. As expected, there was very little in the way of conversation. Instead we disappeared into our various preparations, quietly criss-crossing as we milled through the different rooms. Meanwhile, a pile of kit began to grow slowly in the centre of the kitchen, until eventually we were all standing around it in a circle, each of us wearing our baggy overalls pulled up to our waists.

With that we agreed it was time to leave and headed out into the waking village. When we reached the harbour, we were pleased to find that the surrounding waters were calm and peaceful. A gentle morning breeze stilled the sky and smoothed the icy shallows. It was the first sign that Rán, the Norse god of the ocean, was going to be kind to us. Then, one after another, we mounted the boarded gangway and headed down onto the jetty. We found Theresa's boat at the end of a row of black RIBs, carefully positioned for a swift exit. It was clear she planned to make use of the good weather while it lasted. In fact, no sooner had we arrived than Theresa was standing behind the wheel, waiting for us to be seated. Eager to get moving, I stepped over several coils of rope and stumbled into a seat behind Beth. The seats were built close together, forcing us into a tightly packed huddle, like a band of fluorescent penguins.

When we were settled, Theresa smiled and called for our attention. A little Norwegian flag fluttered over her shoulder. I watched it absentmindedly as she went through her routine safety talk. I didn't even realise she'd stopped speaking until the engine suddenly spluttered in the water. Then it was time to go. Suppressing the nerves, I pulled my fastened collar up with the tip of my nose and held it so my lips were pressed against the material. I often did this when I was wearing a large jacket, partly to keep my face warm, but also because it made me feel more secure.

As we backed away from the jetty, I picked out several early risers and watched them going about their business among the stilted rorbus. Then I looked up at the grey mountains above us, their sloped ridges silvered with streaks of snow. I couldn't get over how alien they looked – so dramatic and unusual.

Some were flat-topped and coloured with foliage, while others, by contrast, were spiked and bare. Together they enclosed us like a tall iron curtain, concealing the distance ahead. Meanwhile, our little boat vibrated gently as we rounded the harbour wall and gradually picked up speed. Our wake cut a path of bow-shaped waves in the otherwise undisturbed water. Again, my eyes were drawn to the mountains, only this time it was their reflection gleaming on the surface around us. Finally, the boat's nose began to lift upwards and a moment later we had passed under a bridge and were bounding out over the open ocean.

For a while we hurtled towards the offing like a pellet loosed from a shotgun barrel. We were breaking free from the confines of dry land and leaving Reine far behind us. I briefly forgot what we were doing and kept my eyes on the lifted nose of the boat. Then Theresa suddenly spun the wheel, causing us to veer sharply, until we straightened up alongside the coastline. After that we followed the long road that wrapped around the feet of the Lofoten mountains. The wind was in our faces and the engine roared and hummed as we cleared little waves.

It was a strange feeling – all of us were swathed together in the on-board chaos of sound and sensation, yet in every direction the leaden water was still and calm. I guess Calum must've noticed this too because, just then, he looked back over his shoulder and grinned at us.

'I wanna get in while it's nice and flat,' he called, straining to be heard above the pounding wind.

We all shared his anticipation. When it comes to a big challenge, especially in sports, I've found that it's the waiting that really gets to you. When you know that you've trained and you're ready, but you're still waiting on the starting line: that's the point when the doubts start to surface in your mind. *Maybe it isn't such a good idea. This is much further than you've ever swum before. Maybe you're not up to it.*

Luckily, it wasn't long until we spotted the island of Mosken, its spiked peak rising from behind a collection of smaller, rocky islands. The sight of our starting point began to allay my concerns. Next, a wave of adrenaline flushed my mind and I clenched the bar in front of me and tightened my foothold on the trembling floor. Without slowing, the boat swept across a choppy six-kilometre strait, which we would later have to swim. Then Theresa had to navigate a ragged channel that wound between the islands. Meanwhile, we kept our eyes on the seabirds overhead, just in case one decided to perform a bombing run. We were told that the nesting gannets and cormorants were protecting their babies from patrolling sea eagles. Hearing mention of those majestic predators offered a momentary distraction. We began searching for their distinct curved beak and slick, dark plumage. Slowly we slipped between sculptured black rocks, fringed with rust-coloured kelp and patched with white, chalky scrawls, courtesy of the resident birds. A silent minute passed before someone suddenly jumped up and jabbed their finger in the direction of an eagle. I leant over the side of the boat and followed their indication. The eagle was sitting perched in a regal pose on the crest of a rock, its golden neck feathers swept neatly downwards, like the scaled armour of an Egyptian soldier.

When we came out on the other side we were greeted by

the towering features of Mosken Island. Rising out of my seat, I plucked my cap, goggles and gloves from my bag and held them bunched tightly in my hand.

'You have a good day for it,' Theresa said as she steadied the wheel.

By now the breeze had dropped and there was little to no chop. Mind you, it did look very cold. We were sharing roughly the same latitude as Siberia, Greenland and Alaska – not the first places that come to mind when you think about swimming outdoors. All around us the sea was black and I couldn't see much deeper than the surface. For some time, I watched the water as it breathed, rising slowly up and down with the gentle ebb and flow of the criss-crossing tides. I knew it wasn't smart to dwell too heavily on what beasties might be lurking in the blackness. I'd seen images that confirmed a lion's mane jellyfish could grow to the same size as a human. I'd marvelled at their pale web of tentacles snaking ten metres beneath a body that glows from within with a pulsating red. I thought they looked like the colossal fighting machines from Spielberg's version of *The War of the Worlds*. The thought of meeting one as it surfaced from the deep was partly exciting, but mostly just unsettling.

Stomaching the nerves, we stood and waited while Theresa guided us up to the shore. Then she cut the engine. For a while we drifted, swaying slowly under the fissured escarpments as little waves lapped against the side of the boat. She told us it was the calmest morning she'd seen all year. Despite the good news, the boat was still beset by a pregnant silence. Carefully, we went about our warm-ups with the grim resolve of a funeral procession. For a while it seemed like there were no other sounds besides the occasional squeak of a wetsuit and the low creak of the boat as it rocked beneath us. For the first time, I also noticed that Robbie and Calum both looked nervous: their mouths hung open slightly and the colour had drained from their faces.

Shifting into action, we peeled our warm t-shirts up over our heads and began to apply Vaseline to the napes of our necks. By now we'd grown used to the various details of our preparation. Next, we zipped each other's wetsuits up and checked the straps to ensure no water could seep inside. Then a few personal additions were added, like Robbie's ear plugs, before we wrapped the floats around our waists and cleaned our goggles. Once we were suited and satisfied that all our kit was in place, we turned our attention to stretching our arms and shoulders. Together, Robbie and Calum went through the motions of shadow-swimming, after which they both lay sprawled over the side of the boat, splashing icy water on their faces and shoulders. The latter activity was something I always opted out of, due to my trusty blubber.

Finally, there was a series of suctioned slaps as our swim caps snapped tight against our foreheads, and just like that we were ready. I picked up my float, hugged Beth and sat on the rigid edge of the boat, dangling my legs into the water. Feeling much calmer, I sat for a moment, kicked my feet and stretched my fingers inside my webbed gloves. Then I looked back as Calum approached me. I could see Robbie behind him, tucking his long hair into his cap. Seeing that they were ready, I spun back and took one last look at the quiet stretch of leaden water ahead of us. Slowly, I measured the distance to the scattered islands where the seabirds flocked.

'All good,' Calum assured me.

Taking a step over the proverbial threshold, I pulled my goggles down, flipped over onto my front and hugged the boat. In this position, I lowered myself slowly into the water, until I lost my grip and dropped backwards, with a rubbery screech, into the ocean.

For a moment, it felt like I'd plunged through a sheet of ice. I dropped down into a flurry of bubbles and the cold wrapped around me like a boa constrictor. Then my chest began to tighten and my heart started pounding. A second or so later I came up, leant back and lay supine, floating on the surface. Taking a moment to catch my breath, I watched the other two as they slid down and entered the water. As soon as they surfaced I kicked off from the rubber underside of the boat, rolled over and began my front crawl. Robbie and Calum followed close behind me, and together we headed to a weathered outcrop, which we'd have to touch before we began our crossing.

When we set off and started swimming we held a steady pace. Unlike crossing the Saltstraumen, this wasn't going to be a sprint. Calum had described it as a *marathon*. We had a window of almost four hours before the tides changed and the maelstrom gathered force. It was our intention to make the crossing in less than three. Nevertheless, none of us felt like dawdling, so we kept our heads down and cut a direct path through the shallows, leaving the island of Mosken behind us. At first it felt like the challenge at hand was immense. I could feel the vast distance of ocean between us and our finish line. Soon, this thought was lodged in my mind and it jarred with my movements. For a short while, I felt uncomfortable, sucking a little too much air in as I came up to breathe and cutting my strokes short. However, as we began to make ground, I felt this uncertainty being swept into my wake. Then Calum took the lead and I slipped back to swim alongside Robbie. I kept Robbie on my breathing side so that I could watch him as I moved through the water. Silently, we both agreed not to exert ourselves and gently slowed into a relaxed rhythm. I find that this particular moment in long-distance swimming is integral to your success. It's the point of letting go . . . it's like . . . Well, have you ever failed to cut loose on a dance floor? There's that stark moment when you look down and realise that it is, in fact, *you* who's dancing. *Wait a minute*, you think, *I can't dance.* Then you start fumbling and tripping as the beat leaves your body. That's what I felt like when we started the Moskstraumen swim. By contrast, swimming with Robbie, I could at once feel my anxiety ebbing away as I began to let go. I could also hear the beat as it rolled around us.

Mind you, it wasn't always easy to swim in that sweet spot, without interruption. Occasionally it looked like we were drifting out to sea, away from the islands. I tried to counter this by edging closer to Robbie, using him as a kind of lubber line to ensure we were both headed in the same direction. In this way, we began to coordinate our paths, as though we were swimming lanes in a public pool. All we had to do, if one of us was veering away from the other, was pre-empt the separation by signalling underwater. The more we did this and the longer we kept this connection, the more confident I became.

We didn't stop swimming until our team called us over. By that point we'd been in the water for just under an hour and Calum had been leading us the whole way. When we reached the boat, they handed us bananas and bottles of water laced with powdered glucose. For a while it looked like it was feeding time in the otter enclosure. We would lie back on our floats and hold our legs up, while chewing our food and sipping the bottles. Even just a small intake seemed to be enough to fill my stomach and warm my blood. Finally, Luke asked us a few simple questions to ensure we weren't hypothermic. It wasn't surprising that we all passed, owing to our thick wetsuits and caps.

'We've been struggling to keep up,' he chuckled as we threw the bottles back and set off again.

The whole Into the Maelstrom team, halfway across the world's largest maelstrom: the Moskstraumen.

I could still taste the strange glucose water as we went on. Soon we gained a stronger pace and bunched into a tighter formation. The next time I poked my head up, unable to resist the urge any longer, I saw that we were close to the first collection of rocky islands. A moment earlier those islands had looked like amorphous ink blots, yet now they seemed to take shape, revealing their knobbled features and the channels between them. Just then, something happened that I won't ever forget. Suddenly, out of the corner of my eye, I noticed a preternatural glow. Turning my head, I discovered a view that froze me in the water. The distant offing was gilded with this beautiful band of sunlight, wedged under the ashen drear that encompassed the rest of the sky. For the first time, I felt like I was truly surrounded by nature. It's impossible not to feel awe in a moment like that. Beneath me the deep seemed to pulse and push upwards against my kicking feet. I could hear the low murmur of the maelstrom and the cawing of the island-dwelling gulls. My eyes were level with the water, which also allowed me to see small depressions and mounds that warped the metallic gleam of the surface. All this combined and helped to remind me just how privileged we were.

Uplifted, I relaxed my strokes and gently swam the short distance to the warmer shallows around the islands. I didn't realise I'd arrived until a single spear of rock lifted through the murk. The shock of nearly being impaled was the first indication that we'd entered the channel. Then patches of shadow slowly formed below me and I saw that I was gliding over tiers of coral-encrusted shelving. In parts the water became so shallow that the sunlight pierced the surface and reflected against the seabed. Meanwhile, I rolled and dug and rolled and dug, sweeping over wriggling tangles of seaweed, dappled with bluish light. Then my eyes widened behind their sealed cases. I marvelled at the cold clarity as bubbles coiled between my fingers, smoothed by flecks of shimmering light. My eyesight seemed almost enhanced, catching details that would usually pass unnoticed, perhaps because the perennial sound of gushing water and the scent-less, tasteless surroundings had limited my other senses. My thoughts slowed and I forgot the ongoing strain of each reaching stroke. Slowly the lovely minutiae poured in, like a shower of mist-wrapped droplets scattering from the tail of a waterfall.

I've always loved being underwater. I think it's partly because my head can be a busy place. I can be obsessive – desperate to right things that I perceive as being harmful to myself or others I love. I can be overly analytical and overtly self-righteous. Sometimes this folly leads me to harm or neglect the people I love the most. Yet there are also times when I am not this person. I am not myself, or anyone, I think. These moments are inexplicable and yet they teach me things – that not everything needs to be written down or categorised in thoughts. Everything is, instead, still. Then you feel the sense of having arrived somewhere peaceful. And there is no explan-ation because no explanation is required. You simply know, down to the marrow of your bones, that what you're feeling is right and true.

I realise now that I never want to forget this feeling, nor

the immensity of nature and the way in which it dissolves the walls of these small worlds and selves we choose to inhabit. I've often sensed this when I'm underwater, exposed to that world of murky silence. It's an alien place, yet at the same time I always feel comfortable there – almost as if I've come home. The experience seems to me to be somewhat paradoxical. You escape and you arrive almost simultaneously. It makes me think of something Garry Shandling once wrote to fellow comic and close friend Louis C. K., shortly before he died: 'Everyone needs to shut the fuck up. The answers are in the silence. Monks set themselves on fire to make this point. Just consider it.'

The answers are in the silence – this was the same conclusion Siddhartha reached in the eponymous novel by Herman Hesse. In the story, Siddhartha embarks on a lifelong search for enlightenment. At the end of his journey, having lived as a beggar, a pupil of the Gautama Buddha and a materialistic businessman, Siddhartha finds contentment in the gentle company of a ferryman. Circling back to where he began, the devoted student immerses himself in simplicity. He learns to study the river and listen to its whispering song as it flows by. Slowly he tempers his frantic intellect with meditation. In time, the natural world begins to nourish his spirit, uncovering that which is timeless and perennial. After years of relative isolation spent ferrying folk across the river, Siddhartha learns to pluck the fruits of a peaceful existence. Ultimately, he discovers that the truth is only complete if one is open to all its various permutations. Therefore each idea must also include its opposite. Though our passage through life seems to have been individuated – channelled through the self – happiness accompanies the realisation that all life is part of the same whole. While that might sound like a pithy, second-hand truth, it took Siddhartha a life of rich experience truly to believe and understand it.

The moment we rounded the last island we were treated to this great, operatic moment as the imposing pointed mountains of Lofoten strode into view, striped with slopes of sandy grass and scree. My eyes traced the snaking counters and found the rocky curve of a beach below. Sadly, I was now imprisoned in my aching rhythms, barred from dry land by the long, choppy strait that lay ahead of us . . . waiting.

Seeing my brothers ahead of me, I lunged forward and started to swim harder. Falling tiers of blue descended into the blackness and passed beneath my fingertips. Soon the lonesome deep was all around me. It became very important to stay calm. Digging hard through the water, I watched the disfigured shapes as they withered and disappeared. I began to feel like an astronaut, flailing untethered into space, while the earthly glow of survival receded from my fingertips. At once I'd lost that feeling of calm to the vast, black ocean. There were no islands ahead of us – nothing but the protrusive fingers of Lofoten. We had entered a stretch of open water that promised more than an hour and a half of swimming. Such lengthy swims in the Arctic Circle are seldom attempted. At this point we'd probably just slipped past the halfway mark as well. I guess you'd say that we were rising over the hump, although I did find it difficult to convince myself we were heading downhill. That's the unfortunate thing about swimming at sea – especially in a maelstrom: you never know when the uphill spells are going to surprise you.

To keep my mind at ease, I had to reach back into that inner depth where thoughts flutter, flicker and flare, but also fade quickly like fireflies. I struggled at first, concerned by the fact that my legs were now numb and the cold was creeping up around my knees. I started to put more strength into kicking, hoping to improve my circulation. It took a while, but eventually the feeling returned, burning through the cold and prickling my skin, until I could finally twitch the tips of my toes. Then my strokes began to spin into a rhythmic cycle and the gasp of each gaping breath faded from my mind.

Gone was the steady splash of my arm piercing the surface. Gone was the whoosh of my hand sweeping through the water. I was about to reach the swimmer's sweet spot again and the pull felt even stronger this time. Then I saw Calum as he came up beside Robbie and matched his pace. We were always aware of each other in the water, but this was different – I could feel their strength as they drew closer. Suddenly, their strokes quickened and wheeled in unison, until their form was almost perfectly mirrored. In that moment, the awesome size of the ocean seemed to stretch around them; they were pinned to the surface, threading through the upper layer of filtered sunlight, dwarfed by the immensity of their surroundings.

Sensing what was about to happen, I dropped back and slowed my strokes so that I could hover on Robbie's flank.

Somehow, I could anticipate the rhythm before we found it. It's like when you sit on a beach and watch the waves coming in. You see them swell and wilt and tumble inwards, one after another. You know the calm joy of that seamless break. You know how pleasing it is to watch and listen to it. If you let it, the motion takes hold of you. It's that point of letting go. I guess you'd call that the threshold to wonder – a liminal space in which the mind lets go and silence reigns.

I awaited our formation as we drew closer together. Then I saw our strokes sliding into a rhythm and noticed my hands cutting through the water at the same time as theirs. After a while my shoulders relaxed and my form improved. As my mind cleared, I felt a wave of calm and realised that we were sharing our energy. My exhaustion was lessened by a sudden sense of community. In fact, I went numb. The water that tore between my fingertips turned to air. The black depths beneath me disappeared. Finally, I forgot that I was swimming. From deep within I felt this embedded sense of calm. I heard a silence, dimly punctuated by each breath as I rolled my shoulders and lifted my arms through the air. Again, and again, my arms followed this cycle, but I couldn't feel it and I was drifting far away – with my brothers.

During that brief escape, I felt like anything was possible. It wasn't an idea I had encountered often in my life. When I was a kid I couldn't ever imagine being able to escape myself. I was a shy and nervous boy. I used to imagine a white wall at the end of the universe. I believed that we were sealed inside the confines of this wall, and that space and everything we knew and would ever know was contained within it too.

*A rare moment of synchronicity when Robbie, Calum
and I find our rhythm in the Moskstraumen.*

As I grew older I realised that this couldn't be so. Your mind
wants a ceiling. Your mind wants a wall. But there is no ceiling.
There is no wall. So there is no limit to what you can achieve.

Several minutes later my eyes blinked into use again and
my mind returned to the water. For a while I kept the same
pace, dividing my attention between each reaching stroke and
the dark descent beneath me. Before long I caught sight of
a peculiar, pulsating shape in the depths below me. Glancing
down, I suddenly noticed that the water was scattered with
translucent spots. Then I delayed my next breath, squinted
through the murk and discovered that these weren't spots at
all, but rather I was passing over a dense bloom of jellyfish.
There were so many that I couldn't even begin to count
them. They just went on and on in a starry mass, trailing

down through the blackness in the same way that fire lanterns drift and criss-cross into the night sky. Mostly they swept by at a safe distance, although occasionally I would roll back under to find one sprawled ahead of me. As soon as I got over the initial fear of being stung I found that the ones closer to the surface were very pleasing to look at. In fact, every time my head went beneath the water, my eyes were drawn to those luminescent rings that encircle their mouths, each one shining clearly like the filament of a light bulb. If they strayed close enough I could also see the thin, fibrous veins of their radial canals, sprouting outwards from the flowing, silken ribbons of their oral arms. In the end, what at first seemed to be a potentially painful hindrance turned out to be a welcome distraction from staring into blackness. Relieved, I swam on in a relaxed stupor, transfixed on the jellyfish bloom. In fact, I didn't stop swimming until I heard a call from the boat, at which point I poked my head up through the surface and noticed, with a slight panic, that I was alone. The other two had drifted onto a different course and the boat was a short distance behind me.

Caught in the inflow of a cold current, I decided to tread water and wait for the support team. While I waited, I propped my head on my swim float, leant back and allowed my body to rock gently over the chop. On either side, the pale horizons stretched out and seemed to bend around me like a silver-banded ring. The cloud-laden sky had started to darken and a sharp wind cut across the surface of the water, biting my bare cheeks. I was struck by the realisation that we were in the grip of the wild outdoors. This was the world we'd been looking for. I could feel us being drawn into it as the currents found their force and the Arctic wildlife started to reveal itself.

When they arrived, the guys on the boat told me they'd seen a puffin and several sea eagles close to the islands. So far, I'd only spotted the armies of red jellyfish and the gulls that squawked and bickered as they circled overhead. I could tell that James, standing fully clad in a thick wetsuit, was now hoping for a pod of orcas to pay us a visit. Of course, we all were – I just hoped they'd give us fair warning if they decided to show up. Also, they would have to hurry, considering we only had a half-hour or so left in the water.

After taking on a few sips of sugary drink and a little food, I kicked my feet and turned towards the Lofoten Islands. Taking a moment, I leant forward with the float straps pulled tight around my wrists. Slowly my legs sank until I was upright. Then I stopped still, wrapped in the numbing cold, and felt the water lapping against my lips and cheeks. Slowly I traced the contours of the archipelago and found the clouded mountains that sloped down to our finishing point. The shore was dwarfed by tall, jagged cliffs, which stood like black bastions with gulls wheeling over the headlands. I began to wonder which one was Helseggen, where Edgar Allan Poe's narrator had sojourned to retell the story of *A Descent into the Maelstrom*. I focused on one of the larger mountains – the lopsided rock face was wrapped in a belt of vapour, shaved and tossed upwards from the inky waves below. Perhaps this was the same view the survivor had seen in Poe's story, as his wheeling ship slipped into the gaping jaws of the whirlpool.

Soon Robbie and Calum swam over and joined me in the water beside the boat. By now the current had settled and we were held in the supple palm of the gentle, rolling ocean. We talked briefly about how we were coping, until the cold caused us to shiver. At that point we dove back under and began our final push towards the finish line. We swam in a loose formation and kicked hard to keep the feeling in our legs. Then Calum started to fall behind us – he was having difficulty keeping warm and his stomach was reacting badly to the intake of syrupy glucose. Meanwhile, Robbie and I were stopping at regular intervals to ensure we were still on a direct course to the beach. It soon became apparent that we'd lost our momentum, although, like a frantic drummer trying to find his way back to the beat, we kept on hitting the water and inching closer to the shore. It was going to be a stretch of hard-earned metres. Now we were pushing through a strong, icy current, which swept around the furthest outcrop of Lofoten. You could feel the waves of cold as they hit your body and wrapped around your muscles. I began to feel like I was swimming in chainmail. One after another my strokes became lazier and heavier, until I was pawing the water and no longer bothering to kick.

Suddenly the sweet spot seemed unreachable. In fact, it looked like the islands were moving away from us. I stopped swimming and kept my head underwater. Taking a moment, I allowed my legs to fall until I was floating upright. My feet pedalled gently over the blackness, stirring coils of bubbles, through which I could see another bloom of jellyfish passing beneath me. This time I noticed that several, larger jellyfish

*Luke watches over us as we swim towards the
Lofoten Islands, while Dave sits at the head of the
RIB with his camera at the ready.*

had been upturned by the current and I had to lift my feet
to avoid their splayed, red tentacles.

I could've rested and watched them for a while, although
slowly the cold was closing in and with it came a chilling
sense of abandon. Slightly panicked, I pulled my head up
through the surface and sucked the Arctic air deep into my
lungs. I could feel my mood shifting. Suddenly I felt heavier.
The waves lapped against my cheeks and salt water lashed my
lips as I steadied my breathing. I began to worry that we were
drifting too far apart. All at once the isolation had sapped my
confidence and seeped into my mind. The undulating ocean
almost seemed to swell upwards and spiral around me. I took
another deep breath and groped the water with my hands,

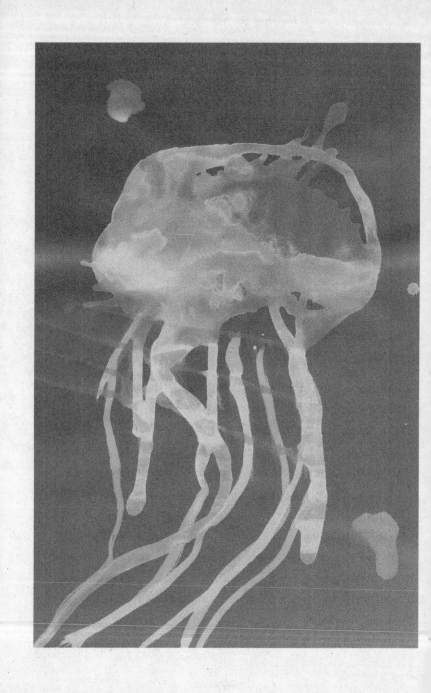

slowing my movements. Perhaps I was being pulled towards the offing or maybe I was about to lose the feeling in my arms. It didn't matter. I was happy to spend a few moments with my fear because it also prickled with excitement. Control was everything I'd run from and, in a way, it felt like a relief to let it go. Just imagine a rickety cart that rolls downhill and suddenly loses a wheel. This cart is likely to be upturned and thrown into a mad succession of pirouettes and somersaults, spinning unhindered as it performs a reckless, rapid dance of destruction. Sometimes the patterns of existence deliver expected forms and we forget what chaos looks like and how it feels. We yearn for order and restitution, but there is pleasure in the sudden disarray. There is joy in discarding the doctrine of normality prescribed by the neatly gathered majority. I felt like I had tapped into that disorder – like I was rolling to the drums of a feral rhythm. As the steady current took me, this feeling warmed my body and attracted my attention. Allowing myself to drift, I searched my thoughts and reached for the source of this warmth. It seemed small and distant, like an enticing flame shivering in the caverns of my subconscious. Then this flame flitted over strands of primitive imagery. I saw gaping jaws . . . a pink tongue . . . rows of large, rounded teeth . . . I saw seals being torn to blubbery shreds and tossed into the air.

That's it, I thought, *that's too much chaos* . . .

Suddenly I was replaying an orca hunt from *Planet Earth* in my head. Or was this a premonition? I couldn't say, although I did know that these images seemed so raw and vivid that they immediately spurred me into motion.

After that I swam with renewed strength and pushed through the onslaught of little, spiked waves. Luckily the current seemed to soften and my strokes lightened as the ache in my shoulders subsided. Then the rugged, green fingers of Helle's coast seemed to lift into view. At last it felt like we'd made it. I exhaled a flurry of bubbles as I cheered beneath the water. This was the moment I'd visualised so many times before. The next thing I knew I was sliding into an expanse of calm, unruffled water, cradled by a salient wall of black rock, which also served as a shield, buffeted and hewn by the rough tidewater.

Feeling suddenly exhilarated, I dropped to a leisurely pace and followed Robbie as he turned towards a sheltered cove. I spent those last few moments enjoying the feel of the still water as it wrapped around my shoulders. Then I watched the seabed slowly appearing through the murk. I saw waving kelp forests sprawled among the pitted rocks. I saw the glinting scales of little fish as they darted out of sight. At the same time, waves of relief pulsed through my body and washed my mind. It was one of those moments of great sweetness hidden amid chaos – a reminder that the natural world holds treasures more glorious than anything you'll find in any catalogue. In the end, there is no substitute for the lamenting howl of the wolf, or any of those other primal delights, which travel down to unravel rich silt in the bed of your soul.

Exhausted, I finally beached myself on a knobbled rock shelf and lay slumped among the limpets. After catching my breath, I used the last of my strength to crawl upwards, clenching handfuls of tangled kelp, like the first slime to leave the ocean. Meanwhile, Robbie had already scrambled up ahead of me. He sat with his arms propped on his knees and grinned as I approached.

'Well done Jackus,' he laughed.

When I reached him we hugged and congratulated each other. Then I dropped down at his side and rolled over onto my back. Together we watched as Calum swung into the cove and snaked towards us. That moment was everything I'd hoped it would be. You train and you train, and you fall and you fall – all for that feeling. You know when you hear about the regime of some mad Olympian who wakes up before sunrise every day and eats and works out like a Spartan warrior? The first thing most people think is why the hell would you put yourself through that, right? For them it makes sense though. Of course, I don't know for sure, but I think the reason can be condensed to that single moment. Jack London said it was the feeling of being God – or being at one with God – and that to feel such a thing, as a lowly, ape-descendant, was a far greater thing than *for a god to feel godlike*. I guess if God is love then you could call it a kind of self-love. I'm not sure what to call it really – I just know that it felt good.

It wasn't long until the three of us were together on that sloped rock, looking back at the grey swathe of ocean we'd crossed from the island of Mosken. Our swim across the Mosstraumen was finally complete, and we'd all made it – we'd crossed the largest maelstrom in the world. We were the first ones crazy enough to do it. Now, should any curious visitor set eyes on this place and ask: 'Has anyone ever swum across it?' the answer would be a definitive 'Yes . . . the Hudson brothers were the first.'

That felt good too.

We were all shivering and laughing as we caught our breath and waited for the feeling to return to our numb extremities. Calum put on a good show, making us convulse with laughter, his crazed, wide eyes darting between us and an excited grin stretching across his face. He was the only one who'd never doubted that we'd make it. He really is one of the *mad ones*. In fact, I remember when he failed his first Double Iron Man, a continuous ultra-triathlon comprising a 4.8-mile swim, 224-mile bike ride and 52-mile run. He later explained what had happened to him during this failed attempt. After almost two days of constant endurance he'd wound up cycling through a dense forest late at night. It was then that he began to hallucinate. Half delirious, he started to see giant horses gathered among the trees. As he swept by, following the dim, sweeping light attached to his handlebars, these horses began to snort and whinny as though they were laughing at him. Suddenly Calum's front wheel veered into a tree stump and he was hurled forward, overturning as he flailed through the air. Then, lying crumpled on the forest floor, Calum slowly began to curse and cry, until another competitor appeared through the darkness, pulled him to his feet and said: 'At some point in the race everyone cries in these woods.'

Despite carrying on through the night, early the following morning, after a seemingly endless cycle of hills and headwinds, Calum wound up too exhausted to continue. I couldn't imagine the kind of grit it must've taken to go back and complete that same challenge – as he did, the following year. For such an endurance event, he said, everyone trains, but those who make it have the outcome set in their minds. They'll pass out before they give up. That was the mind-set he adopted the second time around. I guess you've got to want it so badly that no amount of waking pain can turn you back or make you quit. I love those people. It's easy to listen to someone whose thoughts are carved by adversity. In quiet dreams, I imagine myself having that same resilience to defeat, although I'd probably be off that bike as soon as I stopped freewheeling. And yet, having swum the Moskstraumen, I did get a taste of what it's like to push yourself further than you ever have before. There was something wholly addictive about the way it made me feel.

Back on the boat we dithered to and fro like a huddle of elderly dears at a coffee luncheon. Eventually the others had to sit us down and help us peel our wetsuits down to our waists. Then we wrapped towels around our pimpled shoulders and ate whatever food was still left in the bags we'd brought. At one point Luke poured a cup full of coffee and handed it to Calum. The only problem was that, at this point, Calum was showing early signs of hypothermia, shaking violently and quickly losing the colour in his face. The coffee stayed in the cup for about two seconds before it leapt from Calum's shuddering hands and spilled onto Luke's overalls. Then it became apparent that Calum needed immediate attention and the team huddled around him and provided heaps of jackets and towels until he eventually warmed and stopped shaking.

Before long, Theresa went back to the wheel and eased the engine into a steady purr. I watched the rocks where we'd been sitting and reminded myself what we'd just done. Then I found my seat as the boat reversed over the glassy water and pulled out from the cove. I could feel the weight of our work in my shoulders. I could feel the stinging burn where my cap had been rubbing my neck. I could even taste the salt between my lips. In many ways, I felt drained and beaten, but I was also warm inside my padded jacket and now my mind was still and peaceful.

When we got back to our cosy apartment in Reine, after we'd warmed and cleaned ourselves in the basement showers, the three of us sat at the kitchen table and read some of the messages of support from our phones. One of these messages was from our mum. It was a reminder of the matriarchs who started us on our journey.

The message read:

> *I think on Wednesday this week Grandma Wild and Grandma Martin went and sat either side of Someone-I-Don't-Believe-In, or possibly someone even bigger (Mother Nature/Gaia), and just let them know who was down there braving the mighty Moskstraumen. I think they had a quiet word in their ears from either side about what they would do if any harm came to their lads . . . what merry hell they would unleash should the wind even flutter while their adored grandsons were down there bringing attention to this beautiful planet.*

That evening I wandered back down to the harbour, hoping to reflect on what we'd done. There was a rorbu (a traditional type of Norwegian house used by fishermen) with a grass roof built close to the water's edge. I found Robbie sitting cross-legged on a boat ramp, sketching this rorbu. I went over and stood behind him and looked around to see what kind of spot he'd chosen. I noticed other wooden fishing huts made from large trunks gripped by clumps of moss. Some of the older huts were draped in nets and piles of disused equipment. Still, despite their varying states of disrepair, there wasn't one that looked unhomely or uninviting. There were also a few stilted red rorbues, overlooking patches of cold-water coral. I guessed that this was where most of the fishermen lived. It was a creaking little secret kept hidden from the larger quayside, which usually mumbled with the milling of rugged locals, wrapped in woollen clothes.

After a while I sat down beside Robbie and watched the harbour while he drew. Occasionally a boat would slide into view, trailing a cape of raucous gulls, which would attract my attention. There was also a distinct smell of salt that lingered in the air, no matter where you were on the waterfront. Everywhere you turned there were reminders that you were in a fishing community. In fact, the longer you stayed there the more you realised how dependent the locals were on the sea, as well as the environmental conditions. I read later that the cod travel to the shores of Reine from the Barents Sea, seeking warmer waters in which to lay their eggs. Cod was still the stock fish in this area, ever since it had been used as fuel for the Vikings, enabling them to travel further in their famous dragon boats. Behind us you could see ranks of wooden racks where the cod hauls would usually be air-dried, although today they were empty. If something, like oil drilling, was to alter the number of fish that could be caught in Lofoten, then places like Reine would fade into nonexistence.

Some of the naysayers would have us believe that nothing can be done. They would say there is no way to prevent the destruction of our planet's precious ecosystems. These people are defeatists. You just need to look at the achievements of a few hardy individuals to see how much change one willing person can inspire. Take Lewis Pugh, UN Patron of the Oceans, for example. Lewis wanted to shake the lapels of world leaders and inspire them to be more courageous. With this in mind, he decided to attempt five record-breaking swims in Antarctica, wearing nothing but his Speedos. You might've seen photos of him weaving between floats of sculptured glacial ice. Just to give you some idea of what he went through, the water he was in was a heart-stopping -1°C. In fact, he was swimming further south than any human has ever swum before – a mere hundred miles from the South Pole. Through his efforts, Lewis managed to persuade the Russian government to approve an agreement to transform the Ross Sea into the largest protected marine area in history.

Of course, we would not be so arrogant as to presume we could do anything similar for the Lofoten Islands, although we did set out to draw attention to this part of the world, which is home to the largest cold-water coral reef on the planet, as well as 75 per cent of the Atlantic cod population. The Norwegian energy minister, Tord Lien, has already remarked that we will soon be experiencing 'a new chapter in the history of Norwegian petroleum' – we just hope that this next chapter will have a positive ending.

One of the other things I wanted to promote, when it came to writing this book, was the idea of living more creatively. When you look at a cityscape by nightfall, you see towers, spires, water coolers, cars, monuments . . . everything is organised and neatly slotted together. Then there are rows upon rows of lit windows – an ocean of lights as multitudinous as the stars in the night's sky. I always liked the fact that each light holds a microcosm of human existence. All the worried dreams and hopes of a civilisation, gathered in a serried regiment, dwarfed by the metal and glass totems of business. I remind myself that every light holds the limitless potential of a few human hearts. Together these lights could sprawl and blaze with the tenacity of wildfire.

I am sure this wildfire exists and, moreover, cannot be tamed. Just think back to some of those subversive movements that have drawn followers over the years. Long before I was born, there was the Beat Generation, running on Ginsberg's howling poetry and the heartbeat rhythm of Kerouac's spontaneous prose. I dipped into a few of their novels and poems at uni and felt exhilarated, like they had dreamt up some rampant, unholy gospel, huddled over gallon jugs of wine in low-lit dives, with the heady freeform jazz coursing through their veins. Then there were the Dionysian hippies – laidback, bleary-eyed and riding Hunter S. Thompson's *wave* as it crashed between the rigid white bluffs of American society. Before that, in the 50s, there was also the Civil Rights Movement, evidence of which I found in grainy videos of marches and sit-ins. I distinctly remember sitting at our oversized computer and feeling energised as I listened to

Dr King's sermon in Washington. There's one line I've always remembered: 'No, no, we are not satisfied, and we will not be satisfied until justice rolls down like waters and righteousness like a mighty stream.'

One thing that all these different movements had in common was the guiding goal of freedom. This distinct purpose set fire to flurries of rhetoric, whether it was written or spoken, and stoked the flames of unrest and disobedience. The modern wild swimming revolution – evident in the huge numbers of people who've taken to swimming outdoors – is driven by a similar yearning for freedom. More specifically, wild swimmers seek a closer relationship with the natural world, inspired by the ongoing destruction of our environment. The catalyst for the beatniks was the desolation after the Second World War, the hippies were opposing the atrocities in Vietnam and the Civil Rights Movement emerged to combat racial inequality. In all these examples the status quo had become an anathema, which in turn inspired a radical movement to rise up and challenge it. One of the most dangerous anathemas we'll face in our time is climate change. We are accelerating towards a precipice and some leaders still have their feet on the gas. I guess a cold-water swim might not seem like much of a protest, but it *is* a peaceful way of reminding yourself and others how important nature is.

So, get out there – escape the confines of your routine and remember to share your photos and stories. The wild is unpredictable and beautiful. It might help you to relax and it might also encourage you to think more creatively about what you can achieve in life. If you still find yourself lacking in motivation, then maybe think of your wild swimming journey as a pilgrimage of sorts. This is a chance for you to remind yourself, and those you're close to, exactly why we should value the natural world . . . and, let's not get this twisted, *now* is the time to remember that value.

At this present moment you belong to a species that is facing several self-inflicted catastrophes. First, the Ellen MacArthur Foundation has predicted that by 2050, if we continue dumping waste into the sea at the current rate, there will be more plastic in the ocean than fish. Bear in mind that this plastic won't decay for decades, perhaps even centuries. In our kingdom-topping wisdom, we have taken living organisms out of the water and replaced them with floating, dead material.

Conservation experts and ecologists have also been analysing data from the IUCN Red List of Threatened Species – a kind of global inventory for animals around the world, collected using everything from online crowdsourcing to satellite imaging. This initiative has mobilised millions in a mission to discover exactly how badly different endangered species are faring around the world. Using the accumulated data, experts are slowly discovering the threats these species face and how to protect them from extinction. They have identified two chief concerns that threaten the survival of these animals: habitat destruction and climate change. Their analysis has shown us that, prior to the evolution of humans, less than a single, solitary species per million went extinct each year. Today, as we edge ever closer to the sixth mass extinction in the history of our planet, we're looking at a rapid loss of species that's between 1,000 and 10,000 times higher than the natural rate of extinction.

The responsibility for all this destruction sits squarely on our shoulders.

Just imagine if your children or grandchildren never saw a lion in the wild. Imagine if they looked at pictures of orangutans the same way we look at dodo drawings now. And it's down to *us*. We're taking the wonder out of this experience and stealing these animals from the world. There are now only 20,000 lions left in Africa. Five wild lions are killed every day, just on that single continent. Five thousand leopards are killed each year for their unique coats. One thousand orangutans are killed each year in Borneo and Sumatra, mainly due to habitat destruction. Five African elephants are killed for their tusks every hour and one African rhino is killed every 9.5 hours. Just picture the once healthy bulk of a full-grown rhino left bloodied and hornless, strewn in the dust where it was gunned down. Consequently the rhino is now extinct in Mozambique.

Makes misanthropy easy, right? Well, while we're all complicit in this, there are some who have turned defiantly and are now wading back against the current. On the front-lines of conservation there are thousands upon thousands of individuals who work tirelessly to defend endangered species. There are rangers who die all the time in the fight against armed poachers. The efforts of these brave conservationists have helped to lower the extinction rates of some mammals, bird and amphibians by 20 per cent. At the same time, the Convention on the International Trade in Endangered

Species has been stalling trade and tightening regulations to address the current extinction rates. Recent bans and trade limits have been put in place to protect various imperilled species, including several species of sharks. It is now much harder for the scum of the ivory trade to use the United States as a staging ground for their activities. There are also a few individuals stories of certain species being pulled back from the abyss. In China, the giant panda populations have improved to such an extent that the animal has now been removed from the IUCN Red List and is no longer classed as endangered. Sadly, orangutans are still on the brink, although there is hope in the form of the Borneo Orangutan Survival Foundation's release programme. As many as 250 orangutans, many of them rescued orphans or rehabilitated adults, have been released into safe, protected forests. There are still hundreds more waiting to be set loose from their cages and reintroduced to the wild.

Whether this battle can be fought and won largely depends on our ability to create and maintain large nature reserves. About 13 per cent of land on Earth is now reserved as a refuge for wildlife. However, only 1.6 per cent of the world's oceans are currently being protected and, with 100 million sharks being killed and having their fins hacked off each year, that isn't nearly enough.

As you read this, marine conservationists are fighting around the world to secure globally protected ecosystems. At the moment they are focusing primarily on Colombia, Ecuador, Brazil, India and Sumatra. The idea, centred on protecting the biodiversity of our oceans, is to link isolated regions of habitat, joining them together to create huge, chained habitats, which will then be placed under government protection. New Zealand has just created a 620,000-kilometre MPA (Marine Protected Area) in the South Pacific Ocean. These waters contain the world's longest chain of submerged volcanoes, as well as the second-deepest ocean trench, which descends to depths greater than the height of Mount Everest. It is called the Kermadec Ocean Sanctuary and it will preserve a very significant ecosystem for the future, with thirty-five resident whale and dolphin species and three different species of sea turtle as well.

Another important MPA is also being established around the island of Palau, covering an area of 193,000 square miles. An island smaller than New York City now protects an area of ocean larger than California. In doing so Palau hopes to keep its high rates of biodiversity. Researchers have found that protected waters contain twice the number of fish and five times the number of predatory fish than those left unprotected. A healthy population of predators is a clear sign of an ecosystem on the mend. There have been unexpected benefits for Palau resulting from this. It's common knowledge that in protected areas where fish are undisturbed they will breed, feed and produce more offspring. What's interesting, though, is that as the biomass increases there is a spillover of adult fish into the surrounding, unprotected waters, which in turn means larger hauls for local fisheries. Monetarily, the local government relies on the fishing industry, while also needing to sustain its income from environmental tourism. This is a fine example of how to achieve a sustainable solution, or, as Ray Hilborn, marine biologist and fisheries scientist, put it in his article 'Marine Biodiversity Needs More Than Protection': 'advocates of marine protected areas and those in fisheries management must work together, not at cross purposes.'

Despite these promising examples, the rate at which we are destroying our habitat is still far greater than the rate at which we're protecting it. The obvious question, and the one that we must inevitably ask ourselves, is: *what can we do?*

The answer is simple: *something.*

Just do *something* . . .

Eat less meat, sponsor an animal, give a monthly donation to an organisation like the WWF or WCS. Don't look for excuses not to. Remember that these early steps are everything. Without them there is no momentum. If more people step forward to support the conservation effort, we have a greater chance of saving some of these endangered species and final bastions of natural beauty. We even have a chance of reversing the damage we're doing, every day, to this symbiotic system that pre-dates everything we've ever made by billions upon billions of years. And don't let the defeatists tell you your contributions don't matter. The commitment of every single individual will be essential throughout this century. Jane Goodall, who has given fifty-five years of her life to studying wild chimpanzees, tells us that we possess an 'indomitable spirit'. I believe this is true. Your capacity to do good is boundless, matched only by your capacity to do evil. Use these simple distinctions to propel yourself forward. Feel good about making a small difference and encouraging others to do the same.

For us, there's one thing we know for certain: we're going to keep launching wild swimming expeditions in the spirit of encouraging others to reconnect with nature. So, early in 2018, we're heading way down to the islands of furry-footed folk, painted Māoris and abundant birdlife: New Zealand.

This time we're planning to swim across a deep crater lake, concealed atop the largest active volcano in New Zealand, Mount Ruapehu, the slopes of which were used by Peter Jackson to recreate Mount Doom in *The Lord of the Rings*. First we'll have to meet with a vulcanologist, whose job it is to assess the toxicity levels of the sulphuric water and fumes, as well as the warm temperature, which will require us to adapt our strokes and breathing techniques. We're also organising swims across the Te Aumiti maelstrom, sprinting from the northern fingers of the South Island to the island of D'Urville, as well as including a visit to the island home of an endangered flightless parrot called the kakapo. There are now fewer than 160 of these rare beauties left on our planet. While we're out there we hope to meet the scientists who look after the fifty breeding female kakapos and to mingle with the indigenous Māoris and learn about their traditions and their culture.

That ancient culture alone would be worth the long flight out there. For years I've been fascinated by these island tribes, ever since I first watched the All Blacks and saw bulky Māori descendants, like Tana Umaga, gurning and making those *I'm gonna eat your world* faces during the pre-game haka. Before that I think my introduction to New Zealand was condensed into four separate cinema trips to see *The Fellowship of the Ring*, in which Gandalf and his cronies first appeared on this mythical, alien landscape, traversing snow-capped peaks and tranquil fjords.

Funnily enough, I also remember, during my final year at school, I'd written an unsuccessful history essay on *satyagraha* – a philosophical principle that translates roughly to *holding onto truth*. Supposedly, this idea was integral to the campaigns of civil disobedience led by Mahatma Gandhi to achieve Indian independence. It was then famously channelled by Martin Luther King Jr during the Civil Rights Movement. I remember one of the first sources I found led me to a Māori chief called Te Whiti. I read that Te Whiti was once an astute student of the Māori elders who saved and fed the survivors of the *Lord Worsley* shipwreck, on the fecund coast of Taranaki. In 1867, when other parts of the North Island had been confiscated by the European government, Te Whiti held strong in a village at Parihaka, intent on protecting Māori dignity and preserving their culture. In the years that followed, Te Whiti led the people of Parihaka on a path of non-violent resistance, manifesting *satyagraha* and defying the government. Ultimately, Te Whiti was a pacifist, unwilling to give up Māori land, but equally unwilling to conform to violence.

'They work secretly,' Te Whiti told his followers, 'but I speak in public so that all may hear.'

In time, Te Whiti's village at Parihaka became a stronghold of sorts, defiantly disrupting the legislated theft of tribal land. Then the government decided the Māoris were nothing more than rebels and criminals. Consequently, Te Whiti was incarcerated without trial, which inspired an uprising of Māori ploughmen, who gathered across the country and reoccupied their stolen lands, preventing European expansion. It was a non-violent struggle in which hundreds were peacefully arrested, despite the warrior image of the painted Māori. The story then spread through British media and became a source of inspiration for Gandhi in South Africa.

More stories like that began to resurface as I considered the prospect of travelling to New Zealand. When Calum retreated to his lair to concoct this mad expedition, I sat back nervously and waited with slightly bated breath. His doe-eyed re-emergence was followed by several hours of intense scrutiny. I wanted to know every little detail of what lay ahead. Naturally, part of me wanted to know if our lives were in danger, although another part recognises that an element of danger makes adventure what it is.

In the end, I guess the thing that keeps me interested is a relentless (sometimes smothered) urge to make use of myself. Often, I'll think of pioneers like Lewis Pugh, who recently embarked on a three-year mission to secure additional MPAs in the waters of East Antarctica, the Weddell Sea and the Bellingshausen Sea. If he succeeds, he will have helped to create an MPA covering seven million square kilometres (an area of the waters around Antarctica that's larger than Australia).

None of this would've been possible had Lewis not first overcome his fears and put something on the line, for the sake of something greater. When he stood on a shelf of ice at the North Pole, about to dive into -1.7°C water, he was stomaching the possibility that his heart might stop, at which point his body would sink 4,200 metres, down through the blackness, until it reached the seabed. I mean, how the hell do you get to that point? What is the story that makes you believe it's worth it?

If you read a little about Lewis you begin to get an idea of what drives him. In Antarctica, he swam in shallow waters around an island that was formerly a whaling station. While he was in the water, threading his strokes through the clear surface, it soon became apparent that he was passing over a graveyard cluttered with piled whale bones – huge white jaws, spines and ribs. Suddenly he was surrounded by the skeletons of slaughtered whales, once hauled from the beach and dumped into the shallow coastal waters. The spectre of death was present again when he completed his *Seven Swims for One Reason* – a great YouTube series filmed by videographer Ben Brown – during which he encountered no sharks, no dolphins and no large fish. Instead, he saw dumping grounds dotted with tyres and plastic, and rust-coloured plains of bleached reefs, where the disintegrating coral was shrinking, changing colour and dissolving like rotted flesh.

Lewis has also talked about his motivation in various interviews he's done over the years. The story that stood out for me involved his late father, who, during his time in the Navy, witnessed the controlled detonation of an atomic bomb. When the blast began to mushroom, wreathed in furls of searing white flame, Lewis's father instinctively shielded his eyes. Then the explosion emitted an electromagnetic wave so powerful that it caused him to see an x-ray of the bones in his arm. Many years later, at a crowded TED conference, Lewis would tell a silent audience that the experience changed his father forever. In that moment, he had seen the destruction of gods, in the hands of men. Consequently, Lewis's father ensured that almost every holiday they shared was going to be spent in a natural park. That moment inspired him to raise his son to understand the value of nature, thereby helping to shape a man who would willingly risk his life for the sake of Arctic conservation.

The first time Lewis dove into the black water, for a training swim, he was met by the agonising sensation of being on fire. After swimming for five minutes he clambered back onto the ice and stared at his deformed hands, which were now so swollen that he couldn't even clench his fists. Looking back, he realised that the cells in his fingers had frozen, expanded and burst – the pain was excruciating. Eventually he made it into a hot shower and, inside the cone of spattering water, began to defrost his fingers. He'd lasted five minutes and already suffered immensely. Suddenly he was faced with the likelihood that his dream, to swim one kilometre across the North Pole, was impossible. Thrown into an intense depression, Lewis began to dwell on a story told by Sir Ranulph Fiennes, who attempted to ski to the North Pole. One day, Sir Ranulph had been pulling his sledge across the snow-covered ice when it suddenly hit a weak patch and dropped through into the water. Sir Ranulph had his hand submerged for three minutes before he finally managed to rescue the sledge. When he reached hospital, the doctors informed him that his hand was so badly frostbitten he would have to lose several fingers. The operation was delayed, causing Sir Ranulph to grow increasingly impatient, until – having gained his wife's consent – he went into his tool shed and performed the procedure himself with a saw.

The thought of losing fingers only worsened Lewis's funk. Soon he would be spending twenty minutes in water that was similar in temperature to that which Sir Ranulph had endured. It seemed like their ship was tasked with an impossible feat, ploughing through chunks of sea ice, bound for tragedy. Then a close friend, who Lewis had known since he was eighteen, pulled him to one side.

'I know, Lewis, deep down – right deep down here – that you're going to make this swim,' his friend said. 'I so believe in you Lewis. I've seen the way you've been training and I realise the reason why you're going to do this. This is such an important swim.'

Filled with renewed confidence, Lewis went on to make the distance and completed his symbolic swim, against the current. He defied the odds and proved to himself that he could achieve what had seemed impossible. In doing so he proved to all of us that we can, too.

Acknowledgements

Without certain people, this book never would have been written and published. Before we'd even heard of *wild swimming* Robbie swam the length of Lake Ullswater, which planted the seed for our future expeditions. He taught me to put stock in the logic of trusting your gut, which has proven very useful over the years. Thanks to my unstoppable middle brother, Calum, for dreaming up these mad aquatic adventures and proving that inaction is folly. Also, thanks to them both for their great contributions and illustrations in this book – they are invaluable. Thanks to our family for all their warmth, support and eccentricities. Thanks to our wonderful mum, who taught us that kindness should come before all else. Thanks to Dad, for his deep stores of enthusiasm and encouragement, as well as both our grandmas, matriarchs of the highest order, for revealing the subtle art of ageing without growing old. Thanks also to Iain for helping to raise us and for showing us the joys of a good, lazy backstroke.

Thanks to our trusty team and old mates: Dave, Luke and Sandy, who are always up for an adventure. And, of course, thanks to our Human Swiss Army Knife, James Silson. Special thanks to my girlfriend Beth for being my closest friend and for rounding off my carefully constructed *Things To Do* lists with such comedic gems as: *Take Poop, Think About Said Poop, Smile...* Thanks to my exuberant teachers at UCC and Northumbria, from whom I learnt to work with passion. Thanks to our agent Richard for all his guidance and for taking a chance on that early draft about three Cumbrians fumbling through their childhood river. Thanks to Tamsin, Caitriona, Louise, Liz and the whole team at Yellow Kite, as well as the copy-editor Nick, for helping to shape this narrative, for caring about the story and for taking the edge off the big, imposing London publishing industry.

Finally, I want to say thank you to Mrs Battey. When I left her nursery, aged three, she wrote this line in my leaving report: *I look forward to seeing your name in print someday.*

Well, here it is!

Thanks so much for your encouragement.

Bibliography

Adams, Douglas, *Last Chance To See* (Arrow, 2009)

Attenborough, David, *Amazing Rare Things: The Art of Natural History in the Age of Discovery* (Yale University Press, 2015)

Brooke, Rupert, *The Poetical Works: Poets of the Great War* (Faber & Faber, 2014)

Conway, Sean, *Hell And High Water* (Ebury Press, 2017)

Cox, Lynne, *The Day The Whale Came* (Phoenix, 2006)

Deakin, Roger, *Waterlog* (Vintage, 2000)

Fossey, Dian, *Gorillas in the Mist* (Ishi Press, 2014)

Galdikas, Birute, *Reflections of Eden: My Years With the Orangutans of Borneo* (Little, Brown, 1995)

Goodall, Jane, *In the Shadow of Man* (Weidenfeld & Nicolson 1999)

Hesse, Hermann, *Siddhartha* (Penguin Classics, 2008)

Heyerdahl, Thor, *Kon-Tiki: Across the Pacific by Raft* (Simon & Schuster, 2013)

Kerouac, Jack, *The Dharma Bums* (Penguin Modern Classics, 2000)

Lee, Jessica J., *Turning* (Virago, 2017)

Linden, Eugene, *Parrot's Lament and Other True Stories* (E. P. Dutton, 2001)

Minihane, Joe, *Floating: A Life Regained* (Duckworth Overlook, 2017)

Monbiot, George, *Feral* (Penguin, 2014)

Morgan, Elaine, *The Descent of Woman* (Souvenir Press Ltd, 2001)

Norbury, Katherine, *The Fish Ladder* (Bloomsbury Paperbacks, 2016)

Orwell, George, *Nineteen Eighty-Four* (Penguin Classics, 2004)

Poe, Edgar Allan, *A Descent into the Maelstrom* (Bibliographic Press, 2015)

Pugh, Lewis, *Achieving the Impossible* (Simon & Schuster, 2010)

Rew, Kate, *Wild Swim: River, Lake, Lido & Sea* (Guardian Newspapers Ltd, 2008)

Sprawson, Charles, *Haunts of the Black Masseur* (Vintage Classics, 2013)

Wardley, Tessa, *The Mindful Art of Wild Swimming: Reflections for Zen Seekers* (Leaping Hare Press, 2017)

Wood, Levison, *Walking the Americas* (Hodder & Stoughton, 2017)

Wordsworth, William, *Selected Poems* (Penguin Classics, 2004)

books to help you live a good life

Join the conversation and tell
us how you live a #goodlife

🐦 @yellowkitebooks
f YellowKiteBooks
📌 Yellow Kite Books
📷 YellowKiteBooks